BEING BROWN

BEING BROWN

A VERY PUBLIC LIFE

ROSEMARY BROWN

FREE REVIEW COPY
NOT FOR RESALE

Random House
Toronto

Copyright© 1989 by Rosemary Brown

All rights reserved under International and Pan-American Copyright
Conventions.

Published in Canada by Random House of Canada Limited, Toronto.

All inquiries regarding the motion picture, television and related rights
for this book should be addressed to the Author's representative, M.G.A.
Agency Inc., 10 St. Mary Street, Suite 510, Toronto, Canada M4Y 1P9.
Representations as to the disposition of these rights are strictly
prohibited without express written consent and will be vigorously
pursued to the full extent of the law.

Canadian Cataloguing in Publication Data

Brown, Rosemary, 1930-
    Being Brown

ISBN 0-394-22050-1

1. Brown, Rosemary, 1930-. 2. British Columbia.
Legislative Assembly – Biography. 3. Legislators –
British Columbia – Biography. 4. Women in
politics – British Columbia – Biography.
5. Social action – British Columbia. 6. Jamaican
Canadians – British Columbia – Biography. I. Title.

FC3828.1.B76A3 1989   328.711′092′4   C89-094464-4
F1088.B76A3 1989

JACKET DESIGN: Brant Cowie/ArtPlus Limited
JACKET PHOTOGRAPH: Peter Paterson

Printed and bound in Canada

To women everywhere

who strive to change their world.

Acknowledgments

During the federal leadership campaign, my clearest memory is of the people. Attempting to single out people by name for special mention, in an endeavour such as this, is tantamount to ignoring a sign reading "quicksand" and twice as dangerous. I wish it were possible to list the names of all 658 people who supported me on the fourth and final ballot, but, since voting was by secret ballot, it is impossible for me to be sure who they all were.

It is with caution, therefore, that I will name just a few of those whose efforts touched me personally. Hilda Thomas, the feminist socialist theoretician and wordsmith, who crafted, vetted and honed many of the speeches I delivered, and who chaired the collective that produced the issue papers that were the basis of our educational thrust. Barb and Bob Beardsley, that incredibly calm and solid team, who managed the proceedings at the convention. The entire Manitoba Committee, which treated us all as welcome guests and left no stone unturned that could produce a Brown supporter. Clive Lytle, Mark Bostwick, Jim MacKenzie, June Jensen, who with Hilda and many others teamed up to prepare that outstanding and winning speech it was my privilege to deliver. Bruce Elphinstone and other trade unionists, who brought so many of their brothers and sisters on board; Kay MacPherson, Dorothy Inglis, Vi Thompson, Betty and Tony Mardiros, who kept the issue of peace in the forefront of our agenda. Alexa

McDonough, who broke family ranks to support me; Carl Liden, the MLA for Delta, my office mate and colleague, who delivered his entire delegation and hung in there, despite pressure, through to the last ballot; Gayle and Clare Powell, Marilyn Roycroft, Abe and Beth Arnold, John Rodriguez, for their incredible ability to unearth and round up Brown supporters; Merran Twigg, Candace Parker and Gene Errington for their special brand of sisterhood. Vanessa and Nathaniel Geary for their cheerful willingness to share their time and their mother with the campaign, Gus Wedderburn, my brother, for keeping a smile on my face and having a warm welcome for everyone who came to the committee room. And of course my exuberant sister-in-law, Sylvia, whose infectious laughter and unflagging support reached out to me even in her absence. Muriel Smith, a powerful and highly respected Manitoba New Democrat, and Clive Lytle, a top B.C. trade unionist who had rushed to fill the spot when my original nominator pulled out, my incomparable nominator and seconder, and Robin, who managed to be beside me whenever I needed her, yet somehow was everywhere else dealing with the media, the party bureaucrats and the prowling raiders from other campaigns, doing it all with style, grace and that unfailing New Zealand sense of fair play. The fifty women and men from the Yukon, Northwest Territories and across Canada who signed my nomination form. The people, who will always remain for me the highlight of the campaign.

This book really began in China, when Shirley Sharzer told me that she would call Nancy Colbert. It continued through various and circuitous coincidences; aided and abetted by the support and encouragement of Cleta, Gary, Jonathan and Bill; fuelled by the curiosity of Diana Matheson, the notes, clippings and collective memories of Gene, Hilda, Kay, Barb and Bob, Marianne, Marilyn, Merran and Robin, as well as by the gentle corrective advice of Jane Rule and the "naming" by Ann Crosby. Now that it is all over I can thank them for the proddings and the faith in the book's completion – I doubt that it would have happened without both.

CHAPTER ONE

When I woke I remembered the name, but I knew that he was no one that I knew. So if the legend was right and sleeping with the piece of wedding cake under my pillow meant that I would dream of my future husband, it must mean that I would have to leave the island to find him. Happy with the prospect of a future in a foreign land with an unknown love, I knew that the cake had worked its magic, so I ate it.

Forty-five years later, living in Canada, married for thirty-three years to a man who was born in the United States, I cannot remember the name of the man of whom I dreamt at age thirteen, but I'm content that the decision to leave Jamaica in 1950 to attend university in Canada was made in part because in 1943 a piece of wedding cake predicted it.

I was born on June 17, 1930, in the house of my mother's mother in Jamaica, delivered by a midwife. Family legend has it that I was my father's favourite child — that he doted on me. My memory of him is a hazy mixture of riding high on the shoulders of a tall man who smelled nice, laughed a lot and filled the whole world with happiness.

That is the good memory — the other one is of running around the living room and verandah one afternoon trying to make the grown-ups laugh and play with me—puzzled and frustrated because they wouldn't. The grown-ups were sad and there was nothing that I could do to stop my mother and my grandmother from crying.

I never saw the big happy man again after that—I was never taken on anyone's shoulders for walks, never thrown up in the air and caught, never felt quite so secure nor ever again smelled anyone like that. For years, I never knew what I had done to make him angry enough to leave me—but I always thought that it had to do with my running around and laughing while the grown-ups were crying, and I wished that I could tell him that I was sorry.

Years later my nurse told me that I had behaved badly at my father's funeral, that I had run around laughing while the father who had doted on me was lying in a coffin in my grandmother's living room.

I grew up in my grandmother's house on Portland Road. It was a large place that was filled with the noise of women and children, with their laughter, their joy, their anger, their conflict, their jealousies and their love—but it was a safe place. The men who came and went, uncles, brother, cousins—did so quietly and with respect.

My grandmother's house was big and old and had many rooms. It seemed to be elasticized, because as the number of people who came to live with us increased, rooms would be added on, and bathrooms would be added on, and the kitchen would grow, and the number of small, one-room semi-detached houses where maids and garden boys lived would increase and shrink depending on need. It was surrounded by a big yard with lots of trees and bushes, ideal for playing hide and seek, cricket or doctor with the neighbourhood kids and visiting cousins. My Aunt Leila and Uncle Tommy built and lived in a two-bedroom bungalow at the back of the yard. There was a large garage, big enough to house two cars. And attached to one side of it, under the mango tree, was a large completely furnished one-room dollhouse that was transformed into a house for one of the yard boys when we outgrew it.

A large verandah ran around three sides of the house, and on rainy days we would spend hours racing back and forth around it playing 'catch' or some other noisy, touching, running game. It was also the stage on which we performed for visitors, because the large doors opening onto it from the living room meant that not only could the guests seated on the sofas and armchairs in the living room be entertained by us, but so also could the maids and other helpers, who would sit on the outside steps during our performance.

When I was a child in Jamaica, children were expected to be polite and courteous, and to entertain visitors when they came to call. So I learnt to play the piano and to recite poems. The poems became longer and more dramatic as I grew older and it became clearer that I had almost no talent for the piano.

I loved entertaining visitors; I loved reciting and acting out dramatic poems; I loved the applause, and the way that grown-ups used to predict great things for my future. "That one is going to be a great courtroom lawyer," some would say to my grandmother. The more religious ones would predict a future as a great preacher or teacher. No one mentioned politics until many years later, which is not surprising: although our history records acts of greatness by women during slave and maroon rebellions, in Jamaica in the 1930s politics was not regarded as a traditional arena for women except as helpers and workers.

I never lost my love for dramatic expression, and all through my school years I took elocution lessons and belonged to debating teams. I competed in elocution and debating contests always with outstanding success and, in time, I fell in love with words. I was a voracious reader. I was excited by unusual words or the unusual use of words. I used to like to play with words, using them in unusual and outrageous ways. I can still remember the first time I heard the phrase 'infra dig' – I used it to death, I cherished it, I loved it, I made it mine. Despite this, I never really considered a career in writing as I did not think I had a talent for writing words nor even an outstanding vocabulary; but I loved the poetry of the spoken word and of sentences and phrases skilfully and carefully crafted – I used to spend hours listening to the BBC broadcasts on shortwave radio just to learn new words and new ways of using familiar words.

I loved listening to preachers, politicians, teachers and lawyers – anyone who was eloquent – and I used to lock myself in my bedroom and give brilliant speeches to the mirror, debate against myself and dream of being a great courtroom lawyer, destroying my opponents, not necessarily with logic but certainly with words. Yes, there is no doubt about it, as the saying goes, I was 'full of myself' – the only thing that saved me from being obnoxious was my self-deprecating humour; I laughed at myself and pretended not to take myself too seriously.

You see, I was a middle child, with an older brother (the only boy in the family) and a younger sister (the baby, who was also retarded). This meant that there was nothing special about me, so very early in life I learnt that to capture attention, to be seen, to be heard, I had to make myself special. My humour and my eloquence made me special, especially to my family.

Jamaica of the 1930s and 1940s was a wonderful place in which to live and grow up. Through a child's eyes it seemed to be safe, secure and beautiful. It was not just the sun and the good weather, which we took for granted: for us and for our friends, life was pleasant and without stress.

Years later in Canada, a friend commented that the Depression must have been really hard on us in Jamaica, and for a while I was puzzled as to what she meant. Although I was born during the Depression and was too young to experience it in any meaningful way, because we never wanted for anything or were deprived of anything, we never thought about poverty or allowed its presence to mar our lives until much later – and then it was other people's poverty that concerned us, never our own.

We had many friends, no one and nothing to fear. Children

seemed to be protected by everyone; there were no stories of abuse, kidnapping or murder and no hint of the violence that was to wrack the island in later years. I never learnt of incest until I was an adult, never saw a man strike a woman member of his own family until I came to this country, and never learnt of rape until then, either. In retrospect, I now realize that my sister, my brother and I were shielded from ugliness, pain, poverty and all things evil by a doting grandmother, nurse, aunts and mother. It was an unreal world, filled with people who went to great pains to let us know that they thought we were clever, bright and beautiful. We seemed to have limitless time to read, to swim, to play, and the only fear that existed was in the tales and legends of ghosts, the 'duppies' and evil spirits that existed primarily to see that we behaved ourselves.

The most important concern in our life was to get a good education. My earliest memories are filled with admonitions about the importance of "a good education." Success in life was measured by whether a person had a good education or not; this far outweighed money, property or fame. Knowledge was the single most important ingredient necessary to gain the respect of the entire community. And occasionally, when a person would suffer a mental breakdown, there was always understanding and sympathy if it could be proved that excessive book learning was the cause of the onset of the madness. As a nation, Jamaica in the early twentieth century had two obsessions—politics and education.

My school day started at 6 a.m. with a short walk from my grandmother's house where I lived to the beach (Bournemouth) for a quick swim. When I returned home I would have a shower and dress for school. Combing my hair was a real problem and quite painful because it was, in Jamaican terms, 'knotty'—to distract me my nurse developed a routine. Hair combing time was used to study the collect in the Anglican prayer book or some long passage from the Bible, and everything had to be committed to memory. My hair, which was thick and independent, was tamed by being oiled and braided into three plaits or sometimes two with a large bow attached to the end of the braids.

Breakfast started with a tablespoon of cod liver oil and a raw egg, after which there was a bowl of cooked cereal, usually cornmeal or cream of wheat, accompanied by a glass of milk and toast.

I hated milk. In those days milk was always boiled, then the film of cream was skinned off the top and the milk was chilled. The milk was never really cold enough to my taste, and occasionally some of the cream got stirred in with it, giving the whole mixture a texture the thought of which curdles my stomach even now. I hated it and swore never to drink it once I grew up and left home. Years later when I became pregnant I took calcium pills, rather than attempt to increase my calcium intake with milk. I used to try to trade my milk away to my brother or sister and if that failed I would try to spill it. I guess if I were to be completely honest, I would have to say that drinking milk ruined my childhood.

School began at 8 a.m. but because we lived less than a block away from school we were not allowed to leave too early, for fear of getting ourselves dirty while playing in the schoolyard. Cleanliness was important as a mark of class and status. Very early in life we learnt that people who were dirty were either poor or lazy so, especially for girls, cleanliness was compulsory. Boys were permitted to be dirty so long as it was 'new' dirt recently acquired in play or some form of manly activity. No form of dirt was ever acceptable for girls.

I loved school and found it easy. I made friends easily, and I was very popular with both girls and boys. The curriculum was very basic and very British and the emphasis was on memorizing. In the early years the study of math concentrated on mental arithmetic. The first class was always devoted to some form of mental or memory gymnastics. All the students in the class would be lined up in alphabetical order. Since my surname was Wedderburn, I would invariably be near the end of the line with the Wints, the Wongs and the Youngs. We would then have to answer math questions based on addition, multiplication, division or subtraction. For each correct answer, we were allowed to move one place up the alphabet. For each incorrect answer we would move one place down.

I was so competitive that finishing below the letter B would send me into a frenzy of study and in no time at all the

Wedderburns, Wints, Wongs and Youngs were battling it out for the top spot in arithmetic. Unknown to me two things were happening. One, an unconscious intent was being formed never to marry anyone with a surname beginning with the letter below C, and two, I was being prepared to dazzle my children with my mental arithmetic wizardry. When they were very young I used to astound and fascinate them by being able to add and multiply faster than a calculator. They would brag about this at school and bring classmates home for whom I had to perform – that is, until they were in grade three or four.

In time I graduated to high school, but by then maths had become incomprehensible and defeating. English and literature, however, remained my joy to the end. Soon after beginning high school, I discovered the wonder of boys and was promptly sent to Westwood, a girls' private boarding school, 'for my own good'; my family believed that prevention of contact was the best form of sex education. I loved boarding school. It proved, like my grandmother's house, to be a safe place filled with the energy and sound of women. My teen years seemed to speed by in a blur of books, boys, dancing and an increasing addiction to politics. I returned to Kingston to attend Wolmer's High for Girls for my last two years of high school, so that I could graduate from the same private school that my mother and aunts had attended.

One day during my very early school years in 1938, the whole school was called into assembly at lunch time. This was most unusual, because assembly was usually scheduled first thing each day so that we could sing a hymn, listen to a reading from the Bible, listen to any announcements about rules, changes in rules, special occurrences or whatever, then file out and march to our classrooms to begin the academic day. An assembly at noon meant that something special had happened.

There was much friendly jostling and whispering as we marched into the auditorium. The most bizarre rumours as to what could have caused this unusual event were passed up

and down the lines of students. Finally we agreed that we
were either going to receive an unexpected visit from a
very important personage, maybe one of the princesses, the
Archbishop of Canterbury—or Shirley Temple—because only
something of that magnitude could warrant a special assembly,
or else we were going to be told of the death of someone very
special.

When we were all quiet, Miss Wilson, the principal, told us
to return to our classrooms quickly, collect our books, and
go straight home. She said that there was an 'insurrection' in
Kingston so we were to get home as quickly as possible and to
stay inside listening to reports on the radio until it was safe for us
to leave our house—there would be no more school, she told us,
"until the insurrection was over."

I had never heard the word insurrection before, none of my
friends knew what it meant: we all agreed that it sounded
serious, sort of like resurrection or some other biblical
happening. However, since it was the cause of the school being
closed indefinitely we decided that whatever it was, it wasn't
totally bad. We gathered up our books and ran out of the school
laughing and yelling "insurrection" at the top of our lungs.

It was wonderful. An unexpected holiday, freedom to play.
When I ran into my house still shouting "insurrection,
insurrection," my grandmother told me very sternly that
insurrection was no laughing matter, that there was a riot
downtown, that some people could get killed and that I was to
sit quietly by the radio and listen to the news.

That was the first time that I learnt that people in real life
really did kill and did die because of their beliefs. This was not
stuff in the history books like the War of the Roses, these were
people like us who were angry that they were deprived of the
right to vote because they were not property owners as the law
decreed. They were looting, burning and even killing each other
in the hope that the 'mother country', as England was called by
all of us, would introduce fair labour practices and enfranchise
them.

I did not learn all of this from the shortwave radio, of course,
but from my grandmother, who sat with us and talked very quietly
about the injustices of the system, about why universal suffrage

was a right worth dying for. About J.A.G. Smith and Norman Manley and the People's National Party and about England, the mother country; and about how the meetings that she had been taking us to, the pamphlets that we had been handing out had failed to influence the mother country, and that sometimes the only language that the mother country understood was violence. And how, although she did not condone uprisings, she certainly understood why they occurred and hoped that the army would not be too hard on the rioters. She also added that she hoped that too many lives would not be lost, that J.A.G. Smith would be able to calm the crowds and that this time the mother country would know that Jamaicans meant business.

I became very angry with the mother country that day and remained angry until Jamaica gained independence in 1962.

One question that is always asked of me is when did I decide to enter politics. My immediate response usually is "at the moment of conception." I cannot in all honesty remember a time when politics was not being discussed, argued about, disagreed upon, debated, examined, bewailed or analyzed by some or all members of my family. I grew up thinking that everybody discussed politics every day—certainly in my Jamaica they did. True, there was gossip about the Duke and Duchess of Windsor and about Jack Johnson and his liaisons with white women, but it was just that—passing, idle small talk. Serious talk was about the children's education and the state of the country. Not even the Second World War, although it consumed our interest for a while, succeeded in distracting us from the words and deeds of our politicians.

I suspect, however, that all the political talk that had filled my home and swirled all around me as I grew up gradually seeped into my pores and into my consciousness in my early teens. Yet I cannot actually tell when I decided to become a politician or when I fell in love with politics Jamaica-style. I just know that one day I decided not to become a brilliant lawyer after all, but a brilliant politician involved in my island's destiny instead, and I began to prepare myself.

In my family, politicians were held in high esteem; we admired the way they fought the great British government on our behalf—they were our national heroes.

J.A.G. Smith and Norman Manley, who were the founders of the People's National Party (PNP), based on the British Labour Party model, were giants among the political thinkers of the day. Sir Alexander Bustamante, founder of the Jamaica Labour Party (JLP), although he was their ideological opponent, was no less magnificent in intellect and stature. The heroes and heroines of my youth were not athletes nor even entertainers, they were politicians and political activists.

Politics in Jamaica of the 1940s and 1950s was a wonderfully heady, verbose, eloquent affair—politicians were great orators, heckling was loud and irreverent, but never vicious—there was always loud music, lots of humour, exaggeration, overstatement and crowds. Political meetings were held outdoors at major street intersections at night and everyone turned out for them. These meetings were not just dry speeches and political discussions, they were social events that were attended by both supporters and the opposition, although even in those days, the opposition was always careful not to be too vociferous or belligerent.

Any politician who could not best his or her hecklers with wit and style at such a public gathering was finished even before the ballots were counted. Everyone got into the act, and witty rejoinders and one-liners were repeated extensively, often becoming part of the mento and calypso songs that were an important part of every campaign.

I recall one campaign in which one of the political parties hired a hotshot New York public relations firm to design its logo and motto. The firm designed a large bird in flight with the motto, "We soar above the rest." The other political party immediately responded with an appropriate logo and a motto that, translated into polite language, meant "beware of the droppings of soaring birds." In no time at all the entire island was caught up in hysterical laughter as hundreds of jokes, one-liners and songs about bird droppings sprang up everywhere, destroying the campaign and contributing in no small measure to the defeat of that particular party in that particular election.

Every Jamaican loved politics, *was* a politician and an expert on political strategy. The violence and destruction did not come until the 1970s—in the 1940s, 50s and 60s anger, when it erupted, was directed at the British or some other enemy, never at other Jamaicans. In those days words were the weapons and outrageous promises the battleground—and the women were as tough, as scathing, as bright and eloquent as the men and it was wonderful to be caught up in the excitement of it all.

My grandmother was the first—and most—political person I have ever known. She was a social democrat. Why or how she became one was never clear to me. I doubt that she ever thought of herself in terms of ideologies—her doctrinal system was quite simple and straightforward. She was a member of the People's National Party—she believed in the basic decency of people; she believed that those who had, shared with those who didn't have, and that if a government was run by people who practised these principles, that government would ensure that everyone had shelter, food, employment, health care and the basic necessities needed to cope with and to enjoy life in dignity. She was a profound Christian who experienced politics as an extension of her religious beliefs and always explained it to us in Christian terms—based on the firm moral difference between right and wrong, good and evil.

She had a very special relationship with God. In her home there was family worship every night. We would all sit at the large round dining table with our heads bowed and our eyes closed while she had a little chat with God. She would tell Him about all the irritations of the day, share with Him her concern about our disobedience or other misdeeds, and even tell God of humorous things that happened, and chuckle with Him about them. As she sat praying with her eyes closed, she could tell if one of us children opened her or his eyes or kicked the other under the table or pinched, and she would immediately bring this act to God's attention, as proof of how we tried her patience.

After her little chat with God we would each recite a special verse chosen by her from the Beatitudes. Because I was considered a bit of a troublemaker, my verse was "Blessed are the peacemakers . . . ," my sister's, because she was the baby, was "Blessed are the pure in heart." After saying our verses, we would all recite the Lord's Prayer together, ask God's blessing on everyone, including the King and Queen, brush our teeth and go to bed.

My grandmother was convinced that God approved of her politics.

I am telling you this much about my family because I am so much a product of their collective moulding, shaping and crafting. Imagine if you will a circle, my brother, sister and me huddled in the centre, and all around us these forceful, dynamic persons giving us their best—lovingly, carefully, painstakingly redesigning us in their own image. When I speak of my family I am referring primarily to my mother's family, because when my father died we were so young the responsibility for our upbringing fell to my mother and her family.

My grandmother Imogene Wilson-James was the descendant of indentured workers from India who came to Jamaica after the abolition of slavery to work in the sugar cane fields. She married my grandfather Walter James, known to everyone as Pappy James, a pharmacist, who was the product of the union of a white man and a Black woman. This multiracial beginning expanded until, by the time of my grandchildren's generation, it included Germans, Spanish Jews, Americans, Canadians, Chinese and a member of the Cree Nation.

My grandmother had a talent for acquiring real estate and her financial acumen became the economic basis of our family. She had five children, three girls and two boys. One son and my grandfather died prior to my birth. My mother was the youngest, and being nearly fifteen years younger than her siblings was the baby of the family and was treated as such by everyone.

Aunt Gwen, my eldest aunt, married Stanley Shackleford and went to West Africa where she and her husband established a very successful chain of bakeries through Ghana and Nigeria, the Shackleford Bakeries. It was Aunt Gwen who introduced me to African culture. On her visits home to Jamaica, she would bring beautiful pieces of sculpture, brass trays, paintings, ornaments and other artifacts, which she would donate to the museum in Kingston. She was an elegant woman with a beautiful singing voice who inherited my grandmother's sharp head for business.

The Shacklefords were very wealthy by Jamaican standards, lived in grand style when they visited the island and were very generous. Aunt Gwen, who was herself childless, loved me, pampered me and insisted on taking full financial responsibility for my university education. Because she spent most of my lifetime in Africa, much of my contact with her was by mail. She was a very generous person, whose independence and self-reliance I admired greatly.

Aunt Lil, whose real name is Leila James-Tomlinson, was the scholar in the family. She was the first woman in Jamaica to win an island scholarship to the University of London, England. When she returned to Jamaica upon graduation she was employed by the government to work with Rudy Burke in developing a comprehensive welfare system for the island.

She was called Mrs. T. by everyone and pioneered many of the social services that Jamaicans now take for granted. Upon retirement from the Welfare Service she was appointed to the Bench as a Lay Judge and remained there until she died at age eighty-one. She received many honours during her lifetime, including an MBE from Queen Elizabeth for her outstanding work on behalf of Jamaica's children and families of the poor.

She was an active member of the People's National Party and remained a firm supporter and friend of the Manleys throughout her life. She was honoured by the government in 1975 as an outstanding Jamaican.

I spent a lot of my summer vacations with Aunt Lil, travelling

throughout the island visiting the village community centres
through which the care and welfare of people was administered.
I learnt from her about everyone's right to be treated with
respect regardless of their circumstances in life. I saw poverty at
first hand, and I came to recognize that people work very hard
yet remain poor because they have no control over their lives
and are often the victims of bad, stupid or cruel decisions made
by those who hold power over them.

Aunt Lil, never content just to help people, always took the
time to talk with them about the reasons for their condition. She
always encouraged them to do as much as they could for
themselves, not to blame themselves when things went wrong
and never to belittle themselves or their efforts, but always to
try to identify the real source of their problem. She was a
political social worker who believed that changing society was
more important than changing individuals.

Aunt Lil was always teaching us something. She believed in
the biblical parable of the Talents; she continually exhorted us
children to stretch ourselves, our abilities and our imagination.
She was the first person to tell me how small a portion of the
brain we use in our daily lives and how much more we are
capable of doing than we actually do. She believed quite firmly
that it was a crime to do less than the best one was capable of,
and she believed that failure to use a talent would be punished
by its loss. She was also the person who taught me that the most
valuable gift a person had to give another person was time – she
believed that love and loyalty could not be bought with money,
but were inspired by the gift of time.

To Aunt Lil fell the task of trying to translate my genetic
acceptance of social democracy into an ideological framework.
She described herself as a Fabian socialist; although my
grandmother gave the impression that she did not think that
God played as important a role in Aunt Lil's politics as He
should, she nonetheless gave it her grudging approval and was
always proud when Aunt Lil could clarify some political act or
decision that baffled us. Because of her, I began to read politics
and history, trying to make some real sense of all the political
talk around me. She encouraged the use of the word 'why.'

"Always question," she would exhort me, "always seek to know why."

Her one caution was about going too far, taking extreme positions, because in that direction, she warned, "lurked communism," and the whole point of reading and learning was to have a clear understanding of the difference between these apparently similar political beliefs. To her, communism was a trap to be avoided at all cost since it was just slavery by another name, but unlike my grandmother, she did not depend on God for protection from that pitfall.

My brother, sister and I were known to my mother's family as 'the children.' My grandmother, like so many Jamaicans before the development of a comprehensive welfare system, 'adopted' children. That means that she accepted responsibility for some of their financial needs as well as their religious and moral upbringing. On one occasion when tragedy left three children orphaned Aunt Lil adopted all three of them; and Aunt Gwen married Uncle Stanley, who over the years sired seventeen children, none of them hers. Uncle Karl had no children of his own, neither did he adopt any. After the death of our natural father my grandmother, aunts and Uncle Karl all assumed joint responsibility for our parenting, care and nurturing. No documents were drafted, no papers signed; it just happened. We became 'the children' of the family.

Upon my father's death, my mother and 'the children' moved into my grandmother's house. Our nurse, Baa (whose full name was Violet Thomas), accompanied us and, as was the tradition then, lived with us and remained a part of my family until her death in 1979.

My uncle, as the surviving male child of my grandmother, assumed the duties of father and became the male to whom we all looked as head of the family. The result of this was that although my mother married a number of times after my father's death (five times, to be exact) there were no major adjustments or trauma accompanying the entry and exit of these men through our lives; they remained my mother's husbands—they were never our stepfathers.

All questions of discipline, our future, or matters of any importance concerning us were dealt with by my mother in consultation with my grandmother and my uncle. Until she died, my grandmother's house was always considered our home, and she had more influence and impact on our early life than anyone else with the possible exception of our nurse.

After the death of my grandmother, my Aunt Lil, who was one of my mother's older sisters, assumed the role of matriarch of the family and took on the duties and responsibilities for the children that had been my grandmother's.

While we were relatively young, there was some tension as to where our home should be, since Uncle Karl and Aunt Lil rejected my mother's idea that we should live with her. The children were not included in discussions of this matter. However, we ended up living with Aunt Lil until our late teens, after which we moved to my mother's house. At that time, she had been married to her third husband for many years, the family all liked him, so we guessed that Uncle Karl and Aunt Lil relented and agreed to this transfer.

I was both excited and terrified by my female elders. To me they seemed overpowering, independent, self-assured and strong. I was convinced that I would never be able to measure up to their standards nor carry on in their footsteps. On the other hand, they were very convinced that I could. They had great expectations of me and a very high opinion of my abilities and talents, and like John Donne's God, they encouraged and hounded me, and hound me even now. I guess psychologists would say that I was surrounded in my formative years by positive reinforcement, which did not entice me to rest on my laurels, but which drove me to live up to the expectations of people who loved me.

Today my friends, observing my tendency to be a workaholic, are amused when I say that happiness for me is leading a life of idleness and sloth: their amusement at this protestation is tinged with disbelief. They are right of course, because I suspect that consciously or unconsciously, I am so overwhelmed by the debt that I owe my foremothers and so fearful of my inability to repay that debt in some tangible way, or even to live up to their expectations of me, that my striving will never end.

I am so conscious of the women who are my past that I have come to accept that I see the world through their eyes and react to it as I believe they would. In many ways this makes life much easier for me since it relieves me of having to wrestle with moral and ethical issues in terms of my own selfishness and desires. The response of those foremothers to moral issues was always so clear and absolute that I feel safe in always being guided by their example. This, I believe, explains so much of me that is old-fashioned and traditional as well as why, despite my lack of active involvement with any religious sect, so many of my principles are rooted in biblical teachings.

I find it difficult to imagine a time when I will ever be able to turn my back on any struggle for dignity and human rights anywhere. I guess in time I have rolled all my role models into one person who is represented by my grandmother – my nurse, my aunts, my mother, Sojourner Truth, Mary McLeod Bethune, Angela Davis . . . all those tough, strong, independent women who opened doors for me to walk through, and who by their lives set standards for me to live up to. Those women have given meaning to my struggle and reason to my life – and they are the strength that I always reach back to when I feel myself 'going down for the third time.'

There were two significant males in my childhood after my father died. One was Uncle Karl. Dr. Karl Wilson-James was not the slightest bit intimidated by being the only male in a family of high-powered women. He was himself a high achiever who won a medical scholarship to the University of Edinburgh and went on to become one of Jamaica's leading surgeons.

When my grandmother developed cancer of the stomach and had to go to New York for treatment because there were no adequate facilities in Jamaica, Uncle Karl was very distraught. After her death, he determined to ensure that future cancer patients would be able to receive the treatment they needed without having to leave the island, so he founded the Cancer Institute of Jamaica and opened its first cancer clinic.

He was one of the driving forces behind the development of the University of the West Indies and was one of the members of its first Board of Governors. He firmly believed that a good education makes all things possible and his primary concern was to ensure that the children received the best education the family could afford for them.

He was not and has never been impressed by wealth or title. The only criteria by which he judged people were integrity and intelligence. His pleasure and displeasure with us was measured in direct relation to the grades on our report cards. The Aunts inspired me to explore the universe—Uncle Karl inspired me to hit the books! His favourite advice was "It will still be there when you are through studying." "It" being whatever thing, matter or person seemed to me to need my attention more urgently than studying at any given instant.

He too was honoured by the Queen and received an OBE for his contribution to medicine and the improvement of health care for Jamaicans.

At age eighty he continued to practise medicine, leaving for his office at eight every morning. He treated free of charge as many patients as he could until 3 p.m., taking only a half hour for lunch. His office was located in one of the poorest sections of Kingston, and although he no longer practised surgery he still took refresher courses in general medicine at regular intervals and subscribed to a number of medical journals.

He was an excellent physician who did not believe in retirement: he thought that to abandon the practice of medicine while he was still of sound mind, especially in a poor country like Jamaica where his services were still in demand, would amount to being profligate with the education and the gifts with which he had been so generously endowed.

He remained actively involved in community work, drove his own car, read without glasses and was a vegetarian for more than fifty years. He was proud of the fact that all our family, including his father, who had been a pharmacist, were members of helping professions and saw this as the reason why we have enjoyed financial prosperity and community respect.

He died of cancer in December 1987. My brother and I were able to be with him during those last weeks, and we hope that we were able to convey to him how much 'the children' loved him and appreciated that he had been our 'father' for nearly sixty years.

All the members of my grandmother's family were actively involved as volunteers and activists in the community. Involvement was a family tradition and the children were encouraged to accept that fact as a way of life. My brother, Gus Wedderburn, who is even more involved in his community in Halifax than I am in mine, confesses that he has always assumed that giving one's time in the service of others was what life was all about.

Roy, the other significant male of my adolescent years, sort of snuck up on me and remained my first true love. He was one of my brother's friends – the wonderful thing about older brothers is that they have so many friends. In later years my brother confessed that the reason he had so many friends was that he had two sisters and his friends found him to be the best conduit to them.

Roy was always there, at parties, picnics, trips to the movies – he was just another of my brother's friends and he was a lousy dancer! I was a fabulous dancer, I fulfilled all the stereotypes about rhythm and the love of movement. I could and would swirl and twirl and jump and jive with the best, and boys loved to dance with me. There was nothing romantic about jitterbugging. The slow pieces you saved for the lousy dancers—so I saved my slow pieces for Roy.

I loved to tease him about his two left feet and he would reply that those feet guaranteed him every slow dance with me. That's why I was so surprised when he was quiet and withdrawn at the great birthday party that was thrown for my sixteenth birthday. After some merciless teasing about how quiet he was, he finally said, "Do you really want to know why I'm so quiet?"

"Sure," I said with a laugh and a toss of my head.

"Because I love you and you couldn't care less about me," he said quietly.

I was stunned! No boy had ever told me that he loved me in all my memory. We all kidded and laughed and pretended that life was one long party—I knew that many of the boys liked me, but no one until then had actually said, "I love you," we just didn't speak that way. The silence felt like an eternity. I didn't know what to say. Finally I said, "I'm sorry, I didn't know," then I turned and walked away. He left my birthday party. I can remember little else of that evening except that he had taken all the fun out of it by being serious about 'love.'

Roy became my 'steady' from then until I left for university in the fall of 1950; in truth he was one of the reasons why I left Jamaica to attend university elsewhere.

The debate began the year before I completed high school. As the time grew closer for a decision it became more intense and more family members became involved. There was never any question about 'whether,' only about 'where.' Until then, members of our family had always attended university in Great Britain. It was sort of a family tradition and it had always been assumed that it would continue to be so. After all, all of Jamaica's outstanding public and professional figures had been educated in the mother country—some had returned with accents so British that they were unintelligible, except to other refugees from British institutions of higher learning; this marked them as 'cultured.'

Two things coinciding with my day of decision created the debate. One was my open and outspoken dislike of England's treatment of Jamaica, a situation that led family members to say over and over again that "my mouth would surely get me into trouble" in England; there was some legitimate fear for my safety, since open and blatant hostility to the large influx of Black immigrants to England was beginning to be expressed in violence. For the first time in living memory the attacks on West Indian, African and other immigrants went beyond the verbal and had become physical and often bloody. The polite racism to which early West Indian immigrants had been subjected was fast disappearing, and whereas that early type, though painful, could be ignored, the violence could not.

Second, the University of the West Indies was in its early and formative stage and some family members thought that my attendance there would be the best solution to the problem. Uncle Karl and Aunt Lil were adamant. Travel abroad, leaving the island, had always been part of the educational process of this family. If at some later date I wanted to pursue graduate work at the University of the West Indies that would be okay, but the time had come for me to see some more of the world. In addition, my relationship with Roy was creating some concern as it seemed to them that I might choose to combine marriage and university, which they believed very firmly would cause my education to suffer.

If not Great Britain, then where? The United States was out of the question because Americans were considered to be uncouth and uncultured, and their educational standards questionable. In any event, because of 'my mouth,' I would surely not be safe in such an openly racist country as the USA.

Just when all seemed lost, Dr. Cyril James came to the rescue. I did not know Dr. James, none of us did. We only knew that he was the President of McGill University in Canada and that he had been very helpful in getting the University of the West Indies started. We knew that Canada as a part of the Commonwealth would have high educational standards. The family had heard no wild tales about the treatment of Black people in Canada, so despite 'my mouth' they felt that I should be relatively safe there.

When we began to make enquiries, we discovered that many outstanding Jamaican scholars, doctors and other professionals were McGill graduates. We learnt that there was an active McGill graduate association in Kingston and when we made contact its members painted a wonderful picture of life in Montreal and of Canada's academic institutions.

Gradually, one by one, the family all arrived at the same conclusion—"Send her to McGill, what harm can come of it, after all it's only for four years."

On August 10, 1950, dressed from head to toe in new clothes and accompanied by every living relative in Jamaica, I arrived at the Kingston airport one hour ahead of my scheduled time of departure. As well as relatives, many friends, some of whom had taken time off work, were there to see me off. The night before had been one long send-off party and it carried on until it was time for me to board the plane. I kissed everyone good-bye, leaving Roy for last. As I left, I promised myself that I would return to Jamaica in four years with a Bachelor of Arts degree, then marry Roy and enter the political arena. My future was clear and simple.

I entered the plane, got into my seat, buckled my seat belt and plunged into the most severe case of homesickness that I have ever experienced.

CHAPTER TWO

Living in Montreal, even in the relative seclusion of Royal Victoria College, the women's residence at McGill University, brought me my first contact with racism, Canadian-style. I had been raised on a diet of poems and stories about the oppression of being Black in the United States, but always there was the rider that Canada was different. Indeed, my family thought that by sending me to university in Canada they were guaranteeing that I would not have to deal with what they referred to as the 'ugliness' of prejudice while receiving a reasonably good education (not as good as I would have received in England, but certainly superior to anything offered in the United States).

I must confess that the graduates of McGill, Dalhousie and the University of Toronto I met before leaving Jamaica fed the myth of a discrimination-free Canada by never mentioning prejudice. They spoke glowingly of their Canadian friends, indulgently of their Canadian professors and lovingly of their Canadian social experience. There were many jokes about the weather, some feeble attempts to include French phrases in their conversation and great bragging about the superiority of the academic standards. The only complaint that I remember hearing concerned the shortage of Jamaican girls enrolled at the universities. The boys felt that they had to justify dating white Canadian girls while extolling the beauty and virtue of the childhood girlfriends left in Jamaica, from whom they had extracted promises of fidelity during their absence and to whom they had pledged eternal love.

I read the brochures sent to me by Royal Victoria College and McGill University avidly. I was hungry to add to my limited knowledge of Canada, which did not go much beyond the country's expanse of snow and ice, the dependence of the world on its prairies for wheat, its brave and loyal support of England during the war (unlike the Americans) and the idiosyncrasies of Prime Minister Mackenzie King (and his mother), who seemed to retain power forever.

I conjured up in my mind's eye a community of plain, simple, gentle folk who lived uneventful lives in a cold uneventful country inhabited by very few Black people and a handful of Native Indians who resided on reserves.

I was happy with the prospect of my studying in Canada; so was Roy. We both assumed that I would not have any interest whatsoever in Canadian men, that I would not be distracted by a glittering social life; I would study, complete my four years, and return to Jamaica, probably to attend the law school that was in its infancy at the University of the West Indies. In any event it was obvious to both of us that we were destined to marry and grow old together, and the four years apart would only serve to strengthen our attachment to each other.

Canada was not what I expected. Three weeks after I had settled into a double room in Royal Victoria College, the assistant warden of women called me into her office and explained that I was being given a single room, because the College had been unable to find a roommate to share the double with me. She tried to break the news to me gently, pointing out how lucky I was to secure a single room and how much more private and quiet that would be for studying. I was moved into a single room at the same rate as the double – and two white women students were immediately moved into the double room.

I was stunned! I could not believe that not one of the other students in residence had been willing to share a room with me. Other West Indian women who had been at Royal Victoria College before me shrugged the matter off as not being surprising; having had similar experiences themselves they had known all along that no roommate would be found to share my room. Every year, West Indian women, given the option, requested the cheaper double room, moved in and were later moved into the more expensive single rooms at the lower double room rate. The bureaucracy was embarrassed by the whole procedure, but had not found a satisfactory way around it. It lived in the vain hope that one year things would change and a student would be found willing to share a double room with a Black student, and so it persisted. Despite the fact that that particular form of racism worked in my favour economically, it made me angry and my anger was compounded by frustration. It eventually became clear that the experience would be typical of the prejudice I ran into during my years in residence–polite, denied and accepted.

The dining room behaviour was another example of the peculiar brand of racism practised in Royal Victoria College at that time. Whenever I entered the dining room at mealtime I would anxiously scan the tables, hoping to find a seat at a table with another Black student. If there was none available, I would look for a seat with one of the two or three white friends I had managed to make (I had made some, including Sue Curtis, whose father was the Attorney General of Newfoundland at the time). If that failed, I just sat anywhere, knowing that I would probably complete my entire meal without anyone speaking to me or including me in their conversation.

At first, because I am outgoing, a bit of an extrovert, I assumed that my tablemates were shy, so I used to initiate conversation with the person sitting beside me or across from me–the cold and unfriendly response to these overtures soon convinced me to stop.

I was truly grateful for the people who acted as a buffer against the hurts; although they did not transform Royal Victoria College into a home away from home, they managed to give me a glimpse of that other Canada that existed beyond prejudice and discrimination. Dr. Muriel Roscoe, Dean of Women, and her assistant Marie Madeline Mottola monitored our activities to ensure that we did not withdraw into a lonely shell of self-pity, but participated in social events on and around the campus. Mike DeFreitas, the senior custodian and an early West Indian immigrant who had retired from the railroad, took on the responsibility of surrogate father. He never hesitated to chastise us for staying out late during weeknights and made it his business to meet and to know the young men who dated us. The other Caribbean women were a special source of support, and although Dr. Roscoe encouraged us not to confine our social contact to our immediate and exclusive circle, she recognized the value and necessity of the love and nurturing that we gave and received from each other.

I was neither lonely nor unhappy during my stay at McGill. The West Indian community was large, vibrant and close-knit. My closest women friends were two other Jamaicans, Patsy Chen and Merle Darby, who had attended Wolmer's, the same private school that I had, and whom I knew well. In addition, because the ratio of male to female West Indian students was almost three to one there was never a shortage of dates. Many of the older male students were dating white Canadians but in the early 1950s interracial dating was not as acceptable as it is today and many more of the male students either refrained from doing it or did it clandestinely.

Interracial dating was absolutely taboo for West Indian women. We were all very conscious of the sexual stereotypes that we were told inhabited the fantasy world of white males, and at that time it was still very important to West Indian men that the women they married be perceived to be pure and virginal. The tragedy, of course, was that the West Indian male students internalized and accepted the white criteria of beauty and since the "only life" Black women had to live could not "be lived as a blonde," as a popular TV commercial of the time exhorted, the Black men assumed that white men saw no beauty in us, and therefore their only interest would be in our sexual availability.

Even more tragic was the fact that we Black women students (unlike our counterparts of today) shared this perception of our unattractiveness and consequently closed ourselves off from the world of white males. Tragic because the decision to do so was not based on our assessment of our worth, but on our acceptance of our male colleagues' assessment of our lack of worth.

The real excitement of my academic life at McGill was discovering Hugh MacLennan and Canadian literature. During my voracious reading years as an adolescent and teenager, I had discovered and come to love Mazo de la Roche and Lucy Maude Montgomery, and for me that was all there was to Canadian literature. I had inherited from my English high school teachers the belief that very little of value was being produced by writers in the colonies, so I had no curiosity about Canadian literature. Quite frankly I did not think that there was any.

It was with a sort of bemused inquisitiveness that in my second year I registered for the course in Canadian Literature taught jointly by Hugh MacLennan, the author, and Louis Dudek, the poet. As the works of Gabrielle Roy, Morley Callaghan, Earle Birney and Hugh MacLennan entered my life, they opened up such a rich and exciting world to me that I came to see Canada through new eyes and to develop an addiction to Canadian authors that I have never lost.

In addition, I fell in love with Hugh MacLennan. I found him a kind and inspiring teacher who found the time to talk, discuss and listen as I struggled towards a better understanding of Canadian mores, cultures, attitudes and customs. One teacher stands out in memory from my high school: Lucille Waldron (Mair), my history teacher. One teacher stands out in memory from my university years: Hugh MacLennan, my Canadian Literature professor.

The less polite face of racism remained hidden until later. Although the women who shared the residence at Royal

Victoria College were content just to treat us as though we did not exist, never acknowledging our presence except when necessary and then only with the minimum of courtesy, the landladies and landlords who lived in the neighbourhoods near McGill had no such inhibitions. There was nothing subtle about the racism of the landlords and ladies of Montreal. During the summer the women's residence was closed and we were all expected to return to our respective homes or seek accommodation elsewhere. Of course, my first summer in Canada, I hastened home to Jamaica and remained there until it was time to return to school. I needed desperately to be free of prejudice and discrimination, to see my family, and to reassure myself that I was still a whole and valued human being; and to assess my feelings for Roy. But by the following year, I was in love with one of the male students and wanted to spend the vacation in Montreal to be near him.

Job hunting in Montreal that summer proved to be a nightmare. My Chinese-Jamaican friend Patsy Chen secured a job immediately as a waitress at a golf and country club. Although I applied to the same club that she did, and to others as well, I was never accepted. The employment counsellor kept recommending that I accept childcare jobs or light housework jobs, despite the fact that I explained I was not interested in doing housework or caring for children. She finally explained that although she had personally recommended me for a number of different jobs, only the people seeking domestic servants were interested in hiring me.

The older, wiser, senior West Indian women students, experienced in these matters, had never bothered to seek employment in Montreal. As soon as the academic semester ended, they headed for New York, where they were able to secure any type of work they wanted.

Discouraged by my job hunt, I reported to Gretchen Weston, the assistant warden in residence who was also the designated counsellor for foreign students, that I would be returning to Jamaica for the summer since I had been unable to find employment. Gretchen, who happened to be the daughter of one of the Westons of Weston's financial empire and was herself a student at McGill, was clearly upset by my report; she asked me to allow her to make some enquiries and report back to me in a couple of days. The following day she called to tell me to report to the Weston's plant in Longueil for work the following Monday.

Every summer after that I worked at Weston's Bakeries in Longueil as an office 'gopher.' I started at $35 weekly and worked my way up to $45 weekly by the time I graduated. I enjoyed those summer jobs and made some good friends, although on at least one occasion I'm sure that management regretted its generosity in creating a spot for me. One week, when I was the holiday relief for the person in payroll who computed the work hours of the employees in the plant, I was almost voted most popular person in Quebec when all the workers in the plant discovered that they had received a tremendous raise in pay—it seemed that I had multiplied when I should have added and the results brought loud rounds of applause from all the workers on the plant floor. Management quickly promoted me at the end of that week to filing letters and reports with no responsibility for payroll, although I had earlier been told that I would be working in the payroll department for three weeks.

Marie Mastrojosephs, my friend from those days, tells me that I am still spoken of kindly by many of the workers who were beneficiaries of my brief stint in payroll. And I sometimes wonder as I read about him and see him on TV news if Garfield knows how close I came to wrecking the Weston empire.

Once I had secured a job, thanks to the influence of Gretchen Weston, I had to find an apartment, and that's when I ran into the open, hostile and impolite racism of the landlords and landladies I spoke of earlier. These men and women made no secret of their dislike and distaste for Black people. They were rude, obscene and straightforward about refusing to rent us accommodation, often slamming the doors in our faces to emphasize their rejection of our request. Because I could afford it, I decided that I did not need to live in a shabby apartment near the university, so I sought better accommodation in Notre Dame de Grace and lower Westmount. It soon became absolutely clear that a line had been drawn around the university, in the nature of the U.S. 'redlining' of a neighbourhood, encompassing approximately six blocks in each direction around McGill, that is, effectively making it a segregated neighbourhood. Blacks were not welcome as residents outside that line, except in the St. Antoine district where most of the Canadian Black families of the day lived.

The mild anger and frustration I had felt for the students in Royal Victoria College turned to hatred for the landladies and landlords of Montreal. I fell into a common, irrational habit of including all members of that group in my rage and outrage, rather than just the specific ones who had hurt me. I knew just enough French to understand the obscenities they spat out at me, and various forms of the word Black were present in all of them.

Ten years after graduation, when we returned to Montreal so that Bill could complete his residency at the Allan Memorial Hospital, I found that little had changed. His white colleagues had no problems securing reasonable housing in Westmount and Outremont, while we had to settle for inferior accommodation in the poorest part of Notre Dame de Grace. By then, although the hatred had evaporated, the anger and hurt remained; we were the parents of two small children and the prospect that they would have to face similar treatment because of our decision to make Canada our home added guilt to my feelings of rage.

After that experience, I escalated my efforts to get Bill to decide to leave Canada for some other country, any other country in which our children would be free from racism. He agonized over this situation as much as I did, but always he returned to the conclusion that this was a country whose benefits outweighed the liabilities of racism, and that raising our children with self-esteem despite the experience of prejudice was a challenge we just had to face. I disagreed strongly; I wanted my children to experience my safe, loving and positive childhood, but I was not prepared to take them and return to Jamaica without Bill. So, to my rage about racism was added my anger at being powerless to control my family's choice of country of residence.

But my feelings about landlords and ladies paled in comparison to those I had about another group of people. My nightmares were filled with immigration officers. I hated and feared them because, unlike landladies and landlords, they really had my fate and my future in their hands. They had power. I thought they were stupid and cruel – petty despots who made no attempt to conceal their loathing for Black immigrants and whose sadism was uncontrolled when dealing with us.

Every year at the end of the spring semester West Indian students had to go to the immigration office to ask for an extension of our student visas over the summer. We had to lie through our teeth about not working during this time, saying that we would just be lazing about enjoying the Montreal humidity until time to resume classes in September; as students we had been issued special visas that very clearly forbade us working. Before being accepted as students we had had to prove that we were financially able to attend university without needing to work or receive any financial assistance from Canada, and at the beginning of the academic year we had to show a balance of $1,000 in our bank accounts to cover the year's tuition fees and living expenses. The immigration officers suspected that we were lying about not working but they had no proof, and the frustration drove them into a frenzy. We had to show up at the immigration office with a passport, bank book and letter of acceptance to the fall semester at McGill. We also had to have an address and a phone number, as well as a letter of reference from a respectable member of the community, the Dean of Women for the women, one of the lay preachers from the Student Christian Movement for the men. The officers desperately wanted to find reasons to deport us, and as we sat across from them, watching the rage struggling to erupt as they cross-examined us, we would begin to sweat. For emotional support we would go down to the immigration office in groups.

The day that I was accused of trying to secure two extensions instead of one, because I had had the misfortune to show up the day after my brother, who had been down for his renewal, I thought that my world was about to explode. The agent was furious that I thought I could pull the wool over his eyes simply by changing my name from Augustus to Rosemary—after all, the surnames were the same, the colour of skin was the same, we were both students, both at McGill, both from Jamaica and as far as he was concerned, Augustus was a girl's name. I was unable to convince him that I was Rosemary and that Augustus was my brother, thus making the similarity in name, colour, etc., quite understandable—he refused to renew my visa. Two days later, accompanied by two respectable members of the community, one of them a church minister whom I had met at the Student Christian Movement, my brother and I, carrying passports, bank books, university transcripts, birth certificates and letters of acceptance to the fall semester, returned to the immigration office. This time we had a different officer, who looked at us silently, looked at our documents, looked at us, looked at our documents, stamped the extension in my passport, yelled "next" and dismissed us without addressing a word to us. As I left, something in me snapped and I wept hysterically, right there on the steps of the building.

I used to think that nothing in my childhood had prepared me to deal with this nightmare phenomenon. I was angry at my family for raising me as though racism were a foreign unpleasantness, which I would be spared; I felt that they should have either protected me or prepared me better for this degradation.

I envied Black Americans their access to violent struggle—they could fight back. As Black students in Canada, we seemed to have no options but to rail against our treatment in private and keep our heads down in public, trying to get through the four years to graduation without incident, determined to leave this country without a backward glance or kind thought. Racism seemed to pit me against everyone, including myself—my powerlessness sent *me* into a frenzy.

I was wrong, of course; my childhood had prepared me better than I realized to deal with prejudice. Unlike Black Americans and Black Canadians, I did not become a member of a racial minority group until I was an adult with a formed sense of myself. By then, it was too late to imprint on me the term 'inferior.' I knew that all the things that we were told Blacks could not do, all the jobs that were closed to us in this country, were in fact being done ably, competently and sometimes in a superior way by Blacks at home and in other parts of the world. And I came to understand that my frustration and rage stemmed not from the attempts to make me feel inferior but from a realization of my powerlessness and vulnerability, as a foreigner, to do anything about it. My upbringing had not taught me to deal with powerlessness. I was swamped by the feeling that there was nothing I could do about employers or landlords or students or complete strangers who built fences around me and placed obstacles in my path; and I thought of what it must be like to be born Black in this country and to live all of one's life with law, media, education and every other social institution carrying and reinforcing the message of your inferiority every day of your life. I thanked God that had not been my fate and at that time I swore that no child of mine would ever be forced to endure such a fate. I was determined to leave Canada the day after writing my last exam—not even staying around long enough for my convocation.

Even as I write this, I also recall how each incident would send me racing to the West Indian community in search of succor and to drown the violence exploding in my mind in the laughter and the humour, the music, the dance and the camaraderie that I found there. Anything to forget the glares of hate, the obscene epithets, or the look that just went through me as though I wasn't there—and my own unbearable powerlessness.

When I sit around with friends and reminisce about McGill, it seems that on the surface my life was no different from that of other students. Study and party, party and study—deadlines, panic, fun, anxiety, relief, graduation. Yet in those years I changed in profound and basic ways—for I was never the same after my encounter with racial discrimination, Canadian-style. With the passage of time, the hatred faded and disappeared. But I never lost the rage at the injustice, stupidity and blind cruelty of prejudice.

Before I left home, Uncle Karl decided it was necessary to warn me about some of the pitfalls that awaited me in the larger world outside Jamaica. His sharpest admonition concerned the

West Indian Society at McGill, which he had been told was a hotbed of communism. He advised me to stay out of politics and away from the West Indian Society during my sojourn in Canada. He had always been uncomfortable with my outspoken and radical approach to politics, not because he disapproved but because he feared that unless I put it aside during my student years it could be the cause of my speedy and unseemly deportation from Canada. I agreed to heed his advice because I assumed that I would have many years of political activity on my return to Jamaica after graduation. Indeed, my desire to pursue a degree in law was a preparation for political life.

So on registration day when I was approached by a Black male student with a non-Caribbean accent inviting me to join the West Indian Society, I declined, telling him that I was not a communist and had no desire to be involved with a communist organization. Many years later, after we had been married, when Bill would recount our first meeting he liked to say my response made it clear to him that I was "in sore need of an education." It was the challenge this presented, rather than romance, that triggered his initial interest in me. We both chuckle at that explanation since we recall that although there were at least three other West Indian girls present in the registration line that day, I was the only one he approached and invited to join the Society.

As it turned out another student, Noel Edwards, the nephew of a friend of one of my aunts, who I had met in New York while enroute to McGill, happened to be president of the West Indian Society. He laughed at my fears about communists and assured me that so long as he was president it was safe for me to join. Since I was fascinated by him, I threw my Uncle Karl's admonition to the wind and joined the society forthwith. Bill was annoyed that another had succeeded where he had failed. Noel was amused, and I embarked on the most stimulating and important aspect of my university years.

The West Indian Society was consumed with politics. At home, the islands were caught up in the throes of the struggle to become a Caribbean Federation. Students from all the islands had their opinions about the benefits and liabilities of federation for their own island and for the West Indies as a whole. The Society sponsored visiting politicians and speakers, and encouraged debates, arguments, study groups and disagreements among its membership. Everyone held strong beliefs and feelings ran high. The smaller islands feared that the larger ones would gobble them up, and they all feared the power-hungry bent of Jamaica. In time, as history has recorded, the Federation disintegrated. Nonetheless many of the students who were part of that university experience went on (as *I* had intended to do) to enter political life when they returned to their homes.

The years 1950–54 were an important time of learning for me. Graduate students Eric and Phyllis Valere, two of the brightest and most political minds, guided my reading and fostered my analytical growth. We were all frequenters of the Student Christian Movement, and in that community I came to know a different kind of Canadian. Members of the McGill Student Christian Movement did not fit the stereotype of Canadians that I had developed. They were humane, compassionate, worldly, political, and treated me as though I were a person, rather than a Black person. The SCM house was a place for political and sociological discussion and debate, where much of my Canadian left-wing attitude and commitment was bred, fashioned and expanded.

Slowly but surely I began to mature in my political thought. As Premier Duplessis of Quebec became more repressive, and some of the West Indian students were deported because of left-wing political activity, I became paranoid and careful. It was the era of Senator Joe McCarthy in the United States, when people were guilty when accused and remained so until proven innocent; red-baiting was rampant. I knew that I would receive no sympathy if I returned to Jamaica before completing my degree, so although I read voraciously, listened attentively to all the political debates raging around me, and attended Pete Seeger concerts, I signed no petitions, joined no political party and participated in no political activity concerning Canada.

I deliberately closed my mind to the Canadian experience. I was a West Indian student who cared only about West Indian politics, and although I could not ignore the reality of

Duplessis's Quebec, I went to great pains to demonstrate that I could not care less what the people of this racist country did to themselves or to each other.

By the time I graduated with a B.A., Bill Brown and I had decided that we would get married. He had graduated with a doctorate in biochemistry a year ahead of me and had left for British Columbia to attend medical school there. Before he left we had discussed our relationship, and although we had some doubts as to whether our love was made in heaven, we decided that I would remain at McGill to complete my course to graduation. If at the end of that time we still wanted to make a life together, I would join him in British Columbia, where we would get married. After that, I would work and support us through his years of medical school, then it would be his turn to support me in the graduate program of my choice.

We were both ambivalent about our relationship; although it had passed the stage of wild, heart-thumping breathlessness, we still enjoyed each other's company and shared many beliefs and ideas. I considered myself to be in love. Although he was different from Roy in many ways and I realized that I felt differently about him than I did about Roy, I just assumed that I was experiencing the more mature form of love that comes with age. I have always been attracted to exceptionally intelligent and intellectual men who challenged me and forced me to think, and from whom I could learn. Psychologists tell us that girls seek their fathers in their husbands. I guess I unconsciously sought my Uncle Karl, who remained for me one of the brightest, most intelligent and interesting men I had ever known.

Bill met my criteria, and although he was not as tactile and affectionate as I would have liked I convinced myself that, since I was not perfect, I did not believe that I had the right to demand perfection in him. In any event I was sure that I could change him once we were married.

When he left for British Columbia, neither of us was sure that our commitment would survive a year's separation, although we hoped that it would. As it happened, the separation created a fantasy world in which we both lived, writing long romantic letters to each other, running up budget-breaking phone bills and building up expectations for love ever after that it would have been well nigh impossible to sustain.

It also gave me too much time to think about us. During that year I received two other serious proposals of marriage, and wrestled with guilt and doubt about severing ties with Roy and abandoning my plans to return to live in Jamaica. I agonized over the fact that because our life experiences were so diverse, much of what Bill and I loved in each other was perhaps fantasy rather than reality, in which case marriage could prove to be a disastrous mistake.

I began to question whether I really knew him well enough to want to spend the rest of my life with him, despite the fact that we had dated each other relatively exclusively for at least two years. True, I knew all the biographical data about his birth in the southern United States. I knew that he had one sibling, a younger brother. I knew that his father worked for the railroad and that they shared a deep love of trains, that his mother owned and ran her own restaurant and small hotel in Georgia. I had learned that some of his family were farmers, others teachers and small entrepreneurs, that his maternal grandfather had been murdered by the Ku Klux Klan, and another older cousin had barely escaped the South with his life and now lived in exile 'up north.'

I knew that his childhood, though happy, had been 'segregated' and that his ambition had been to be a railroad engineer. This dream was thwarted by the Jim Crow practices of the South that closed such jobs to Black men, so as an alternative he had attended Tuskegee, a Black college in the southern United States, while he pondered what to do with his life. An interesting comment made by the governess in the movie *The Sound of Music* is that whenever a door closes on our dreams, a window opens somewhere else. Such was his experience because in his first year at Tuskegee he met a professor, a graduate of McGill, who encouraged him to do two things—to transfer to McGill University in Canada, and to pursue a more academic program of study.

I also knew that his bright, carefree manner masked anger at a world that would permit him to be a doctor but prevent him from being a railroad engineer, that would make the colour of his skin a prison to limit his options, proscribe his movements and direct his choices.

I also knew that he spent so much time with the West Indian students that we came to forget that he was an American and accepted him as one of us. I knew that I loved him as a kindred spirit who shared my love of dance, music, books and laughter, as well as my hatred of injustice, my reverence for life and, alas, my hopeless addiction to flirtation!

I worried about repeating my mother's experiences, because although I am convinced that I have not been damaged in any obvious way by my mother's many marriages, I had nonetheless formed the intent to marry once and once only, and to make that marriage work. Choice of mate, therefore, was crucial to me. So, as the days approached for my journey to Vancouver, my physical and emotional need for Bill wrestled with my doubts about our ability to create and sustain a permanent monogamous relationship and face the challenging demands of family life. Yet I made no move to cancel or postpone my plans, and looked forward with anticipation and pleasure to being with him again.

In retrospect I am appalled that all the life options that I considered on graduation revolved around my relationship with the men in my life. As well as Bill, there was one friend who suggested that I apply to law school in England, where he would be, so that we could be together – I actually did that and was accepted by Lincoln's Inn (lovingly referred to by foreign students as the Colonial Inn) to study there. Then there was the old childhood friend who suddenly declared his love and suggested that if we married I could do a graduate degree in social work at McGill while he did his graduate work, and, viewing this as another option, I submitted my application to the McGill School of Social Work while I mulled over his proposal. And there was my other friend who suggested that we marry and return to Jamaica where he would attend medical school and I would study law at the University of the West Indies.

So there I was, an adult in my final year at university who was willing to go anywhere, study anything, depending on which man I thought I was in love with at the time.

Often when I speak to women students today, I am struck at what a difference feminism has wrought in their thinking and their attitude. I am always pleased and relieved to meet these students who are planning their lives according to their own goals and their aspirations, rather than the goals and plans of the men with whom they are involved. I recognize that these women are still in the minority, but I am glad that they exist and I hope that their numbers will increase.

In the end I chose to follow Bill to Vancouver. I like to tell the story that he promised to make me happy ever after if I followed him to British Columbia and married him. I also like to tease that I kept *my* end of the bargain! There have been times when I have wondered how my life would have been different if I had accepted one of the other marriage proposals. In any event, there is no doubt in my mind that I would have hated to miss the exciting rollercoaster that life with Bill has been, and the challenges he has encouraged and supported me in exploring.

CHAPTER THREE

I arrived in Vancouver on the evening of August 7, 1955. I was so nervous that I sat frozen in my seat and was the last person to leave the plane. Bill was so happy to see me that my fears immediately vanished. The following morning we went to the B.C. vital statistics office on West 10th Avenue, picked up a marriage licence and submitted to a venereal disease test. The law in B.C. at that time was that if either of us proved positive on the VD test we could not marry each other. Bill seemed sure that his Wassermann would be negative so I decided not to worry about it.

Sophisticated as I considered myself to be about most things, when it came to venereal and other kinds of sexually transmitted diseases I was truly ignorant. In retrospect I am horrified by the ease with which I relinquished responsibility in all matters pertaining to sex to Bill. I just accepted that he was more knowledgeable and expert in those matters than I was, and that since he proclaimed verbally as well as in writing that he loved and cherished me, I could feel secure that he would take care of my best interest in these things.

When we arrived at the office of vital statistics, the clerk told us to return on Friday for our results; after that, if we were disease-free, we could marry on Saturday, August 13. My response was instantaneous. "No way," I said, "I will not marry on the thirteenth day of any month, we'll have to wait until

41

Monday." Bill, who was not superstitious, disagreed; he was not prepared to postpone our nuptials until Monday. He wanted to marry immediately after we got the results, because he had already waited a year for our wedding and that was long enough. Bill proceeded to get into a long and heated argument with the clerk concerning the reasons for waiting until Saturday to get married if we knew on Friday that we did not have VD. "Wasn't there a risk that we could get VD by Saturday," he asked. It seemed to him that the sooner we married after receiving the results of the test the safer the province would be from the possibility of either of us catching any dreaded sexually transmitted disease. The clerk conveyed his suggestion to her superior, who came to the counter and joined the discussion only to inform us that it would be against regulations for us to marry on the day we were diagnosed as being free of VD.

At that point Bill explained that he was a medical student, that he had studied venereal disease at great length and in detail and that his medical opinion was that it was far safer for us to marry immediately that we were proven VD-free rather than a minute later. At this point the superior stated that, in fact, our results would be received in the office on Thursday. Bill expressed horror at the increase in risk if we waited two days after the results were received to marry, and urged her to reconsider her ruling. After some thought she agreed that, although it was highly irregular, if we arrived to pick up our results by 9 a.m. on Friday, since that was actually one day after the results were received in the office, we would be permitted to marry that same day.

Since the marriage registry was in the same building as the VD clinic, right across the hall actually, we thanked her and arranged to pick up our results at 9 a.m. on August 12 and to marry in the registry across the hall at 9:15.

Our marriage exposed me to another face of Canada. One of our witnesses was Bill's landlady, Mrs. Olive Reid. I was surprised to meet a Canadian landlady who was nice, decent, and appeared to be completely non-racist. She certainly challenged my stereotype and over the years she and her husband, children and grandchildren all became our very close friends.

Worried that we would have no wedding guests, one of her sons, Jack, his wife Doreen and their two babies as well as Olive's husband Cecil all attended the very small ceremony in the Registrar's office. Our other witnesses were Joyce and Jason Routtenberg, who were friends of friends from Montreal, and Ozzie Dawkins, a Jamaican medical student who was in the year ahead of Bill at the University of British Columbia.

A reception was organized by Ozzie at one of the fraternity houses, and he invited all of his classmates to attend. A few of Bill's classmates attended too. But I knew no one except the Reids, the Routtenbergs, Ozzie and Bill. Despite that, we received many gifts, and the reception became a roaring party that we were later told continued long after we left on our honeymoon.

I was pleasantly surprised and puzzled by the warmth and affection of everyone. In all my years in Montreal I had never experienced anything like that—it was as though these people were colour blind. Over the years I came to know that they were a special and unique collection of human beings who were no more examples of the perfect Canadian than racists were the example of imperfect Canadians; and in time I learned that as in Montreal, racism was alive and well in British Columbia.

Because my initial contact was such a surprisingly happy one, I fell in love with British Columbia and its people, and I thanked heaven that the memory of Canada I had been carrying around in my head was being changed and widened to include decent landlords and landladies, friendly fraternity brothers and sisters, and people who cared enough about others to share happy and special moments with them, regardless of race.

I had wanted to be married in Jamaica among my family and friends, but Bill could not afford such a luxury, and even though my family offered to finance his trip down to the island for the wedding, he declined. He was adamant about not accepting money from my family. It was a matter of pride with him then and later that we never sought any financial assistance from my family. I admired his principles at the time, but despite everyone's kindness it was a lonely wedding for me. At what appeared to be the height of the reception, we left the fraternity house on West 8th Avenue to catch the CPR midnight ferry to

Victoria, where we planned to enjoy the two-day honeymoon our limited budget permitted. On board we settled into our tiny stateroom with the same sorts of doubts and anticipation that I suppose other honeymoon couples have about the years ahead – and about our sexual compatibility and ability to survive the hours ahead.

I opened my fancy luggage and lovingly unfolded my beautiful white lace negligee, bought specifically for that night. Bill opened his luggage and pulled out a bottle of rye. Panic gripped me. I suddenly felt that I did not really know the man I had married – I knew the fantasy, but what if the reality was that I had married an alcoholic with no pajamas? I controlled my fears, performed my ablutions, donned my white lace negligee, and waited. Bill removed his clothing, performed his ablutions and opened his bottle of rye. Even as I write this, I am reliving the panic as I remember the shock of realizing that not only did he not have pajamas but that, although he thought my negligee was pretty, he certainly did not think that I planned to sleep in it.

Over the years, throughout my relationships with boys or men there had always existed two Rosemarys. There was the cool, sure, sophisticated woman on the outside and the inse-cure, old-fashioned little girl on the inside. There was clearly a great deal of confusion around my sexual identity, and the submissive, dependent Rosemary I secretly believed to be the real me was always struggling to remain hidden behind the assertively smart, independent Rosemary, true to the role the women in my family had created for me. And though I admired my mother for never staying in a marriage that oppressed her, I envied my friends and relatives who lived in stable, traditional families, and secretly dreamed of such a family for myself.

Much of the ambivalence and anxiety I had about getting married was rooted in the determination that for me there would be only one marriage and that it had to work. I was determined that my children would not be subject to the economic and emotional stress I had come to know went with a 'broken home,' nor experience the loss that, in an almost intangible way, I had felt growing up without a father of my own.

Let me digress here to tell you that until my honeymoon, Coca Cola had always been my drink of choice. I seemed to be able to get as high on it and have as much fun as people who were drinking alcohol. Years later when it was revealed that the original Coca Cola had traces of cocaine in it, Bill remarked that that would certainly explain my behaviour at that time. I am so allergic to so many drugs that it is quite possible that one drop of cocaine in a bottle of Coke was all that was needed for me to experience an advanced state of euphoria. In any event, that honeymoon night, in my determination to appear 'cool' and 'with it,' I downed two straight ryes in succession, felt the warmth of the liquid spreading slowly through my body, climbed out of my white lace, virginal negligee and tried to fit into the lower bunk with my spouse.

Just as I was thinking that maybe everything was going to be okay there was a loud knock on the door followed by a chorus of loud male voices singing "We know what you're doing." Suddenly we remembered that Bill's landlord and the veterans from his regiment were also on the boat, on their way to a reunion in Victoria. I died with embarrassment as I lay there listening to Bill laughing and whispering to me that we should at least shout a response, as the voices in the corridor sang louder and louder "We know what you're doing!" The following morning, I insisted that we get off the ferry early before any of the other passengers awoke, and head for the old Dominion Hotel on Blanshard Street where we planned to stay during our two-day honeymoon.

I enjoyed our honeymoon. We walked through the city with its little shops and restaurants all striving to look like replicas of English buildings — the flower baskets hanging from the lamp standards were a mass of colour, high tea at the Empress Hotel was impressive, the weather was perfect. We went to a movie, lost our marriage certificate and then found it, to my relief, since I was convinced that no one would believe that we were married because we were so happy, and I needed to have it as proof of the legitimacy of our union. I thought Victoria was the cleanest and prettiest city I had ever seen. I knew that I would return to enjoy it on many other occasions, but I never dreamt that one day I would be an elected member of the legislature, and serve in the imposing legislative building, which looked like a fantasy castle when its hundreds of light bulbs were turned on at night.

Immediately on our return to Vancouver, I began job hunting. It soon became clear that the reluctance of employers to hire Black people was even more entrenched here than in Montreal. Indeed, the front page story of the day was of a teacher at an exclusive private school who had married a Jamaican woman who was Black, and the consternation that this caused despite her protestations that she was only one-fifth Black and therefore more white than Black. The Black population here was small and scattered, and the unwritten rule seemed to be that, aside from entertainment, the special jobs open to them were domestic work for women, and portering on the trains for men. There were, as with all things, a handful of exceptions, but for the most part when I showed up for job interviews at banks or offices, personnel managers seemed very surprised that I had responded to their advertisements.

I explored every avenue in my job search. I used the services of employment agencies as well as the newspapers. An employee at one of the employment agencies finally confessed that she wished that she could return my fee, because she was sure that she would never be able to find me a job except as a domestic. Part of my job search included a visit to UBC to file an application with their employment office. Things became so desperate that Jason Routtenberg, a friend from Montreal who had been one of the witnesses at our wedding, decided to create a job for me in his two-person accounting firm. I refused to accept his very generous offer; I was determined to find the one person in the whole city of Vancouver who would look beyond the colour of my skin and would hire me solely on the basis of my competence as a typist and my Bachelor of Arts degree from McGill.

It was an economic boom period in Canada, there were more jobs than there were workers to fill them, and I decided that if this was a city in which people would rather survive without an employee than hire a Black person, then it certainly was not a city we would want to live in. Bill and I would have to explore alternative ways of surviving the three remaining years of his education — even if that meant we had to be separated, and I had to return to Jamaica in order to secure employment.

We were not destitute, of course. We had savings from our summer jobs plus $1,000 that my family had given us as a wedding present; as well, Bill received a small monthly cheque from his parents. So by 1955 standards there was really more rage than panic in our situation.

Since I spent all my time job-hunting, Bill decided to take responsibility for finding us an apartment. Moreover he had been in Vancouver for a year and knew exactly where he wanted to live. He wished to be near the university since most of his classmates lived there; it was cheaper to be able to walk to classes rather than use the bus and it was convenient to the library and labs. Again, it soon became very obvious that like the Montreal landlords and landladies, those in Point Grey were unwilling to rent us even a basement suite.

In 1955 Black students were a rarity at UBC and Dr. Gordon Shrum, who was in charge of student housing, found that he had to give them priority in university housing, because the neighbours of the university were certainly unwilling to do so. However, because we had not anticipated a problem, by the time we realized how critical our situation was, we were too late for university housing that semester, so our name went on a waiting list and Bill kept searching. It was desperate, depressing work and after many failures we decided that job-hunting and house-hunting were draining too much of our time and energy. It was clear that the racial barriers in the city were too intact to respond to our feeble assault, so we accepted defeat and agreed that we would stop trying to find decent, good quality shelter and live wherever we could find housing, whether it was suitable or not. Clearly this was not our town so we would remain here only as long as necessary, then arrange to leave this province within five minutes of Bill writing his final exam, never to return.

Despite the efforts of white friends and classmates who

themselves had no difficulty finding housing, since there was actually a glut of apartments on the market, we found that we were not welcome in the West End, nor in the neighbourhood around Vancouver General Hospital. We finally managed to rent a bachelor suite in an old converted house at the corner of 6th Avenue and Spruce overlooking a dirty and sluggish False Creek, which at that time gave no hint of its trendy, fashionable future. The rent was $40 a month and accommodation consisted of one room with cooking facilities and a bathroom down the hall that we shared with two other tenants on the same floor.

That experience was the beginning of our bathroom fetish—we swore that if we survived that situation, we would never share a bathroom with anyone again. We furnished our suite with a double bed, two bamboo armchairs, a coffee table and a small kitchen table with two straightback chairs. We had received dishes and saucepans and linen and everything else as wedding presents, so we were very comfortable as we settled in to get through the next three years of our life.

A week after we moved into our apartment I answered an ad placed by the Registered Nurses Association of B.C. for a clerical worker. When I arrived for my interview, I was introduced to Miss Alice Wright, the president, who spoke happily of her visits to Jamaica and of the friends she had made among the nursing community there. She asked why I was applying for such a junior position despite my clerical experience and university degree. I explained about the difficulty I was having in securing employment. She was genuinely upset by my story and offered me the job although she felt that I was overqualified for it; she insisted that I treat it as a temporary placement until something better came along.

I worked at the Registered Nurses Association office on Cypress Street for one year at $130 per month, until I was hired to work as a library assistant at UBC for $181 monthly. I remained in that job until a month before the birth of our first child and only daughter, Cleta.

As employment goes I was lucky; other non-white immigrants with more skills and better education have had to work a lot harder under worse conditions for less money. I have always been grateful to Miss Wright and the RNABC for being 'the one person' willing to employ me despite the colour of my skin.

Over the years I developed the 'one person' theory, on the basis that no matter how many people in a situation are willing to discriminate against you for racial, religious or other reasons, there is always 'the one person' who will refuse to go along with the pack. So the secret to living with discrimination is to hang on and keep fighting until 'the one person' in any given situation is found – because that person always exists. Certainly the story of my life in Canada is the history of these 'one persons' who always marched to a different drum when prejudice and discrimination surfaced.

A friend once asked me whether the Jamaican McGill graduates who encouraged me to attend university in Canada had discussed Canadian racism with me, and I realized with some surprise that no one mentioned the topic even once during all of our briefings. Even more surprising was the realization that on similar occasions when I had spoken to students planning to attend Canadian universities, I had never raised the question of racism either.

Everyone knew of and spoke openly and at great lengths about racism in the United States; everyone spoke openly and at great length of our sense of betrayal at finding racism in the mother country – England – but for some strange reason we did not discuss racism in Canada.

Part of the reason, I guess, is because of the subtle and polite nature of Canada's particular brand of racism. We often found it difficult to describe to each other racist experiences because, except in the case of housing and employment, their form was so nebulous – a hostile glance – silence – being left to occupy two seats on the bus while people stood because no one wanted to sit beside you – being stopped and questioned about your movements by the police in daytime in your own neighbour-hood – the assumption of every salesperson who rang your doorbell that you were the maid. How do you protect yourself against such practices? How do you tell someone to beware? How do you explain that sometimes you feel ashamed to be the recipient of such treatment and that the reluctance to acknowledge its existence is somehow linked to lowered self-esteem and self-worth?

I believe that if you are going to be a Black person living in a racist country, it is best to be born a middle child. The sense of humour you develop to compensate for the fact that you are neither the first-born (with the attendant privileges of that position) nor the youngest and pampered, stands you in good stead when racial stupidity intrudes on your life. I developed humour as an armour and I learnt in time how to use it as a teaching tool to turn insensitivity into a crash course in tolerance. When the saleslady in the exclusive dress shop who was waiting on me as I tried on a very expensive ultrasuede suit asked with a smile whether I was a singer, I replied with a smile that no, I was not, neither was I a boxer! We both laughed at my response, and the message was sent and received that Black people earn their living like everyone else in a variety of different ways. Humour doesn't ease the pain or deflect the hurt of the victim, it just penetrates the mind of the perpetrator because her or his defences are down.

After two years in our bachelor pad, my pregnancy precipitated the need for us to seek larger accommodation, and once again we were faced with the tedious reality of anti-Black and anti-children landlords and landladies. Pregnancy compounded our dilemma: now we could be refused housing, not because we were Black but on the ground that we were about to have a child. Many landlords were relieved to be able to tell us how much they wished they could rent to us because they really like 'our people,' but unfortunately the other tenants would rebel at the prospect of a baby in the building. That experience was the beginning of a fear that has grown over the years, namely that Canadians as a people do not like having children around and often just barely tolerate their own.

In any event, once again just when it seemed that there was no hope, 'the one person' in all of Vancouver willing to look beyond our colour and my pregnancy and rent us accommodation appeared. In this case, it was Margot Ney, a school teacher who had given birth to her daughter in July, one month before Cleta, our daughter, was born, and her husband Phil, a medical student in the year behind Bill. They described themselves as Christians, who believed that because all people are created in God's image, no one person or group of persons was inferior to any other person or group, and that to hold a prejudice against anyone would be to hold a prejudice against God. We had been discriminated against by so many Christians over the years that we had ceased to think of Christianity as having anything whatsoever to do with humanity.

Phil and Margot were truly special. We became their tenants. Our daughters became and remain fast friends and, despite differences in belief and commitment on very basic and fundamental issues, we all remain part of a loving and extended family—a really strange fact considering that Phil, a psychiatrist, is opposed to feminism and the right to reproductive choice; that Margot returned to university to study law at age forty and is one of the leading legal supporters of the anti-abortion movement in B.C. I remain firm in my belief that the control of one's reproduction is an inalienable right that should not be wrested from women by government or law—and that, if women lose that right, their enslavement will be complete. The Neys and the Browns never discussed abortion during the years both families lived together, and during which our respect and love for each other grew. So, by the time the abortion debate began to divide friends and relatives, we already had too much respect and love for each other not to accept the right of each of us to her or his personal belief and commitment. Even today, although we oppose very strongly each other's opinion on this controversial issue, and even though we would dearly love to convince each other of the rightness of our positions, we accept our differences and our love survives.

By 1956 the Black population at UBC was increasing, albeit slowly. More students, especially from Trinidad, were coming to take advanced degrees in agriculture and other sciences. They were also coming to understand and appreciate the similarity of their on- and off-campus experiences. Bill and Ozzie Dawkins, the Jamaican medical student who had planned our wedding reception, decided that the time had come to organize a West Indian Society. They were both disappointed that there was no centre to the West Indian community, and, although they appreciated International House for the haven that it was, they longed for the peculiar rapport and camaraderie of a West Indian Society like the one at McGill and other eastern universities. They hoped that such a society would create a place where consciousness-raising as well as political debate would combine with fun and socializing, bolstering the self-esteem and combatting the loneliness of being a 'foreign' student.

The Black West Indians flocked to join the organization, but they soon made it clear that they were primarily interested in the social aspects of the club. The legacy of Senator McCarthy hung heavy in the air and everyone took great pains to steer clear of any political discussion or involvement. In the Caribbean, the Federation of the West Indies had disintegrated, and individuals were focusing more on the politics of their own particular island than on global issues. Bill and I were desperate for political debate and discussion and we really missed the engrossing and stimulating discussions that had been so much a part of our life in Montreal. It seemed that in Vancouver, everyone was caught up in studies and personal or superficial concerns as well as the nationalistic chauvinism that is so much a part of people from small countries. The West Indian Society was not our only social contact. We also became part of a small group of the married classmates of Bill's year who partied together and shared our concerns about children, mounting debts and the future. After our daughter was born, I stayed home until she was six months old, then returned to work, this time for the Faculty of Commerce at UBC. For us, life revolved around our daughter, my work, Bill's studies and our friends.

Although we occasionally saw other Black people in the city and would always smile and say hello, it was not until Bill's third year in medicine that we actually became acquainted with any members of the British Columbia Black community. During a hospital rotation at the Vancouver General Hospital, Bill met a patient named Dolores Collins. He was so excited that he phoned me on his lunch break that day to tell me of this first meeting with a real live Black Canadian in Vancouver. Mrs. Collins seemed genuinely pleased to know him, and they chatted every day that she remained in the hospital. On her discharge we were invited to her home for dinner and there we met Frank, her husband, and their children, and learnt about the B.C. Association for the Advancement of Coloured People, which was just in its formative year—Frank was the president.

It was the beginning of a truly wonderful friendship that changed our life in B.C. Bill was especially happy. He was tired of being surrounded by West Indians, much as he loved us, and he longed for contact with American Black people. He found that the Collinses and the Holmeses, two couples in the Black community, and their friends had more in common with him than West Indians did, and he embraced the Black community of Vancouver with eagerness and joy. We joined the BCAACP immediately and became very involved in its struggle against racism in British Columbia. In the process we learnt much about what it was like to grow up as a true visible minority person in this province.

The BCAACP was patterned after the American NAACP. It was neither the oldest nor even the most powerful Black organization in B.C. at that time. The Union of Sleeping Car Porters had a larger membership than any other Black organization. The Marcus Garvey Movement, although still in existence, was small and not very active. The Black American Church had lost most of its members, and its preachers, like its congregation, drifted away to join other mainline churches. There was no highly visible Black ghetto as in Montreal and in many American cities, but with one exception all of the Black families lived and owned homes in the east end of Vancouver. The exception was Mrs. Ruby Sneed, who lived with her husband and two daughters on West 8th Avenue near Alma and taught piano lessons. We soon came to know that many members of the Black community were members of one large extended family that included the Ramseys, the Sneeds, the Collinses and others who had migrated here from Edmonton, Alberta. In the late 1970s when I was invited to speak at a reunion of the Alberta Black community, I discovered that just about all our friends in the Vancouver Black community were in attendance.

The BCAACP under the leadership of Frank Collins was an active and aggressive organization. It established a few priorities for itself and pursued them vigorously. It was determined to open up housing and employment to Black people and to ensure that young Black people pursued education and professions as one means of fighting discrimination.

Over the years I sat on the executive of the organization, and both Bill and I worked with it in its efforts to force the provincial government to introduce human rights legislation and a human rights commission. Neither of these goals was achieved until after the election of a New Democratic Party government in 1972, an election in which Emery Barnes and I became the first Black people to be elected to any provincial parliament in Canada's history.

The BCAACP was responsible for raising the consciousness of the Vancouver community around Black issues and for increasing the pride of the community in itself. It was not a radical organization and it enjoyed a lot of support in the white community. The daily newspapers were very cooperative in reporting its activities, and in time it became the organization that spoke for all Black British Columbians, its opinions being respected by all levels of government. In later years more radical Black organizations took over its place in the limelight, but none of them has equalled or surpassed the BCAACP and its lasting impact on the quality of life of the Black people of this province.

By the time Bill graduated in 1958 either our painful memories were fading or Vancouver was changing. In any event we were expecting our second child and planning to purchase a house and put down roots in Vancouver. I still longed to return to Jamaica, and especially so that my children could grow up in a warm and loving Black environment, and Bill had nostalgic longings for the stimulation and excitement of Montreal.

Bill's career plans ruled out both options. At a time when internships were becoming difficult to secure he was fortunate to have been accepted at the Vancouver General Hospital. By that time, also, he had decided not to return to research but to pursue the specialty of psychiatry. When in addition he had been assured of a position in the UBC residency program under Dr. Jim Tyhurst, we accepted that we would be living in Vancouver for a long time.

Before marriage, Bill and I had spent hours exploring the options of where we would settle down. We desperately wanted to live and raise our children in a Black environment, I because my experience had been such a positive one and he because growing up a Black child in the southern United States had been so fraught with anxiety and tension. Despite this, wherever we looked, it seemed that political instability, economic underdevelopment and lack of social resources were the lot of the English-speaking Black countries of the world. Bill believed that we owed our children the best education, the best health care and political stability. He was convinced we could compensate for their minority status through teaching and example.

I disagreed on every point except the one of political stability. I was not willing to expose the children or myself to civil wars and violent uprising. However, I believed that the building of self-respect and self-esteem that comes from living as a member of a majority group was more important than health care or education. Also, because I came in contact with racism later in life I knew that there was a qualitative difference to life for a Black person in a white community. Because that Black person is always 'on guard.' A seventh sense is developed that is always alert, a radar scanning for hostile signals. I remember reading somewhere that Black women in North America never let their babies out of their sight when away from home—not in a shopping buggy or on a playground swing—not because they were afraid their children would fall, wander off, or get into mischief, but because they feared that someone would hurt them.

Black people have a sense that one is always in danger. And conveying to one's offspring at the earliest possible time the importance of always being 'on guard' had always been the primary responsibility of Black parents raising children in a white environment. Black parents overprotect their children in the same way that women overprotect their daughters. They know that for them the world is a truly dangerous place.

The discussions about a place to live escalated to arguments, but Bill was adamant. He believed that it was important for our children to live and survive and excel in this country. I have always felt that there was no substitute for a Jamaican childhood and that my children were deprived because they did not have that experience, although I must confess that they seem none the worse for the lack. Eventually, the compromise we worked out was that at the completion of his medical training, we would return to Montreal. He would complete his residency and establish a practice there, and I would return to McGill to study law. We would be close to Jamaica and to his family in Georgia and our children would have easy access to both these Black communities.

Like so many of our life plans, the future took on a direction of its own. The subtle magic and beauty of British Columbia, combined with the FLQ uprising in Quebec, convinced us that British Columbia was home and that we should put down our roots right here.

My second pregnancy, in 1959, also precipitated a rethinking of my own career goals. I rejected the study of law as no longer feasible for a number of reasons. For one, I would be quite old by the time Bill completed his four-year residency, and each year that I was away from university my doubts about my ability to handle a long, rigorous academic program increased.

With each passing year Bill had contributed less and less to responsibilities around the home since his studies were so demanding, and I began to doubt my ability to juggle parenting, homemaking and studying. So I decided that I would have to pursue a program that was shorter and less demanding than law, but I had no idea what it would be. Bill repeated his commitment to support me during my course of study in return for the four years I would have to work while he pursued his psychiatric residency, plus the four years he had studied medicine and interned. I found myself negotiating for eight years of educational support, even as I was deciding that I would have to restrict to less than four years the time of study I could pursue.

We accepted that B.C. was home—in 1959 we applied for and received our Canadian citizenship. For better or for worse this was our country now. We were Canadians and what happened to this country was part of our responsibility since we now had the right to become actively involved in its workings.

CHAPTER FOUR

One of the most important memories of my youth was the visit to Jamaica by Paul Robeson, when he addressed thousands of Jamaicans who had gathered at Racecourse, an open air arena, to hear him sing and speak. He gave the concert free of charge so all who wanted to could hear him.

Paul Robeson had always been a larger-than-life hero to Black people. We were proud that his talent and brains, his athletic achievements and artistic triumphs had not led him to escape into glittering vulgarity. We were proud that he had recognized the need that Black people had for him to be a role model and to speak out on our behalf against injustice wherever it existed. Unlike Jack Johnson and some other high-profile Black performers, we felt no ambivalence about him; we loved him openly and worshipped him shamelessly. Bill clings to his memory of a visit Paul made to Montreal to sing at a concert, when he found the time to sit and speak for hours with a group of students from the West Indian Society at McGill.

The attack launched against him by the government of the United States, which was determined to destroy him and his livelihood, filled us with pain and anger. His communist politics did not tarnish him in any way in our eyes and we followed his exile from America, and his eventual death, with sorrow. We were left with a sense of loss, and deeply depressed.

We moved into a small, rented two-bedroom house, and our second child, Gary, was born soon after the death of Bill's mother in 1959. Her death had a profound impact on him. She had hoped that he would return to live in the United States, and he had always felt guilty about not wanting to do so. He dreaded the day when he would have to tell her that he would be relinquishing his American citizenship to become a Canadian. She became ill and, after a short but painful bout with cancer, died soon after a visit to Vancouver. She adored her granddaughter, who bears a very strong resemblance to her. Bill's father also died of cancer a year later, and Bill felt that with his death the important ties that had held him to the United States were severed. It was nearly twenty years before he visited his homeland again, although his brother, aunts and other relatives visited us in Vancouver and his family maintained close ties via the telephone and letters.

On the surface, our life was uneventful, but the birth of children mobilized us into wanting to change the community and world in which we lived. All around us Canadians were organizing to protest the worldwide testing of nuclear weapons; women across Canada linked their forces in the powerful Voice of Women organization, which called on Canadians to raise our voices against the threat to our children and our world that was inherent in the fallout from the continued testing of nuclear weapons.

A small branch of the Voice of Women was formed in our neighbourhood. We used to meet regularly in our homes for the exchange of ideas and information and to develop lobbying action directed at the federal government. We collected our babies' teeth and sent them off to be part of research about the presence of strontium-90 in breast milk and cows' milk. We prepared briefs, participated in marches, signed petitions, wrote letters to newspapers and politicians – all with the one goal of bringing an end to nuclear testing.

This was the first involvement in the peace movement for Bill and me. Through it we met people who shared our concerns not only for peace but for human rights and justice as well. It was also our first involvement in Canadian politics. Because we were now Canadian citizens, we were not afraid of deportation;

and because we were parents, we were prepared to take any risks to ensure that the world was safe and secure for our children. Involvement with the Voice of Women helped us break through the paranoia and the fear of the McCarthy hearings in the United States, which had frozen us into inaction, and for the first time we were prepared to take risks. On two occasions eggs were thrown at our front door; this time, however, the attack was not because we were Black but because we were working for peace.

In time internal friction blew the Voice of Women organization apart: in Vancouver, we saw it as an Eastern Canadian struggle, so we continued working within our neighbourhood group. Some of the original members of that group—Igna Heiden, Jim and Irene Foulkes, Ross and Olive Johnson, Hillary and Geoffrey Bursill-Hall, Joyce Routtenberg—became close friends. In 1986 when my granddaughter Katherine, aged two years, joined me on her first peace march along with my youngest son Jonathan, aged twenty-one, and nearly 100,000 other Vancouverites, I could not help but remember those first early marches for peace when Bill and I and two babies (Cleta and Gary) were part of a tiny group of less than 1,000 participants.

As our second baby grew older the time approached for me to return to work. I would have returned to UBC except for one of those accidents of fate, which at the time seem unimportant, yet prove to be pivotal. Our friend Joyce Routtenberg, who had been one of the witnesses at our wedding and who was very active in our neighbourhood peace group, decided that she wanted to be a foster parent. In applying to the Vancouver Children's Aid Society for a foster child she recommended me as a personal reference.

One of the social workers from the Children's Aid Society visited me to discuss Joyce's application. After she had completed her interview about Joyce, we had tea and discussed social work and the work done by the Children's Aid Society. I spoke of my interest in social work and my dilemma in deciding on a career. She suggested that prior to making a decision about what I wanted to do, I should work as a social work aide at the Children's Aid Society. The prerequisite for the job was a general arts degree. If after working for a year I decided to become a social worker, I would be given a leave of absence to secure my degree. Bill and I discussed this suggestion and we agreed that it seemed like a good idea while I was trying to decide what other career options to explore.

Before this I had been toying with the idea of becoming a writer and had enrolled in a creative writing course taught at UBC by the writer Jane Rule. It was a night course, which I could attend while Bill cared for the children. My legacy from the course was a wonderful friendship with Jane and an armload of rejection slips from some of the most prestigious magazines in North America. Jane thought that one way of accurately testing my ability was to have my writing appraised by the best magazines in North America; so I had wonderful warm letters rejecting my stories and poems but encouraging me to keep writing.

But, because of my relationship with my Aunt Leila, the idea of social work intrigued me. I had always admired the way she had mobilized people to change their lives in positive ways; in some ways social work did not seem too different from the profession of law, since it was a way of helping the defenceless to defend themselves.

I explored all these ideas with Bill. This was a period of great closeness between us. He sensed my growing frustration with homemaking, and he really wanted to help me to become more involved in interesting pursuits. He has always been unusual in that respect. Because his mother and all the women in his family had professions and worked outside the home, he seemed to accept that this was the norm for women. He did not believe that homemaking offered sufficient intellectual stimulation and reward for a woman, any more than it did for a man, and he never expected or encouraged me to make motherhood and homemaking a full-time job. He believed that all women were like his mother, and he assumed that it was natural for those women who wanted to work outside the home to do so. I later learned that his view of the world through his mother's experiences skewed his appreciation of feminism in strange and subtle ways. Because he had never lived in an equal relationship with a feminist – and because what is acceptable in a mother is not necessarily so in a spouse – the difference between the intellectual acceptance of women's equality and the reality proved problematic for him in many ways.

I applied and was accepted as a social work aide at the Children's Aid Society. My salary was $185 monthly and I was responsible for a general caseload that included children in foster care and group homes, and unmarried women in private placements as well as at the Salvation Army Maywood Home. I remained at the Children's Aid Society for two years; I learnt much about the suffering of children. Foster parents who were in the business because they loved children were a rarity. More often fostering was perceived to be a way to make a few extra dollars while a woman was at home rearing her own children. However, because government, then as now, computed the accurate cost of raising a child and paid the foster parents considerably less, expecting them to subsidize the cost of that child's care, foster parents found that caring for these children was an economic liability rather than an asset, and the drop-out rate was high.

On many occasions I would go home and plead with Bill to adopt one baby or another that had come into care, especially if the child were Native Indian or Black. I knew that the future of such babies was bleak and meant the transfer from one foster home to another while they awaited an adoption that would often never happen.

At the same time, I was angry with both the Native community and the Black community for allowing their babies to be the wards of the white community. I developed migraine headaches and stomach problems, both as a result of my frustration at being unable to do anything to help the children and because of my anger at what I considered the neglect of the children by both of these communities.

I had grown up in an environment where people who could always took care of children in need. My grandmother, mother and all of my aunts adopted children – not legally, they just took them into their homes and assumed responsibility for them. Uncle Karl never did, but all the women in my family did, as did many other families in Jamaica at that time. Bill was adamant in his opposition to either formal or informal adoption. He felt that our responsibility was to our own children, and he vetoed every attempt I made to open our home to those children.

(During that time at the Children's Aid Society I made many friends, including Allan Fotheringham, who was enamoured of a beautiful social worker; to his chagrin, she chose later to marry Eric Nesterenko, the hockey player, and moved to Detroit. Allan displayed his passion for Barbara by generously leaving his red convertible sports car with her whenever he had to go out of town. She would take a couple of us tootling off to the beach on our lunch break, with the top down when the weather was good. Allan was writing a travel column for the *Vancouver Sun* at that time, which was wonderful, because it meant that he travelled a lot, giving us generous access to the little red bomb.)

The experience of my two years at the Children's Aid Society convinced me that every child who is born should be a wanted child, and that to throw a child on the mercy of the state should be the absolute last and most desperate resort of a parent.

The Children's Aid Society did a superhuman job of caring for the unprotected children of Vancouver, and the decision to phase out its service was a mistake. Today there is much concern about the trend of young girls who become parents to keep their babies—I share that concern, because of the immaturity and the lack of financial resources of these young women. However, I am not convinced that those babies would be better off adopted or placed in foster homes than they would be with their natural mothers, if more resources were available to help these mothers discharge their parenting responsibilities.

My experience has convinced me that as a society we would benefit if we educated young women about the real hardship of single parenthood and the need to take full responsibility for their sexual acts and reproductive choices. However, if and when they do become pregnant, we would also be better off to ensure that the resources are in place to assist them to be competent and able parents. The decision of the Social Credit government in British Columbia in 1988 to force single mothers with babies over the age of six months to work outside the home was vindictive, stupid and dangerous. Parents, not governments, know what's best for a child, so the decision of women who choose to remain at home with their children should be respected. As a nation we pay for a government's cruelty and stupidity with increased pressure on our mental health, social service and penal systems. More importantly, the decision unleashes on our society a large number of adults who have been the victims of sexual and physical abuse and neglect, and no nation can begin to compute the destructive impact of such a phenomenon.

At the end of my two years at the Vancouver Children's Aid Society I applied to and was accepted into the Bachelor of Social Work program at UBC. That was a very difficult year for me. All my fears about juggling parenting, homemaking and studying proved well grounded. Bill was giving less assistance at home and spending less time with the family. As he became more engrossed in his work, tension developed between us. I was always tired, overworked and fighting a cold.

On one occasion when I had an important school deadline to meet and felt yet another cold coming on, I took two penicillin tablets and headed for my desk. Bill had gone to the movies after putting Cleta and Gary to bed, so that I could have absolute quiet in which to work. In a few minutes my heart began to race, my throat began to close and I was gasping for breath. I thought that I was dying. I staggered upstairs to kiss my babies good-bye and headed back downstairs to telephone the neighbours. I must have passed out on my way down, because when I opened my eyes I was in Emergency at the Vancouver General Hospital.

Bill tells me that he had been standing in line at the Dunbar movie theatre waiting to purchase his ticket when he suddenly decided that he didn't want to see that particular film after all. He immediately returned home and found me unconscious at the foot of the stairs. He had no idea what had happened to me except that I had a very slow pulse, so he gave me a shot of adrenalin, called in the neighbours and asked them to keep an eye on the kids, and rushed me off to the hospital Emergency ward.

The doctors there, concluding that I had had a massive allergic reaction to something, did what they could and waited for me to wake up. That was the first inkling I had that I was allergic to penicillin. I remained weak, with swollen feet and fingers, for some time, but the swelling in my throat receded and I returned to school to complete my year. At the end of the academic year, when we moved to Montreal for Bill's final year of psychiatry residency at the Allan Memorial Hospital, I went to the allergy clinic for tests and learnt that I was allergic not only to penicillin, but to all forms of local anaesthetics and to anything with any derivative of cocaine in it.

I really hated the year we spent in Montreal while Bill completed his residency in psychiatry. Once again I was working, this time at the Montreal Children's Hospital. Because of the prejudice of apartment managers and owners we were forced to settle for substandard housing in Notre Dame de Grace, and while Bill blossomed at his work and his social life grew in this, his favourite city, I was trapped between work and the care of two small children. After life in Vancouver with its parks, free libraries, beaches and beautiful surroundings, Montreal proved to be a nightmare. We had to walk blocks to the only decent park, which was in Westmount. The children had to play indoors or on the street because there was no yard around our apartment block. There were no libraries within walking distance for me to use, and our limited funds curtailed my access to books.

Bill controlled the use of the car because his working hours were unpredictable, which meant that I was often caught in the worst weather, having to depend on public transit. In general our relationship deteriorated at an alarming rate. I felt old, fat, ugly and desperate.

I survived because I made friends at work and found my job challenging and interesting. I worked with the families of children who were brain-damaged. The condition of many of these children was the result of encephalitis, but more often it was caused by automobile accidents. I soon learnt that many children who were struck by cars died, that many children who were thrown from cars in an accident died, but that most of the children who were thrown around inside an automobile during an accident lived with damaged brains for the rest of their lives.

That lesson made me a committed and fanatical proponent of seatbelts for children. When the Social Credit government in B.C. introduced compulsory seatbelt legislation in 1977 it excluded children under the age of six on the grounds that parents should decide what was best for the children. I was thunderstruck by the monumental stupidity of that reasoning. And every year throughout my term of office I begged, pleaded and lobbied for an amendment to that legislation to include the protection of children. My pleas fell on deaf ears and my private member's bills were ignored.

It was not until the B.C. Medical Association took up the challenge that the government backed down and amended the legislation to make the wearing of seatbelts mandatory for all people in the province regardless of their age. That amendment remains one of the highlights of my political career and is numbered among the very few successes of my political struggles.

Although we tried to ignore them, the unexpected racial incidents kept gnawing away at me. And in Montreal, as was not the case in Vancouver, I seemed absolutely powerless to insulate either myself or my children from them.

On one occasion when I was having a particularly severe toothache, Agnes Sunderland, who used to be a neighbour in Vancouver before moving to Montreal, suggested that I see her dentist. She phoned and asked him to see me as it was an emergency and he agreed. I waited in his office until he had completed his day's appointments. Then he called me in to his work area: he launched immediately into a tirade, shouting at me about waiting until I had severe pain before telling my employer of my dental problem, forcing her to call him. He accused me of taking advantage of the fact that since she was one of his regular patients he would be forced to work beyond his already long work day to see me so as not to jeopardize his relationship with her.

As he continued to shout and rant at me, I sat there stunned. I realized that he thought I was Agnes's maid and that that gave him the right to abuse me. When he finally finished his hysterical harangue, I apologized for the intrusion and explained that I would have to seek the services of another dentist. Of course, by then my toothache had disappeared – I was growing aware that my sanity was about to snap and that in the process I would kill the dentist. As he launched into yet another tirade, I removed myself from his chair and went in search of my coat.

His nurse, who had been embarrassed and terrified by his behaviour, suggested to him that I be referred to another colleague. She explained that she had already called another dentist; he had agreed to see me immediately. She had in addition called a cab to take me to his office. The dentist calmed down and agreed that that was a good idea. As he began to explain to me about the referral, I interrupted to inform him that he had not heard the end of the incident and that Mrs. Sunderland would certainly be given a graphic recounting of his behaviour. I was shaking as I left.

When I arrived at the office of the other dentist, I told him that my toothache had stopped and that I did not need his services. I described my encounter with his colleague and told him that in my present state of mind it would be better that we not proceed with the appointment. He was stunned, apologized profusely on behalf of his colleague and assured me that he would pursue the matter with him.

He no doubt did, because early the following morning I received a phone call from a very chastened dentist apologizing for having mistaken me for a maid. Despite my explanation, he never understood that my rage was not at being assumed to be a maid because I was Black and female, but at the fact that he dared to speak to me with such rudeness just because he believed the colour of my skin and my economic status gave him the right to do so. The incident added to my misery and increased my urgent need to get out of Montreal. Bill wrote a formal letter of complaint to the dentist with a carbon copy to the dental association, and as far as we can tell that was the end of that.

Bill received his certificate in psychiatry, and one August morning in 1964 we set out in our brand new Buick Wildcat to drive back to British Columbia. I was very happy to leave Montreal, but not just because it had been such an unhappy year: a year earlier, before leaving Vancouver, we had used $5,000 of Bill's inheritance from his mother to put a down payment on a home at 3863 West 11th Avenue, and I was eager to move into our first house. Although daunted by the prospect of a $15,000 mortgage, we were anxious to take possession because for us it meant freedom from ever having to face another landlord or landlady. Although we had run into some racism in the purchase of the house, there had also been an unexpected act of wonder. Oliver Kuys, the realtor, an immigrant from South Africa, had responded to the vendors' concerns about our race by explaining to them that he had left South Africa to escape racism, so he was not going to tolerate it in Canada. He added that if they were going to refuse to sell their property to us because of racial considerations, he would not continue to be their realtor. The vendors backed down and said that as Christians they had wanted to be sure that *we* were Christians before they sold the house to us, and that their concerns had nothing to do with race.

By that time we were running into less racism in our daily lives. More Black people were moving into B.C.; our improving economic status made it possible for us to avoid the environments where racism was most prevalent, and Black activists in the United States were beginning to send shock waves across North America as the Black Power movement began.

Another reason I was glad to leave Montreal was that the struggle for Quebec separation was moving beyond rhetoric into a violent phase. The explosion of mailboxes in adjoining neighbourhoods made us very nervous, since we never knew where the next bombing would occur or who the next targets would be. At the end of my work day at the Montreal Children's Hospital, I would pick up Cleta at Queen's School in Westmount where she was attending kindergarten and we would walk the many blocks home to our apartment on

Northcliffe. We had to pass at least three mailboxes enroute and, once the mailbox bombing began, as a precaution we would detour away from them, adding at least another three blocks to our walk.

Bill and I followed the debate about separation with great interest and sympathy for the French cause. We agreed that the French in Quebec had been oppressed and exploited by English-speaking Quebeckers, and we hoped that their struggle for equality would have a successful resolution. However, we did not want to get caught up in the civil war we feared was pending, so we heaved a sigh of relief as we drove away from Montreal.

The timing of our departure proved to be lucky because after we left Montreal, matters got worse. The news of the kidnappings of James Cross and Pierre Laporte and the invocation of the War Measures Act remains a frightening memory of that time. The proclamation of the War Measures Act seemed to us to herald the onset of a short, though bloody, civil insurrection. Many of our friends in psychiatry, who had spent their residency year in Montreal at the same time we did, were at a party at the home of Conrad Schwartz in Vancouver the night the news broke of Pierre Laporte's murder. Many of us were closet sympathizers with the Quebec revolutionaries, and we were sad and quiet as we gathered our coats and left the party as quickly as possible, stunned by the bloody turn of events.

In the following months Bill and I took heart from and pride in the fight that Tommy Douglas and his little band of New Democrats put up in Parliament against Prime Minister Trudeau's invocation of the War Measures Act. I have always admired and respected those few brave voices who voted against that legislation, and I've never forgotten the names of the three NDP members who broke ranks and supported the government.

Our motor trip across Canada was one of the happiest periods of our married life. The kids loved the excitement of new motels and adventures every day, and we loved being alone as a family with no contact except with each other. Since Bill loved driving at night, we would travel until about 1 a.m., check into a motel, sleep late, then spend the day at a playground or somewhere where the kids could play. We would head out at about 4 p.m., stop for dinner at six and bed the kids down on the back seat; they would be fast asleep by 8 p.m. Then Bill and I would settle down to quiet hours of conversation and happiness as we drove along the nearly deserted highway. We loved every moment of it.

The return to Vancouver and moving into our home proved to be wonderful. To our children's delight there were twenty other children living on our block, at least six of them within their age group. There were twelve Doyles, six Clarkes, Munroe Pickering, Tommy Harris and Paul McKnight. One of the Doyles was a girl the same age as our Cleta and six of the boys were within a year or two of Gary. Our children just could not believe their good fortune.

I became pregnant with our third child just before leaving Montreal to return to Vancouver. I welcomed the pregnancy as an opportunity to get a break from working. I seemed to be exhausted all the time. Working, homemaking and even taking that year out to attend university were taking their toll.

Bill plunged into building up his practice, and I lost myself in fixing our home and awaiting the birth of our third child. Before long I was back working with the B.C. Association for the Advancement of Coloured People and the peace movement. Bill bought me a car, an old pink Plymouth, and it seemed that life would be happy forever. We decorated the room for the new baby and exulted that, for once, a new baby would not be a burden on us financially.

We decided that the time had come for me to take our two children for their first trip to Jamaica, because they were old enough and it would be cheaper and easier than travelling with three children later on. We were exceedingly happy.

Cleta and Gary loved Jamaica. I could actually see them relax—the tension, the 'on guard,' dropping away and the mounting joy at being surrounded by friends, relatives and even strangers who were Black. I too relaxed and wished that I never had to return to Canada—I was home, and for the first time in years I felt safe! It was not the perfect Jamaica of my youth, of course. My relatives complained of the changing values of the islanders, the increasing use of drugs, the growing disrespect for elders, traffic congestion, crass modernization, chasing of the tourist dollar, and so on. But to my children it was paradise and to me it was home.

About a week after we arrived in Jamaica, as I was putting the children to bed one night, Cleta confessed that she had always thought the stories her dad and I used to tell her, about places in the world where most people were Black, were really fairy tales. She thought we had made those stories up, and that in fact everyone in the world was white except our family and some of our friends.

I was so depressed and sad when she said that, I phoned Bill in Vancouver and told him that we just could not raise our children in Canada, that it would be cruel and selfish of us to do so. He was very sympathetic and suggested we discuss the options when I returned to Vancouver.

One morning about a week before the baby was due to be born I was sitting in the rocking chair I always had in my kitchen, relaxed and planning the day ahead. Cleta and Gary had both left with the six or seven children from our block who walked to school each morning. I was tired, as always at that time of day, after preparing breakfast and getting two children and one spouse off to school and work, carrying around a nearly full-grown, about-to-be-delivered baby. But I knew that for a few minutes at least I could sit and rock, looking at the mountains in the distance, before beginning my round of bed-making and housework. Suddenly the baby within me heaved and a searing pain shot through my body, then all went still. My heart was racing and an immense sense of doom settled over me. I knew that something had happened, I didn't know what, and I was immediately gripped with panic.

I took some deep breaths to calm myself, waited for the pain to recede and waited to see what would happen next. At that moment my neighbour, Billy Clayton, phoned to say she was on her way grocery shopping and she wondered whether she could pick up anything for me. I immediately told her about my experience and she came right over. We decided that it was probably false labour and made arrangements for her to take me to the hospital in a hurry if necessary, and to contact other neighbours to care for Cleta and Gary until Bill got home.

Greatly calmed, I proceeded with my day's chores, but something was different. My previously hyperactive baby was not moving.

By noon I could control my anxiety no longer and contacted my obstetrician, who suggested that I come in to see him immediately. Two days later I delivered a beautiful, full-grown, stillborn daughter, with the umbilical cord tightly wound around her neck. Bill and I clung to each other and wept for hours.

I will never forget returning home from the hospital, getting out of the car, my heart breaking because my hands were empty. I stood rooted to the spot, whimpering that my hands were empty and that I couldn't walk because my hands were empty, because there was no baby in my arms. Bill, sensing my desperation, tried to encourage me to move, but I was paralyzed. My legs would not move. Finally, on a gamble, he handed me one of the pots of mums we had brought home from the hospital and said, "Here, carry that." With tears streaming down my face I walked into the house clinging to that pot of flowers.

The loss of my baby gave me my first encounter with 'sisterhood,' even though that word was not in common use then. I was almost never alone. Women I hardly knew, but whose children attended school or played with my kids, women in the neighbourhood, with whom I had not exchanged more than a polite greeting, showed up at my home. They brought baked goods, home-cooked meals, casseroles and sherry, and stayed to visit. Many of them spoke of their own losses—of miscarriage, stillbirth, death of a small child or other loved one. They surrounded me with love and warmth and nurtured me through my mourning and depression.

Bill and I grew closer together as he loved me and monitored me carefully to ensure that I did not plunge into and remain in a state of self-pity. We agreed that I would not return to work, but would enrol in the Master of Social Work program at UBC the following fall.

Before that, however, another twist of fate occurred. A friend, Joyce Lockhart, heard her friend Gordon Bryenton speak of looking for a back-up social worker for a CTV panel show, *People in Conflict*, on which he was a panelist. Joyce suggested that such a job would cheer me up and pull me out of my depression. When Gordon approached me with the offer, I wanted to decline, but Bill encouraged me to accept. He pointed out that I would only be working one day each month, since the station filmed one week's programs in a day, and that it would be fun to work with Gordon, whom I knew and liked; and of course I would be earning a lot more money than I would as a social worker. All my friends joined in encouraging me, and after a visit with Rae Purdy, the producer of the show, I agreed to try out for the back-up spot.

I loved being on the show and remained with it almost until the birth of our son Jonathan two years later. *People in Conflict* was a national show, and even now, nearly thirty years later, I run into people who used to watch it and who were sad to see it terminated.

The format was very simple. It consisted of a panel of three professionals: a lawyer, the flamboyant H.A.D. Oliver, who was always running off the set to check with his broker; a psychologist, my friend Gordon Bryenton, who was also a marriage and family counsellor; and a social worker, the position I occupied one week each month. Our job was to respond in a helpful and positive way to people who appeared before us with problems. There were no written scripts or professional performers. People off the street volunteered for the show. They were told the problem they were to present to the panel, and they were left to act out and present their stories in their own way. Before the show the panelists would be briefed as to the nature of the problems, but we were never sure what twist or turn a story line would take.

The show was aired at 3 p.m. because the station wanted to be sure that it was nearly over before children got home from school. We dealt with problems of infidelity, impotence, rape, family violence and a number of topics that station bureaucrats thought would be too steamy for young eyes and ears. Nonetheless we heard stories of whole classes of kids rushing to the home of a classmate who lived close to school to catch the show. So we revised the program to deal with the most sexually explicit issues first, since that meant the kids would arrive just in time to hear the good advice of the panelists, but would miss the details of the problems. Bill and my friends proved to be correct, and *People in Conflict* did help me survive one of the down periods of my life. I soon became pregnant again and, with the birth of Jonathan on November 13, 1965, we decided that our family was complete.

I was thirty-five years of age, had had four pregnancies, three live births and one stillbirth, and for emotional, health and economical reasons we decided that we wanted to concentrate on raising these three children. We knew that we would have to explore a more reliable form of birth control since all my four pregnancies had occurred while we were using one form of birth control or another. We talked at great length about our future and decided that I would try taking 'the pill,' but that if it failed, or if I proved, for some reason, unable to continue its use, we would try the other methods, including abortion if necessary, to prevent any further pregnancies.

When Jonathan was a year old, we sold our home on West 11th and moved into our 'dream house' on Belmont Avenue. We decided it would be home for the rest of our lives; politics intervened, however, and fifteen years later we moved. The circumstances surrounding that decision are so painful that I will postpone discussion of them until later.

It was time once again to go job-hunting. I now had a Master's degree in social work and I was confident that finding employment would not be difficult. Over the years we had insulated ourselves more and more against racial discrimination. Our children had the occasional taunt to deal with, but for the most part they were making friends and seemed happy enough. We made sure that they had the best of everything—whether cultural, educational, material or emotional—that we could afford, and that they were exposed to Black history and literature.

We spoke to them about Black people in positive terms and kept reinforcing that being born Black they had much to be proud of. Our task was made easier since the civil rights movement in the United States was receiving a lot of media coverage, and they could see bright, articulate young Black leaders fighting against the barriers to their advancement.

Cleta, as the eldest child, had always had a more difficult time than the others, because in every case she was the first Black child in her school and remained the only Black child until her brother joined her two years later. She was a very serious, sensitive child who asked searching questions and spent long periods of time just quietly observing the activities going on around her. Nonetheless, she always had friends and never seemed lonely. I am convinced that she suffered most of all the family from having to grow up not just in a country steeped in racism, but in the bizarre situation of being in an environment where she was the only person of her race. I have always believed that it was too stressful a situation in which to place a child; I do not believe that anything we did altered the fact that, to her, life must have been a nightmare. I stand in awe of her strength and power. I have never envied her and know that I could not have survived her ordeal as well as she has.

I have a different kind of relationship with each of my children. With Cleta I have shared the unspoken fears of being a Black woman living in a white country. I worried that, surrounded by all the messages of beauty being white, blond and blue-eyed, she would internalize those criteria and come to see herself as being ugly and unlovely. She grew up during the period when all Black women were straightening their hair, and although I wanted to keep her hair in its natural state as long as possible, I found that I had to give in to her importuning to have it straightened at an early age. I knew that the process would damage her hair and, as her role model, I felt guilty because I was straightening my own hair and so could not advise her that her natural hair was beautiful. Bill and I told her constantly how beautiful we thought she was, but our words were continually contradicted, by TV, comic books, movies and other images in her environment.

We worried that as she grew older her feelings of being unlovely would be exacerbated by difficulty in having dates, and by seeing her brothers, and other Black men in the community, dating and marrying white women. We explored the possibility of sending her to school and university in either the West Indies or the United States, and we prepared to build an elaborate shield around her until she was mature enough to recognize that she was beautiful, bright and very, very nice. Time proved that our worries were exaggerated; Cleta has always dated, had lovers and enjoyed a social life. Nonetheless my antenna remains tuned for the slightest sign of dysfunction in her life.

Gary was an outgoing, happy child who made friends easily; he found that often in incidents of racial teasing, his friends would surge to his defence. Jonathan was loved, pampered and spoilt by all of us.

While I was thinking about returning to work, I was approached by Bea Lipinski, from Simon Fraser University, and told about plans to develop a suicide prevention and crisis centre in Vancouver. The idea intrigued me and I assured her that I would be happy to become involved. I offered to help design the volunteer training program and to train the first batch of volunteers. It seemed like a good way for me to ease back into the work force.

Before my volunteer stint with the suicide prevention centre was complete, Bea asked whether I would be interested in joining the counselling service at Simon Fraser. She was the director; the service was large and growing, with a psychiatrist and a number of psychologists on staff. She found that a number of students were coming to the service because of problems with the provincial Department of Social Service and thought that it might be a good idea to have a social worker on staff part-time, to whom she could refer these cases. She also wanted me to be involved with some of the group counselling programs.

I was excited at the prospect, especially since she agreed to allow me to develop a volunteer outreach program that would encourage students to volunteer for community work. Little did I know that once again my life was about to change and that this job was literally the first step of a fourteen-year adventure.

CHAPTER FIVE

The day that Malcolm X was assassinated in 1965, Jonathan was conceived. Bill and I clung to each other, stunned that one of our own could have pulled the trigger to end the life of someone who spoke so clearly to us of our condition and our oppression. We had anticipated that someone from the white community would snuff out his life prematurely, but in our naiveté we assumed that the Black community would have been a haven of safety for someone so important to us as a people. We were immobilized by a mixture of rage, despair and a sense of betrayal, by the realization that our prophets and our revolutionaries—even those who dwelt among us—would never be protected or safe from their enemies. We wanted desperately to do something about the situation, because, although we did not endorse Malcolm's call to arms, we certainly identified with his appeal to us as a people to reject oppression and discrimination and to believe in our value, our talents and our rights. Many years later, a political acquaintance visiting our home noticed the large framed portrait of Malcolm on the wall of Bill's library and commented that he had not realized that we were 'the sort of people' who would have liked Malcolm X, thus revealing once again the ignorance about the relationship of Black people to Black people that survives and pervades even the political community.

It was the year 1967. The Black Panther party was achieving greater visibility in the United States, and Eldridge Cleaver was emerging as one of its most articulate spokesmen. In Canada a small group of us was beginning to meet from time to time to discuss the formation of a national Black coalition, and the Royal Commission on the Status of Women was established by an Act of Parliament.

Bill's practice was thriving. Our children were healthy and happy. I was depressed. I took Cleta and Gary to Expo '67 in Montreal, where we met my mother and other relatives and friends who had travelled up from Jamaica for the fair. It was one of those down times in my life when the whole world seemed to be spinning in the opposite direction. I had a very clear sense that the Black Panther movement was pushing the United States into a bloody racial conflagration. Ever since the assassination of Malcolm X two years earlier, I had concluded that white America would never permit or tolerate justice or equality for its Black citizens. I believed that the Civil Rights Movement was doomed, and I was being crushed by the realization that my children and grandchildren would face a life of prejudice and discrimination.

I gave up all hope and began to question the point of living. I was not really suicidal, however—I knew that I dared not face my dead grandmother and aunts on the other side with the excuse that I had killed myself because I had been defeated by life.

Up until this point the major influences in my life aside from my grandmother and my aunts had been Angela Davis, Paul Robeson, Malcolm X and W.E.B. Du Bois. From them I had drawn the strength and the inspiration needed to survive in this country. I now found that they could not help me through a depression that was deepened and exaggerated by a hysterectomy and approaching forty.

Someone, I can't remember who, loaned me a copy of *The Feminine Mystique*, by Betty Friedan. Suddenly it was all there, the story of my life—as I read the book, I became more and more agitated; I realized that I was not unique, that there were women all over North America, women of all colours, who were experiencing the same sense of being unfulfilled in their personal lives. Learning this fact should have depressed me further, but it didn't. The effect was the opposite. The fact that I was not alone reassured and mobilized me.

The Feminine Mystique, with its simple examination and revelation of the lives of women in North America, was one of the three 'jolts' that have hardened my commitment to feminism; the other two were Marilyn French's *The Women's Room*, a book about the sometimes brutal relationship between men and women, and a strange little TV drama called *The Stepford Wives*, which depicted the ideal wife as a robot programmed to respond with unquestioning obedience to her husband's wishes. Once the programming of the robot is completed the real-life wife is murdered. I know that none of these are profound analytical works of great import – but for me, each in its own way shocked me and reminded me that the dislike and distrust of men for women touches every aspect of our life, even the most petty and superficial. In later years Alice Walker, through her poems and writings on the experience and condition of Black women, was to put it all into perspective and remind me of the legacy of strength and resilience with which my ancestors had inoculated me.

I began to read voraciously everything that dealt with women's life and women's struggle. In Canada the pressure for a Royal Commission on the Status of Women was successful. I followed the hearings and its progress with great interest.

And I felt more a part of Canada as I listened to reports of the briefs being presented, so many of them seeming to be the story of my life and my experiences. Suddenly, the 'click' of which feminists speak came, as I realized that my sisterhood with those women was greater than whatever divided us; and by the time the Royal Commission had completed its task and tabled its report in the House of Commons, I was a committed feminist.

At Simon Fraser University, Bea Lipinski encouraged exploration into sponsoring workshops and courses in women's studies. Consciousness-raising groups were springing up everywhere and I attended as many as I could. I was intoxicated with the concept of sisterhood and eager to learn as much as possible about women's history, and about how we came to occupy our present place in the economic and social structure of our nation. Prior to these years, sexism was not an issue to which I had given any thought, but gradually I came to see how my concerns about racial injustice had blinded me to the sexism that existed even within the Black movement. I am grateful to those women in the Civil Rights Movement in the United States who spotted the discrepancy between the principle they were fighting for and the way they were being treated by their male comrades, and who began to speak about the sexism within that movement. Their writings triggered the conflict in me that had been heightened by the growing hostility of both Black men and women in the Civil Rights Movement in Canada to the involvement of Black women in the feminist struggle. Black Canadians insisted that feminism was a white ideology and the women's movement a white, middle-class movement. They saw it as yet another attempt to drain the energies of the Black struggle, and to siphon off the commitment and weaken the determination of the small band of activists working against prejudice.

I agonized over this conflict. As a Black person, I believed that every criticism they leveled at the women's movement was correct. Indeed, I realized that they had not gone far enough in their censure. Yet as a woman, I knew that much of my exploitation and oppression would continue even if the colour of my skin turned white, so long as I remained a woman. I could not turn my back on the women's struggle, yet I did not enjoy being perceived as a traitor to my race when I spoke out about the sexism of the Black male.

So I continued to be active in both struggles, trying to reconcile and justify my involvement in both. The relationship between white women and Black women in North America has always been fraught with suspicion, anger, distrust and dislike. Black women resented being cast in the role of servants to white women, being unable to live up to North American society's criteria of beauty, and being the last choice Black men settled for when they were unable to have white women or women of any other race or colour.

Black women believed that their rejection by Black men was

what undermined their self-esteem and reinforced their perception of their status as inferior. They had come to live with the knowledge that any white woman, regardless of whether she was uneducated, less talented, less skilled, unendowed, less intelligent, or unattractive, was preferred over any Black woman regardless of *her* qualities. And although the Black Power movement had established that 'Black is Beautiful,' Black women never trusted that slogan nor developed the self-esteem it was supposed to engender. The preference of Black men for white women was one of the painful realities that remained a part of their daily life.

The women's movement triggered the latent hostility that always existed between these two groups, and Black males exploited the hostility and distrust in an attempt to keep Black women out of the women's movement. Black women knew also that the success of the feminist movement would be measured in terms of how many previously barred doors would be open to white women. The early women's movement displayed as little interest in Native and visible minority women as it did in poor and working-class women. Nonetheless, as a Black woman I concluded that I did not have much to lose in either and had much to gain from both movements.

If either the struggle against racism or that against sexism was won, the victory for me would be a fifty-percent solution. To achieve one hundred-percent success both struggles had to be successful. And so, quite frankly, I could not afford to turn my back on either one. The challenge that faced me was how to articulate my position in a positive and convincing way to the Black community.

I must confess that I was not concerned by the radical wing of the women's movement that denounced all men, and declared that women had to separate themselves completely from men in order to be free. I was too emotionally involved with my two sons to give that idea serious consideration; moreover, there had been other men who had enriched and influenced my life in positive ways and I did not intend to deny that fact. I was not even concerned or surprised by the racism that I knew existed in the women's movement. I knew that I could extract enough from the analysis and ideology to strengthen me, and my contact with some women in the consciousness-raising groups had taught me that sisterhood was possible between Black and white women.

I must also confess that I was not genuinely concerned about convincing Black men of the rightness of the women's movement. I still carried within me resentment and anger concerning their traditional denigration of Black women, and the trivializing of our contribution to the civil rights struggle by men like Stokely Carmichael, who had stated that our most valuable position in the movement was prone. I frankly didn't care whether they endorsed and supported our efforts or not.

I was, however, very deeply concerned about my Black Canadian sisters and wanted urgently to convince them that feminism could be a liberating experience for us. I knew that I needed to get beyond their appraisal of the movement as a white women's movement, and beyond their fear that the struggle for equality could damage the tenuous and fragile relationship they had with Black men.

North American Black women have been indoctrinated with the belief that our salvation was tied to the liberation of the Black male—that his ego, his rights, his needs were paramount; and that it would be up to him, once he had improved his position in society, to raise that of his women and children. They were brainwashed into accepting that their role was to support and work for the rights of their fathers, husbands and sons, and that they should not compete with them because the struggle for racial justice would be weakened by such an act.

In truth, many Black men have lived up to this dream. They have protected and cared for their women and their families; however, in increasing numbers Black women in Canada were finding that benefits that accrued to Black men did not necessarily benefit them.

What I had learnt from feminism was that women's place had as much to do with the social and economic system as it had to do with race. I believed that Black women had to take control of their lives, establish their priorities and pursue their goals. I also believed that an independent, secure woman had more to contribute to any struggle than an insecure, dependent one, and that the battle against racism would be fought more effectively by women and men standing side by side as equals, rather than by an unbalanced, lopsided team of unequal partners.

In addition, I had to combat the wariness of those Black women who perceived me to be a privileged woman who, because I enjoyed a degree of economic security, could afford to take risks with my personal and marital relationships.

I was determined to continue my efforts to convince Black women, particularly those of us who were mothers of daughters, of the importance of both the Black movement and the women's movement to our search for dignity, self-esteem and rights. I believed that we had a responsibility to undermine and destroy the socialization that maintained and supported the powerlessness and oppression of Black women. I continued to read, explore, study, analyze – and to pray for an opportunity to confront this issue. Through the National Black Coalition and the BCAACP I tried to raise and push the issue on a number of occasions.

However, it was not until I was invited to deliver the keynote address at the Annual Banquet of the Negro Women's Association of Ontario in 1973 that the opportunity I longed for occurred. The Association suggested that I speak on any topic of my choice, so I prepared myself carefully and extensively to deliver what remains for me the most important speech of my lifetime, entitled "Black Women and the Women's Liberation."

In preparation I developed a rationalization I have used whenever I have been faced with controversial speaking engagements since, namely to assume that such a speaking engagement offers a once-in-a-lifetime opportunity. Hence, I cannot waste it by speaking to the audience of what it wants to hear, but instead I have to use the opportunity to speak of truths that have to be told. That way, if a second invitation is not forthcoming, there are no regrets, since I have said it all the first time anyway.

This was definitely such an occasion. On the night of the banquet there were nearly 300 people in an audience that included the Governor General of Ontario, the Mayor of the City of Toronto and a large number of white Canadians. Although the topic was one of which I would have preferred to speak to an exclusively Black audience, because once again I feared being accused of betraying private family secrets to the other side, I decided that this opportunity to speak out could not be ignored.

My anxiety and nervousness about the occasion shut my stomach down and I was unable to eat anything at the banquet. My heart raced, my mind went blank and sweat oozed out of my pores. Despite this I tried to smile and chat throughout the meal, appearing to all the world relaxed and confident. Nonetheless, I was a shaking, nervous wreck as I walked towards the podium, anticipating the hostility that my words would generate.

However, as I began to deliver the speech, I became caught up in the urgency of the content and the force of my conviction; I heard my voice move out and across the room and capture the attention of the audience, I saw the intentness in the faces before me, and I knew that they were not just listening but were actually hearing what I had come to say:

> . . .Whenever anyone – male, female, Black or white – asks me why I am part of the women's liberation movement, I always reply "because I am a woman." Then I wait for the significance of their question to dawn on them – for in reality, what they have said to me is that since I am a Black person, Black oppression is the only oppression with which they expect me to concern myself.
>
> But for me not to participate in the women's liberation movement would be to deny my womanhood – for indeed I am twice blessed. I am Black and I am a woman – and to be Black and female in a society which is both racist and sexist is to be in the unique position of having nowhere to go but up! And to be in the unique situation of learning about survival from being able to observe at very close range the Achilles' heel of a very great nation.
>
> Indeed, my Black friends who congratulate me for speaking out on racial issues chastise me for being a feminist. And my sisters who love me for speaking out

on the issues of the movement chastise me for being preoccupied with my race. Add to all of this the fact that I am a socialist living in a capitalist country and you will wonder what worlds are left for me to conquer or be conquered by.

Yet I enjoy a strange kind of freedom – because in order to survive I have had to learn and learn well about racists and about sexists and about capitalists. And the wisdom that I have gleaned from these studies is that all people depend on all people, and that unless all of us are free – none of us will be free, and that indeed when I fight for your freedom, I am also fighting for my own and when I am fighting for my freedom I am also fighting for my sisters and brothers and for all of our children.

I learnt also that this country, this Canada, is beautiful and strong only because of the people of both sexes, and of all races and political persuasions who have lived in it and contributed to its culture and its soul and its growth. And that its strength and its beauty will increase only to the extent that it is able to accept and respect all of its people equally.

But what did I learn of us? Of you and me – the Black women who through choice, or luck or by birth make this our home? Where do we fit into this space and into the changes and developments that are taking place about us?

Well, if you read the traditional history books, you will find that we have never been here and indeed are not here even now – the invisible people. Because where judicious prodding might unearth the names of one or two of the males who made contributions in the past – the digging has to be deep indeed to find the women.

So, I left the history books and went back to the school of survival, and there I learnt that there are a number of liberation movements sweeping this land – racial, economic, and of course, the feminist movement. And I asked myself, "Where do Black women fit into the women's liberation movement?"

And I learnt something very interesting – namely that unless the women's liberation movement identifies with and locks into the liberation movement of all oppressed groups it will never achieve its goals . . . that unless it identifies with and supports the struggles of the poor, of oppressed races, of the old and of other disadvantaged groups in society it will never achieve its goals. Because not to do so would be to isolate itself from the masses of women – since women make up a large segment of all of these groups.

I believe that Black women do fit into the women's liberation movement. I believe that through the movement we can fight for Black women as well as for all women of all other races. Even as, when we fight for Black people, we fight for Black men as well as for Black children and Black women. . . .

April 7, 1973

At the end they very graciously accorded me a standing ovation, but I was so exhausted and wrung out that I barely made it back to my seat. The applause was sustained long after I sat down, and in the back of my mind, as the thumping in my heart, which had been drowning out the applause, subsided, I heard my grandmother and the aunts saying "Not bad, not bad at all, girl."

One of the perks of working at Simon Fraser University was that staff members sometimes had their way paid to attend conferences at other universities and educational institutions. Because I was a part-time employee, however, I was not eligible for the exotic trips to the United States or Eastern Canada. I was really pleased, therefore, when Bea Lipinski, my boss, approached me and asked whether I would be interested in attending the conference to discuss the recommendations of the Royal Commission on the Status of Women that was being sponsored by the UBC Department of Continuing Education and the University Women's Club.

I was ecstatic. I had wanted to attend the conference anyway as the representative of the B.C. Council of Black Women, a very small and impoverished group of which I was the president, and of the National Black Coalition, of which I was the western representative. Bea's offer to send me meant that SFU would pay the registration fee and I could represent all three groups at the same time.

The conference, held at Hycroft, the elegant home of the University Women's Club, was a great success. There were at least 500 women in attendance, and at the end of the day June Dunlop, one of the participants, asked those women who were interested in being part of an ongoing organization to work for the implementation of the Royal Commission recommendations to stay behind. Needless to say, I was one of those.

The Vancouver Status of Women Council was born that evening, and Anita Morris was chosen its first president. The goal of the organization was to ensure that the 167 recommendations included in the final report, which had been tabled in the House of Commons on September 28, 1970, not be ignored. We knew that during its tour across the country, the Commission, headed by Florence Bird, had received 468 briefs and more than 1,000 letters. We believed that the recommendations reflected accurately the wishes of most Canadian women, but we also knew that Royal Commission reports had a history of languishing on shelves collecting dust and generating little or no action.

The women who remained behind after that Hycroft meeting were determined that that would not be the fate of this particular report. The founding members of the Vancouver Status of Women included a cross-section of all political parties and included many of the highly visible and outspoken feminists of the day—such as Joan Wallace, Nancy Morrison, Anne Petrie, Pat Thom, Carole Anne Soong, to name a few—all of whom in one way or another have remained faithful to the feminist cause.

Soon after that initial meeting I was approached by Anita Morris and asked to design and develop an advocacy structure for women, along the lines of the Ombudsman concept. I was delighted and excited to do so. I subsequently discovered that Anita had overstepped her jurisdiction and had acted without the mandate to appoint me to such a position; however, in the interest of harmony, the organization decided not to challenge my appointment, confident that a year later when the position was open to election I would be defeated quite easily.

The Ombudservice was the challenge I had been preparing for all my life. A small grant from the Department of the Secretary of State paid for a post office box and the purchase of an old typewriter. The media gave the service generous and free coverage, and soon women in Vancouver knew that there existed a place to which they could bring complaints against government, the law, unfair labour practices or whatever, and that every effort would be made to work for a positive resolution of their problems.

Like all other positions in the Status of Women Council, mine was a volunteer one; I worked on those days when I was not at Simon Fraser University. There was a committee that worked with me. We were the first Ombudswoman's service in Canada, and the committee felt like freedom fighters — determined not only to protest bad laws or the absence of good laws, but also to tender recommendations for the introduction of 'equality' legislation.

As Ombudswoman, I soon found that most of the complaints that came to the service concerned unsatisfactory divorce settlements, non-payment of maintenance, and the startling impoverishment of women as the result of divorce. The service investigated many instances where divorce had caused the immediate economic descent of women from middle-class status to that of welfare recipients, instances where the awards of the courts were arbitrary and inconsistent, and where enforcement of support orders was virtually nonexistent.

The second largest area of complaint concerned older women who found that their pensions ceased immediately upon the death of their spouses, thus plunging them into complete poverty. Gradually, as the body of cases grew, the unseen and unfair disposition of justice to women became obvious, and we were able to make clear links between women's poverty and women's dependency status in marriage.

The other area of complaint and a practice that contributed to women's poverty was the lower pay they received for the jobs they did. It became clear that these lower wage scales resulted in lower pension contributions, and guaranteed poverty in old age even for those women who spent their entire lives in the work force. The Ombudservice handled a number of high-profile equal pay cases that we lost; and at least two of the ones that were successful actually contributed to the defeat of the NDP provincial government in 1975.

Soon after the Ombudservice was established we were approached by some women who worked as dietary aides at Riverview Mental Hospital, the largest mental health facility in the province of B.C. We were asked to investigate the wage gap between their earnings and those of the cooks' helpers. They explained that both groups did exactly the same job, except in two instances: cooks' helpers chopped vegetables and cooks' helpers could eventually be promoted to cooks. Dietary aides, on the other hand, could not become dieticians unless they had a university degree, and they were not permitted to chop vegetables because that task took place in the kitchen, and dietary aides were not permitted to work in the kitchen. The other difference between the two groups was that cooks' helpers were all male and dietary aides were all female; for these reasons the hospital felt justified in maintaining a different pay scale for the two groups.

Our investigation confirmed that the complaint was indeed valid. However, the hospital justified its differential wage policy on the grounds that because the pay scales of both groups had been negotiated by the unions through the collective bargaining process there was nothing they could do to change them. It was up to the union, they said. Discussion with the union failed to resolve the issue; so the Ombudservice decided to place it on our political agenda to be dealt with at the next election.

Not long after that failure, we were approached by representatives of practical nurses who worked in one of our larger hospitals; they complained that the differential between their pay scale and the pay scale of the orderlies was unfair. Our investigation found that, although orderlies were sometimes called upon to do some lifting, which was not required of the practical nurses, there was no training required for their jobs, whereas practical nurses had to be graduates of a course of study. Again, the hospital in question maintained that its hands were tied because a union contract bargained for and protected both wage scales.

Equal pay was one of the platforms on which the NDP campaigned in the 1972 provincial election. After its victory, Dennis Cocke, the new Minister of Health (and spouse of Yvonne Cocke, one of the founding members of the NDP Women's Rights Committee), moved to deal with the dietary aides at Riverview and the practical nurses in hospitals across the province.

When, as a result of the government's initiative, the practical nurses' pay scale was raised to equal that of orderlies, it set off a wave of protest: the registered nurses suddenly discovered that they were earning a little more than $20 monthly above the practical nurses' wage, despite the facts that their training was three years in duration and that they had much more responsibility for patient care than the practical nurses did. They were enraged, and they demanded that a wider wage differential between themselves and the practical nurses be negotiated immediately. Although they had been willing to accept a mere $20 monthly more than male orderlies, they were not prepared to do so in the case of female practical nurses.

In the case of the dietary aides at Riverview (again on the initiative of Dennis Cocke), their jobs were rolled into the category of cooks' helper, the position of dietary aide along with its different pay scale was eliminated and the job became open to members of either sex. The resentment engendered by these two attempts to enforce an equal pay policy, as well as the incredible monetary costs of the new policy, created hostility that festered and resulted in the efforts of many workers in the health profession to defeat the NDP government in 1975. In addition, the rift between registered nurses and practical nurses never healed completely and, when the Social Credit government moved to eliminate the practical nurses' profession in 1988, very few registered nurses came to their defence.

Those experiences taught me about another aspect of feminism, namely its potential to be a two-edged sword. I began to study the impact of any change as far into the future as possible before working to institute it; and although I never retreated from any struggle, I learnt to prepare more carefully to deal with the consequences of my actions.

The efforts of the Ombudservice on behalf of married women in the province led us to oppose a particularly flawed amendment to an Act regarding wives' and children's maintenance in 1971. It was introduced by Grace McCarthy, Minister without Portfolio in W.A.C. Bennett's Social Credit government. Mrs. McCarthy was infuriated by our actions, but we were adamant that what women needed was a completely new bill that reflected their equal status with their husbands within the marriage and their right to fifty percent of all the family assets. A delegation of us appeared before the standing committee of the legislature on health and welfare to formally present our arguments in opposition to this Act, and our alternative recommendation.

The Bill was eventually defeated; but I remember the day of our presentation for another reason. At the conclusion of the meeting Dennis Cocke, the NDP member for New Westminster and a member of the Legislative Committee, approached me. He said that he wanted me to meet Dave Barrett, his leader, and he wanted me to run as a candidate for the NDP in the next provincial election. I thanked him for his suggestion and assured him that seeking political office was not part of my life plan. I thought that was the end of the matter. However, as our delegation was leaving the legislature to catch the ferry and return to Vancouver, we ran into Dennis at the door with Dave in tow. Dave said he was impressed with what he had heard about me, and wanted to encourage me to seek an NDP nomination for the next provincial election.

Bill and I had a good chuckle over that at home that evening, because we knew that no Vancouver riding would choose a person who was Black, female and an immigrant to be its elected representative.

CHAPTER SIX

The primary goal of the Status of Women Council was to secure the implementation of the 167 recommendations of the Royal Commission Report on the Status of Women. It was foremost a political organization, which transcended party politics in pursuit of this goal. The membership included women of all political parties, although no member allowed party affiliation or lack of it to obscure her objective of changing, albeit superficially, the condition of Canadian women.

The Council divided its goals into a series of tasks and struck committees with responsibility for expediting each task. All the standing committees, whether on education, finance, media, the Ombudswoman or the speakers bureau, knew that their real function was to ensure the success of the political aims of the Council and support the work of the political committee. No case on which I worked as the Ombudswoman was ever dealt with simply as a personal psychological problem; each person's crisis was discussed in economic, social and political terms, as well as in personal ones. There was always a linking of the experience of the individual and the status of that person as a woman in our society.

Invariably, when a solution to a given problem eluded us, as in the case of the Riverview dietary aides, we would put it into a political context and seek a political solution. For me it was a crash course in consciousness-raising, and this process was repeated throughout everything the Council said and did. The Ombudservice unearthed the cases of family violence, unequal pay, unfair divorce settlements, lack of pension benefits and other discriminatory labour practices, as well as the issues of poverty, inadequate childcare facilities and demeaning welfare demands, that constituted the reason for our involvement in the liberation struggle.

Right from the beginning the Council members decided that we would not be satisfied to have the concerns of women remain in the hands of male politicians. We wanted to elect politicians of our own. We agreed that to continue to focus solely on lobbying, supporting, even educating male politicians to translate our issues into public policy would be a waste of our time and energy. Our focus, therefore, was to find women of all political parties who had even the faintest desire to run for public office and to build the support and infrastructure that would translate that desire into reality.

Our only requirement was that these women support the findings and recommendations of the Royal Commission Report on the Status of Women. Women who shared that goal needed only seek our endorsement and support to be assured of the willing and full cooperation of the Council members. Many of the ideas, techniques and strategies being used by 'Winning Women' groups across Canada today in their thrust to get women elected to public office by 1994 were pioneered by the political committee of the Vancouver Status of Women Council.

Because of the open and aggressive political thrust of the Council, for many years the women of B.C. were perceived by feminist groups across Canada as being in the forefront of political action and awareness in the women's movement. Long after groups in the rest of Canada were saying "let's keep politics out of the women's movement," we were saying "politics is what the women's movement is all about."

So the education committee proceeded to study, research and expand on the rationale behind the Royal Commission recommendations. The speakers bureau continued to groom its members to carry the message of the Report and its recommendations to organizations, schools, institutions and any group in the community willing to listen or curious enough to learn of it. The media committee was mandated to keep our activities in the public eye, and the finance committee, which was really the fundraising arm of the organization, launched an appeal to convince both government and community that the funding of our activities was in the best interest of women throughout the province.

The Council ran on high-octane energy. We were all convinced that we could change the world, and we were determined to do so. Members of the political committee monitored the decisions of all levels of government and, through the very effective media committee, maintained a steady barrage of critical comment on all areas of their performance.

Meantime, the search for women candidates continued. By the time Premier W.A.C. Bennett called a provincial election for August 30, 1972, the Vancouver Status of Women Council was ready. Three members of the Council had won the nomination of their parties as well as the endorsement of the Council. All Council members were exhorted to become actively involved in the campaign for the woman candidate of their choice; fundraising was accelerated, and the money was distributed equally among the three members who were running. A major all-candidates meeting for female candidates was sponsored and organized at the downtown YWCA. The Vancouver Status of Women newsletter carried full reports on the three candidates and urged that all members give them their support. The three publicly declared their membership in the Status of Women Council and their support for the Royal Commission Report and commitment to its implementation.

The Council was seen as a force to be reckoned with by three of the four political parties, and commitments of support were given by all except the Social Credit Party. Since one of the women candidates supported by the Council was running for the Liberal Party, and the other two were New Democrats, the Council was confident of some success in achieving its goal as long as the Social Credit government was defeated. Since all the membership shared the common goal of defeating the Social Credit government, there was much sharing of workers and materials between the Liberal and NDP women's campaigns.

The Status of Women Council was also the incubator for a small but extremely effective group known as Women in Teaching (WIT), headed by Linda Shuto, a teacher. The teachers of B.C. were very unhappy with the Social Credit government and determined to launch a highly visible province-wide opposition in the upcoming election. Linda, a member of the Council, had convinced us of the importance of raising the consciousness of women teachers, not only about the sexist content of the curriculum and of textbooks with which they worked, but also about their own unequal status within their profession and employment. We were happy to support her endeavours and to include WIT under the umbrella of the Council.

In Victoria, the provincial capital, another group of women had organized the Status of Women Action Group (SWAG), headed by Kathleen Ruff. This group shared the goals and aims of the Vancouver Status of Women Council and mobilized the women of Victoria in opposition to the Social Credit government members in that city.

Feminists in the rest of Canada looked on in disbelief at the audacity of the actions and pronouncements of the Vancouver Status of Women. It contributed to the Canadian myth of British Columbians as unusual, and although they admired our organization no province moved to duplicate it; all were convinced that such an organization could not survive outside B.C. There is a certain political recklessness about British Columbia that is manifest in its ability to support far right and far left parties with equal fervour. The only thing that it lacks is the ability to be middle-of-the-road. The women's movement is no different, and the aggressiveness of the Vancouver Status of Women Council was accepted by British Columbians as quite normal.

The 1972 election was the first time since the disintegration of the Voice of Women that the women of urban areas of B.C. had united and mobilized against a government. Although the opposition parties treated the efforts of the women seriously, the Social Credit people, with the particular arrogance that is their trademark, underestimated both the commitment and the determination of B.C. women.

The Social Credit government was defeated in that 1972 election. The Status of Women Council enjoyed success with the election of the two NDP women candidates. Joan Wallace, the defeated Liberal candidate, who was president of the Council at that time, was not daunted by her defeat and went on to run in other elections. The two NDP women began to work for the implementation of those recommendations of the Royal Commission that fell under provincial jurisdiction, as well as for the development of other resources and services that had been identified by the collective women's community as being necessary to improving the condition of women in B.C.

Those two successful NDP candidates were Phylis Young of Vancouver-Little Mountain riding, and Rosemary Brown of Vancouver-Burrard.

The 1972 NDP government became the first provincial government in Canada to fund rape relief centres, transition houses and women's health collectives. The government also expanded childcare services, from 2,500 spaces in 1971 to 18,603 by 1975, and introduced the Women's Economic Rights Branch in the Ministry of Economic Development. It created the committee to eliminate sexism in textbooks and curriculum in the Ministry of Education; it appointed Kathleen Ruff (past president of SWAG) chairperson of the Human Rights Commission, and Gene Errington (Ombudswoman of Vancouver Status of Women Council) coordinator on women's rights to the government. During its three-year term in office the government also established the Berger Commission on the Family, and introduced Bill 100, the Human Rights Code, which prohibited discrimination on the basis of sex or marital status.

Many of the women appointed to new commissions, boards and directorates had been active members of the Status of Women Council; the irony of the Council's successful sortie into electoral politics was that it disseminated its leadership ranks. Within twelve months of the election, Nancy Morrison, an outspoken feminist lawyer, was appointed to the Provincial Bench; Carole Anne Soong entered the employ of the Secretary of State; Linda Shuto became head of the Status of Women Committee of the B.C. Teachers Federation. Gene Errington, Reva Dexter, Jillian Riddington, Kathleen Ruff, Anne Marie Sweeney, Anne Petrie, Hannah Jensen and many other founding members had all left the Council to head feminist programs now supported by the government, to accept positions on boards and committees, or to pursue other careers. Phylis Young and I were now newly elected feminist members of the legislature.

Gradually a shift began to take place in the goals and focus of the Council. In the euphoria of the moment, there was at first relief that a government biased on behalf of women had been elected, that political action at the provincial level would now simply be a matter of helping the government; this was followed by a panic that perhaps political affiliation or support with this or any one government would hurt the relationship of women's organizations with future governments. By then, the Council was being heavily funded by all three levels of government, federal, provincial and municipal, and many of the workers were on salary. The autonomy and independence of the organization was undermined. The organization became so dependent on government funding that the fear of the loss of funding began to affect its activities. By 1975 the political voice of the VSWC was lowered to a whisper, and its goals became more diverse and diluted.

Despite its cautious stance, however, future Social Credit governments withdrew all funding from the organization under the pretense that it constituted a threat to the family and was really a hotbed of lesbianism. The Council survives and carries on very important work in the service of women today, but it has never recaptured the power and stature that it enjoyed and then lost after it decided to absent itself from active and visible political involvement.

However, its spirit was captured by the women of Canada when, as Penney Kome described it, "a political earthquake occurred . . . in 1981." They mobilized to force a recalcitrant group of male political leaders to rewrite Canada's Charter of Rights and Freedoms. Gathered in a kitchen in the Ottawa Convention Centre, in a last-ditch attempt to finalize the bargains that would result in the nation's Constitution, those gentlemen forgot the fifty-two percent of the population that is female, and failed to protect their equality. At that point, women and women's groups of all political ideologies united to create the powerful force that convinced them to include the equality sections, number 15 and number 28, thus enshrining the equality of all of Canada's women before and under the law.

The first time my friend Marianne Gilbert spoke to me about seeking public office I was pleased but dismissed the suggestion with a touch of humour. Coming as it did just a week after Dennis Cocke had made a similar suggestion, it seemed that the fates were teasing me. At the time, I desperately wanted to be elected to the federal House of Commons. Most of the Royal Commission recommendations dealt with the federal level of politics and my involvement in the Black movement and the women's movement convinced me that both struggles had to be fought and won on the national level if they were to benefit all Canadian women equally. After that, the national government would have to take its enlightened policies onto the international stage and link itself with movements in other countries, particularly those of the Third World, in order for the true spirit of sisterhood to be realized. Although municipal and provincial politics touched many of my own day-to-day concerns, I had never really seen either arena as addressing the need I had to translate my political action into a benefit for people in Africa, Jamaica and other nations in the developing world.

Despite my Canadian citizenship and the fact that I had spent more years living in Canada than I had in my place of birth, Jamaica, I still felt obligated to make my work serve and benefit Jamaicans and other Black people in some way. In retrospect I realize that working for OXFAM or CUSO or some other development organization would have brought me closer to my goal. But in 1970 I believed that when I worked for peace in Canada, or for women's rights, or against racism, or for the elimination of poverty, Canada as a positive force in international politics would convert these benefits into advantages for the developing world, too.

However, although my real political interest was international in a national context, I was realistic about the slim possibility of the Canadian people electing an immigrant who was Black and female to Parliament. So I thanked my good fortune for my appointment as Ombudswoman and determined to continue to make that position a political and social force in the life of B.C. women.

Marianne was persistent in her pressure on me to run, never missing an opportunity to point out the contribution I could make to various groups as an elected representative. My part-time job in the counselling service at SFU pitted me directly and continually against Phil Gaglardi, the Social Credit minister responsible for welfare, and the frustration of my position and my anger at the government combined with Marianne's suggestion. In time, I began to 'wonder if. . . .'

Just a word of explanation about my job. The government of British Columbia had a policy that forbade welfare recipients to attend university. They were encouraged to take short-term training courses and programs, although such training inevitably led to low-paying jobs that often left them no better off than when they were on welfare. Recipients were actively discouraged from pursuing any career that required an extensive time of study, as this was seen to be an abuse of the system.

From time to time people would defy this regulation and secretly enrol in university. They were inevitably discovered, and it was my responsibility as a social worker to plead their case with the Ministry of Rehabilitation and Social Improvement, as it was called despite the fact that it crushed all attempts at either rehabilitation or self-improvement. The method I used was to develop a financial statement that forecast the cost to the government of continuing to support the student for the four-year course of study in university, and to include the almost certain tax-paying employment the student could secure upon graduation. I would compare this with the long-term cost of continued support for the student without university study, or on a short-term training program. Since there was never any additional cost for a recipient attending university, it was simply a matter of comparing the cost of support for the recipient to attend university with the cost of years of welfare dependency. Since a person without skills would remain on welfare until her children were grown, the duration of support could be eight, ten or twelve years. As a social worker, I also knew that extended support could mean that in time the children too would become dispirited, defeated welfare recipients.

In every instance, I was able to prove that the dollar return to the government in taxes, human labour and productivity for a student in university far outweighed the other two options. The government would invariably permit the student to continue and complete her course of study—with the understanding that a special exception had been made in her particular case and that its action was not to be considered a precedent.

This procedure was frustrating, a waste of time and money. However, I was never able to convince the Social Credit minister to amend the regulations governing this matter. Later, when the NDP formed the government, it concluded that the community at large would be resentful of poor people on welfare enjoying a benefit that was not available to everybody. It decided that it would rather suffer the increased cost of maintaining people in poverty indefinitely than provide an avenue out of their economic condition that could be construed as a privilege or special treatment. So it too failed to change the regulation.

In any event, the chance to run against and defeat the Socred government grew increasingly tempting as Marianne continued to weave a scenario of its possibility, and my sisters in the Status

of Women Council added their voices in support of the idea. I
continued to hesitate, however, about committing myself to
the task.

Sometime in 1970 the education committee put forward the
proposal that the Council should sponsor some women to run
for the University of British Columbia Board of Governors.
After some discussion it was agreed that Carole Anne Soong
and I, as UBC alumnae and Council members with relatively
high profiles, should be put forward as candidates. I was eager
to enter the contest for a number of reasons. If I won, I would be
able to represent visible minority students at the same time that
I was fighting for women, and it would be an opportunity to test
my electability; I would be able to perform the part-time service
required of a board member without too great a disruption of
my family life and without leaving the city. The last
consideration was very important, since at that time my
children were aged thirteen, eleven and four. Although Bill was
very supportive, I was loath to embark on any career that would
necessitate leaving the children, especially Jonathan, the
youngest, while they were still quite young.

The Council ran a very vigorous campaign, and as feminist
challengers to the UBC establishment we were sufficiently
bizarre to get excellent media coverage. However, we were both
soundly defeated, I much more so than Carole Anne. That
experience was all the proof that was needed to confirm my
belief in my lack of electability; so I put electoral politics out of
my mind and resigned myself to working for political change
behind the scenes. However, my rollercoaster year was not
yet over.

My work as Ombudswoman brought me into constant contact
with the law and with lawyers. Many young female lawyers,
Nancy Morrison among them, were active members of the
Council and volunteered their services generously for the
Ombudservice. My own latent interest in law began to
resurface, so I jumped with enthusiasm at the suggestion of
Michael Jackson, a young activist professor of law at UBC and

a VSWC volunteer, that I should apply for entry into UBC law school.

Bill and I had long discussions about the fact that I was forty, with three small children, but that law had once been my career goal and that I was becoming increasingly interested in it. I needed to know the law because many of the limits on women's equality, as well as many of the barriers erected against Black people, were embedded in law. Without much effort I managed to convince myself that a joint social work/law degree would make me twice as effective in the role of advocate for these two groups.

Bill reminded me that he still owed me about six years of education, since I had worked eight years to support his medical specialty and my Master's degree had only taken two years. However, because I had been away from studying for so long and was so much older I felt very insecure about my academic ability, and I thought the course would prove to be beyond my capabilities. Bill and Michael were joined by Joan Wallace, June Dunlop and other members of the Council who encouraged me, insisting that I had nothing to lose by trying.

That same year at almost the same time, at the other end of the country, my brother Gus Wedderburn, aged forty-two, was approached by the Dean of Law at Dalhousie University with the suggestion that he should pursue a career in law. My brother, who had a Master's degree in education, was the vice-principal of a high school in Halifax and an outspoken human rights activist. He felt that this was as far up the education system as a Black person would be permitted to rise in that province. The racism in Nova Scotia was legendary. It was the province in which a Black child was refused burial in a cemetery because of an old law prohibiting the burial of Black persons in that particular graveyard, until the National Black Coalition mobilized the collective rage of the country about that law and forced the government of the day to rescind it, very reluctantly.

My brother had begun his teaching career as a principal in an all Black school in East Preston, and he was later transferred to the Halifax school system. He was very active in the Black community: president of the Nova Scotia Association for the Advancement of Coloured People, a vice-president of the National Black Coalition and a high-profile, outspoken opponent of racism. At the same time that the Halifax school board had hinted that they would prefer that he lower his public profile and he became aware of his vulnerability as an employee, Murray Fraser was encouraging him to pursue the study of law so that he could be in a position to contribute even more to the struggle for justice.

When he agreed, the Dean of the Law School waived the requirement that he write the Law School Admission Test (LSAT) and immediately accepted him as a student.

My experience was quite different. Along with my application to the UBC Faculty of Law, I was asked to submit transcripts going back to the beginning of time; and when I asked for an interview with the admissions professor, he expressed the opinion that my age would be a liability in meeting the admission requirements of the school, and added that in any event the deciding factor would be my score on the LSAT. In the end my score on the LSAT was so mediocre that UBC had no problem in rejecting my application.

Professor Michael Jackson was furious, and suggested that I should have been accepted under a special category reserved for students who had made an unusual contribution to the community, and for whom the study of law would result in further benefit to society. The year I was rejected, two businessmen, both older and with fewer academic qualifications than I, had been accepted without being required to sit the LSAT.

The rejection of UBC law school plunged me into a depression. The difference between the way Dalhousie had treated my brother and the way UBC had treated me highlighted for me, not the difference between the two universities, but the sexism of the UBC law school.

A number of the faculty at the law school protested my rejection so strongly that the school agreed to consider my application under the special category if I reapplied for the fall of 1972. But that proved to be too little, too late – by fall 1972 I was involved in other, more pressing business.

With the defeat in the UBC Board of Governors election and the rejection by the law school, 1971 began as a down year for me; I felt stymied and blocked in every direction. Jonathan was almost ready for kindergarten, Cleta and Gary were settled in school, Bill was enjoying his profession and it was once again time for me to seek full-time employment. I knew that I could remain at SFU forever on a part-time basis and continue my job as Ombudswoman, but my frustration with Phil Gaglardi, the Minister of Rehabilitation and Social Improvement, and his government was beginning to get me down. My depression didn't last for long, however, because Bea Lipinski, my boss, became involved in the possibility of having women's studies introduced at Simon Fraser; and the NDP was increasing the pressure on me to consider a nomination in an election it knew would not be long in coming.

When Marianne Gilbert approached me to join the NDP and run for public office, that was the first inkling I had of her party affiliation. She had been a member of the VSWC political committee since its inception, and had always seemed very knowledgeable about the workings of government and the various political parties. I made the mistake then (as I had on other occasions) of assuming that, like many other members of the Council, her interest in politics had developed as a direct result of her contact with the Royal Commission and its report on the status of women.

I had come to learn over the years that British Columbians kept their party affiliation a closely guarded secret; this created the impression that, although people voted in an election and some people even worked for political parties during an election, politics, like religion and sex, was a clandestine activity and not a topic for casual discussion or explanation.

Often in my early years in B.C. I used to make the mistake of assuming that British Columbians were really not very interested in politics. To me, this was truly bizarre! In the Jamaica of my youth, although one might not know where a person lived, or what a person's income or marital status was, one certainly knew whether that person supported the People's National Party and its social democratic ideology, or the Jamaica Labour Party and its conservative ideology.

Indeed, there is a ritual that every Jamaican goes through on meeting another Jamaican for the first time; it involves subtle and polite probing and sharing of information with the single goal of establishing in what part of Jamaica a person grew up, what private school that person attended, and whether that person is a PNP or JLP supporter. This information is crucial to the decision to either pursue a friendship with each other or just allow the relationship to end after the first contact. So to live in a province for sixteen years without ever having met, seen or heard of a person who voted for a Social Credit government was one of the strange happenings I had had to learn to accept as part of my B.C. experience. (The Socreds had won every provincial election during my life in B.C. until then.)

I was baffled by this phenomenon; it was important to me to know people's political affiliation. My emotional and social connectedness with people was influenced by their political and ideological commitment; indeed one of the problems Bill and I had in developing friendships while settling down in B.C. was the superficial nature of the friendship that many of our acquaintances seemed to want to maintain. Politics was so much a part of our life that we found it difficult to develop deep and sustaining friendships where political bonding was absent—in time we learned how.

I was relieved to learn that Marianne was an NDP supporter, because I really liked her and hoped that we could be friends beyond our VSWC contact. On one of her visits to me at SFU, Marianne brought an NDP membership card with her. She explained that, whether I ran in the next election or not, I should join the party. I agreed without hesitation, filled out the card, wrote a cheque for my dues and became a party member. The year was 1971.

"I have spoken to some people in the Vancouver-Burrard constituency and they are interested in meeting you," Marianne said afterwards. "They will know whether you can win an election in that riding or not. The last NDP members were Tom Berger and Dr. Ray Parkinson. Tom, as you know, is no longer interested in running for public office. Ray Parkinson is, but we are not supporting him. Please agree to meet with them."

I blanched (to the extent that I'm able) at the information. Ray Parkinson was a partner in Bill's medical office. He and his wife were friends of ours. We once sublet their cottage in the Gulf Islands when they were away in the summer, and we had supported him financially and otherwise in the 1969 election. I explained all this to Marianne, saying that to challenge him for the nomination would jeopardize his partnership with Bill and the friendship of the two families. I categorically refused to consider running in Vancouver-Burrard. Marianne was disappointed but told me to think about it.

Once again Bill and I had one of our long discussions. He assured me that my political plans and Ray's should have nothing to do with their medical partnership, and that if I wanted the nomination, then I should go after it.

By this time, Joan Wallace had declared that she would be running for the Liberal Party and invited me to do the same. I received a number of phone calls from other prominent Liberals asking me to be their candidate. I had to decline on the grounds that, as a democratic socialist, I just would not fit into the Liberal Party. Needless to say, I was flattered by all this attention but did not take any of it seriously.

Bill and I decided that my running would increase the profile of the Ombudservice and the Vancouver Status of Women, *and* get the election urge out of my system, but that was all. He was adamant that I should not expect to win, nor go into a depression if I lost.

Marianne again asked me to meet with the small group from the Vancouver-Burrard constituency that she had mentioned earlier, just to give them the opportunity to meet me. I agreed. When the Saturday arrived for the meeting, I was so nervous I felt physically ill; I knew that this was not a simple social gathering, that I was going to be probed and examined and analyzed for my worth as a candidate and a spokesperson for the NDP. Despite my protest about not wanting to run, I certainly dreaded being told that I was not electable. I wanted to cancel the meeting. And I wanted to attend it. In the end, as I knew I would, I presented myself to them.

I learnt afterwards that the seven people who met and grilled me in Astrid Davidson's apartment that Saturday morning were considered the left-wing radicals of Vancouver-Burrard; this meant that they were extreme indeed, since Vancouver-Burrard, despite having elected such luminaries as Grace MacInnis and Tom Berger, was considered a part of the radical wing that kept the party on its toes.

Moreover, I was not their first choice. They had wanted Ray Haynes, Secretary-Treasurer of the B.C. Federation of Labour, to be their candidate, but party leader Dave Barrett was wary of too obvious links with labour and did not want a high-profile trade unionist on the NDP ticket in the upcoming election. The party leadership put pressure on Ray to abandon his plan to seek the nomination on the grounds that it would be in the best interest of the party if he withdrew. The particular group of seven who interviewed me were bitter at the interference and determined to find a substitute for Ray without any party intervention.

To me the group members appeared to be very intense, very serious, totally humourless political analysts in search of the 'perfect' candidate. Although I could sense Marianne's nervousness, she concentrated on reassuring me that nothing was at stake and that I should relax. Bill's attitude had been exactly the same. "If they find you imperfect," he reassured me, "that means they don't know a winner when they meet one."

Despite these reassurances I was tense and anxious. I knew Ray Haynes, admired him and felt inadequate to fill his shoes. I also knew that I was not Dave Barrett's choice either, but that did not bother me unduly as my priorities did not include his approval. However, on that fateful day I decided to be open and straightforward, whatever the consequences. I arrived at the address on 14th Avenue, took a deep breath and climbed the stairs.

The meeting lasted three hours. I was tense, alert and on guard throughout. Marianne told me afterward that everyone had been impressed by my relaxed and assured manner. I left the meeting not knowing whether I had made a favourable impression or not but very relieved that I had survived. Later that evening Marianne phoned to say that the group wanted me to run for the nomination on a ticket with a young man named Pat Dodge, and was ready to go to work on my behalf.

The Vancouver-Burrard Dodge-Brown nominating machine was a flawless, precision-built, accurate, energy-powered, politically sophisticated and astute organization, which was truly impressive to behold! It was absolutely state-of-the-art.

However, before accepting their invitation and endorsement, more agonizing, soul searching and discussion ensued between Bill and me about the conflict and trials that we knew awaited us. My friend Gene Errington, who was also a social worker and succeeded me as Ombudswoman at the Council, was especially enthusiastic; she pledged to sign up every friend and relative living in the constituency to support my nomination. The executive of the Vancouver Status of Women Council was ecstatic. The hierarchy of the New Democratic Party was furious.

I received phone calls suggesting that a decision to run in Vancouver-Burrard would be divisive, that Ray Parkinson had 'paid his dues' and deserved the right to the nomination, that he had chosen Norm Levi as his running mate, that Burrard was a swing seat that had been lost to the party in the last election and could be lost again unless the 'right' candidates were nominated. Some of the same party people who had telephoned to encourage me to run now telephoned to exhort me not to run. Emery Barnes, the other Black hopeful in the party, phoned to offer me his place on the ballot in Vancouver Centre. Gary Lauk, his running mate, phoned to withdraw the offer on the ground that 'a woman' could not win that riding. Norm Levi, the other hopeful in Burrard, phoned to suggest that he and I should run in Vancouver South so that Ray Parkinson could choose another person to win with him in Burrard.

My phone was ringing continually; for every person who phoned to tell me not to run in Burrard, there was one who would exhort me to do so. I was torn by all the conflict swirling around me. I had not yet decided whether to seek the nomination in any riding, yet Bill was beginning to feel tension growing between him and Ray Parkinson in the office. There was tension developing between the party hierarchy and me, and once again Burrard was at war, both internally with its membership and externally with the party brass.

While I was being buffeted by this turmoil, the Dodge-Brown

machine was quietly making lists, signing up new members, lobbying old members and preparing for the nominating fight of its life.

I must confess that the excitement set my adrenalin soaring, and I was probably off and running before I knew it. The act that confirmed my decision was almost anticlimactic when it occurred. One evening Ray Parkinson telephoned me. I remember very little of the conversation except that it was tense and it was brief. He explained why he thought that I was not electable and he asked me not to run since I would surely lose the seat for the party. I pointed out to him that he had already done that in 1969. When I hung up the phone, Bill explained that he had had a similar conversation with him, that Ray had asked him to 'tell' me not to run, that he had explained to Ray that he was unable to compel me to do anything and wouldn't even if he could, so Ray had told him that he would phone me himself.

Bill added that none of that mattered now that I had decided to run. When I told him that I had still not made a decision, he told me that in my conversation with Ray I had made it quite clear that I would not be influenced or deterred by his assessment of my electability, thus leaving the clear impression that I was seeking the nomination.

I was stunned to realize that without being aware of it I had formed the intent and declared my entry in the race.

Allow me to add at this point that I do not believe in the principle of 'paid dues.' I believe that a nomination is an opportunity open to any hopeful to contest and I deplore the practice of reserving seats for someone just because they have been active in the party for a long time. My credo is that if you can't win a contest of your political peers, then you shouldn't be representing them on the hustings.

That night Bill and I had yet another of our long discussions; and once again he assured me of his full support and repeated that his partnership with Ray Parkinson should be of no concern to me. However, he also repeated that he did not want me to build up any false hopes since, with the party establishment against me, I could surely well lose.

I spent about two seconds worrying about taking three losses

in a row, since the loss of the nomination would follow on the
heels of the law school rejection and the Board of Governors
defeat, and decided that despite the possibility of a loss this was
a once-in-a-lifetime opportunity. I decided that it was the
chance that my grandmother had never had, that it was the
opening every Black person in Canada dreamed of. It was
the goal of feminists who supported the Royal Commission report, and it was the possibility that Bill and I had worked to
bring within reach of our children. It was unthinkable that I
should turn my back on it.

When I broke the news to Marianne that I was interested in
seeking the nomination, she expressed relief and pleasure but
no surprise. She had done her work well and had known that
her perseverance would pay off. She arranged my first meeting
with the Dodge-Brown Committee so that I could meet Pat
Dodge, a young man of whom I knew absolutely nothing, and
go over my role and responsibilities in the campaign. I
requested and was granted permission to add Gene Errington
to the committee. The committee, which had been meeting
regularly for some time, outlined its expectations for me.

1. I was to submit the name of every potential NDP member
   living in the riding.
2. I was to acquaint myself with party policy on issues affecting
   the riding as well as on any issue that might crop up during
   the course of the campaign.
3. I was to visit every existing NDP member of the riding to
   seek her or his support.
4. I would be handed a list of new members each week and I
   was to telephone, introduce myself and ask for their
   support.
5. I was to be accountable to the constituency as well as to
   the party.

The committee divided itself into subcommittees. Cliff
Andstein, who later became the Secretary-Treasurer of the B.C.
Federation of Labour, and Ed Livingstone were responsible for

policy development. Astrid Davidson and Marianne were responsible for scheduling my visits. Peter Dent, June Jensen and Bethoe Shirkoff were responsible for organizing the new members, and Jill Holter and Melodie Corrigal were responsible for phoning the existing members. Joe Killoran and Lorne Hanson were responsible for preparing two leaflets for distribution, and Gene Errington, although not a resident of Burrard, made good on her offer to sign up as many supporters as possible on behalf of my campaign. Pat Dodge and I were not expected to attend all meetings of the committee; we were expected to be out canvassing the membership.

For the next two months my schedule never varied. Every day I would get home from work by 3:30 p.m. I would spend some time with the children, prepare and eat dinner with the family, then leave to visit NDP members in Burrard; Bill supervised the older children's homework and prepared Jonathan for bed. The routine never changed except on Saturday and Sunday. On Saturday during the day I would sometimes do visits. I would often take Jonathan and Gary with me; Cleta was usually too busy and too 'cool' to want to tag along.

It was a slow, time-consuming process, but well worth it, because I had the opportunity not only to knock on doors, but to actually sit and visit with the membership. I learnt a lot of the NDP history of Burrard and made some good friends.

I soon learnt that Burrard New Democrats were straight-talking people. A number of them raised concerns about my race, and we talked about the possibility that it could be a liability, which we would have to work very hard to overcome in an election. Others were more concerned about the public perception of me as a radical feminist and wished that I would tone down my outspoken women's liberation ideas. Others expressed regret that they could not support me, either because I had not 'paid my dues,' for I had not been a member of the party long enough, or because my decision to challenge Ray and Norm was divisive. It soon became clear that Pat Dodge and I had a tough fight on our hands.

The worst thing that you can call an NDPer is a communist; the next worst thing is a liberal. About halfway through the campaign, the rumour started and spread quickly that I was really a liberal and Bill was a communist. The committee, after some debate, decided that we could not afford to take time away from our assigned tasks to fight the rumour, so I would have to address it head on whenever it was raised; and the pamphlet prepared for the night of the nominating meeting itself would have to stress my Jamaican social democratic tradition along with my early peace activities.

Pat, on the other hand, had all the right credentials: a white, anglo-saxon, male, long-time party member who appeared upbeat all the time and sure of victory. At the regular committee meetings there was a continual updating and recounting of delegate commitments and for some time it seemed clear that the Parkinson-Levi ticket was heading for success.

Gradually an unusual phenomenon began to take shape. It seemed that Norm Levi, the carpetbagger, was leading Ray Parkinson, the ex-MLA, by a wide margin. For some unknown reason, our committee was greatly heartened by that sign and redoubled its efforts.

The preparation for nomination night was the worst part. Vancouver-Burrard was a double-member riding; that meant that each delegate voted for two people. The first two candidates to gain fifty percent plus one of the votes cast would be the winners. Everyone wanted to win on the first ballot for a number of reasons. First, at least ten percent of members who promise support will fail to attend the meeting for one reason or another. Then, of the ones who do attend, another ten percent or more will leave after casting their ballots without waiting to hear the results or to vote in the event of a second ballot call. There is also the fear that people may change their minds between the time they give their commitment and the time they vote. Strange things happen on second ballots; they are a wild card and totally unpredictable, and no politician cares for them unless they have been carefully factored into the strategy.

The format of the meeting was as follows: after the opening preliminaries about voting procedure each candidate was given fifteen minutes to speak, including time for the nomination. After the speeches would come the balloting; then, while the ballots were being counted, there would be a keynote address and fundraising, followed by the results, and the winners' acceptance speeches.

In April 1972, the Burrard nomination was held in the old Indian Centre on Yew Street. The press, smelling blood, were out in full force. They had been excited about the idea that an ex-MLA might be defeated, curious to see whether the Status of Women Committee endorsement would be a liability or an asset to me, and intrigued by the prospect of a Black woman being nominated for the first time in Canada to run in a provincial election. They were not alone—half the provincial New Democratic Party membership also turned up to view the spectacle.

I was a nervous wreck. I could not eat for days and I could not sleep. Two weeks earlier I had decided that I needed a buffer against the depression that I knew would surely engulf me after the loss of the nomination, so I went to visit my friend Toni Cavelti, the jeweller. He had always admired my hands and would tell me that I should model rings. I asked him to design for me an inexpensive ring of gold that would lift me out of my impending melancholy. That April morning I picked up the very simple ring of bold design that he had crafted for me, and its classic modesty lifted my spirits immediately.

One thing that seems to calm me when I'm tense is water, so on the afternoon of the meeting, I decided to relax in the shower before dressing. After I had been in the shower for what Bill claims was an inordinate amount of time, he came in, turned off the water and said "Let's go get this thing over with so that life can return to normal." I dressed, put on my anti-depression ring and headed for the meeting.

The children were excited at being allowed to attend. Cleta and Gary, being nearly fifteen and thirteen respectively, had lived through all the discussions and agonizing and were just bursting with anticipation. Cleta shared my nervousness, but Gary was confident of my victory. Jonathan, at five, was supremely oblivious to anything but the excitement generated by the crowd and the prospect of staying up past his bedtime.

The building was packed to overflowing, mostly with

spectators. Every NDPer in the Lower Mainland was there, including the 'heavies': the future attorney general, Alex MacDonald, future minister of finance Dave Stupich and future minister of health Dennis Cocke. Many members of the Status of Women Council and the B.C. Association for the Advancement of Coloured People were there, as well as every relative and friend that Pat Dodge, Norm Levi, Ray Parkinson or I could muster.

At the last meeting of the committee, Pat and I had been told that the number of undecided votes was high and that we needed to capture most of them in order to win. That meant that our success rested on our speeches. The decision was that I was to be nominated by a woman, and gentle, soft-spoken Bethoe Shirkoff was chosen to perform that chore.

I had determined not to read my speech, so I fell back on an old technique that I still use occasionally. After writing the speech, I practised its delivery over and over until I was satisfied that I had the accents in the right places and the tone and timbre of voice correct; then I recorded it, and recorded it, and recorded it until I had a perfect version. The cassette of the perfect version accompanied my every move, and I played it until the words and the tone and the sound of it were seared into my brain.

There is only one danger I had found in memorizing a speech and that was that a lost word could paralyze me and blank my memory out. So to avoid this I would choose four 'trigger' words that I would write in large bold letters on a small card that fitted into the palm of my hand. In the event of a memory blank, a quick glance at the card would trigger my memory to another idea and away I would go. I never tried to recapture a lost thought or remember a forgotten idea; I would just pass on to the next. My entire family heard my speech so often that even they knew it by heart.

Despite my preparedness my legs were trembling so hard that when my nominator announced my name, I was afraid to stand in case I might fall. The applause that greeted my ascent to the platform, however, was deafening and sustained. That proved to be all I needed. I began to speak, got caught up in the words, the memory drive kicked in, and I never missed a beat.

When I was through, I could tell from the applause and grins on the faces of my committee that, although I might not have converted any opponents, I had held my supporters and picked up the uncommitted vote. The results proved me correct.

That night, on the first ballot, Norm Levi and I were nominated to represent the riding of Vancouver-Burrard in the upcoming provincial election. Six months later Bill and Ray Parkinson severed their medical partnership.

CHAPTER SEVEN

I suspect that each of us carries inside a memory that is so startling, so vivid, that it remains alive long after all our other recollections fade. The memory may not be tied to any heroic or profound experience, but may be more in the nature of a miracle, a surprise, the receiving of something for which one had longed but dared not hope – sort of like the "for me?" query and joy that lights up my granddaughter's face at the unexpected receipt of a coveted treasure.

August 30, 1972, was my miracle. That was the day when Canadians living in the area of Vancouver bounded by 16th Avenue, Fraser Street, Waterloo and the Pacific Ocean elected me to represent them in the British Columbia legislature. Because it made very little sense to me that people who had for years refused to rent me accommodation or hire me for employment would entrust me with the responsibility of representing them in the place of power, where laws governing their lives were drafted and enforced, I had run in the election with my intellect but not with my heart. Don't get me wrong; the race for me had not been a casual one. I had run hard, run to win, but deep inside I had known that racism – that faceless coward that dogs the endeavours of all non-white people in North America – would strike at some time, barring the way and putting an end to the dream.

So in this election, as on so many other occasions, I had

prepared myself for defeat. Together with Bill I had constructed the defensive shield, part rationalization, part extrapolation, that would protect me against despondency and self-blame. Even as I campaigned, I was exploring career alternatives, having learned that for a Black person a contingency plan was the best defence against defeatism and despair.

The decision of the Vancouver-Burrard voters stunned me. Not since 1858, when Mifflin Wistar Gibbs sat as a councillor in the City of Victoria, had a Black person held public office in British Columbia. So, on August 30, 1972, when the voters overturned that tradition and included Emery Barnes and me with the thirty-six other New Democrats chosen to form the first social democratic government in B.C., they were not just making political history but writing Black history as well.

I do not believe that our election resulted from any revolutionary decision on the part of the voters to strike a blow for racial equality. Rather, their discontent with the existing government and their determination to turf it out of office overrode their prejudices, and resulted in the temporary colour and political blindness that allowed them to support us despite the fact that we were both New Democrats and Black.

My miracle encompassed a triumph not just over racism but over sexism as well. Despite the fears expressed by the more traditional elements in the party that my outspoken support for the women's movement would cost me votes, I had held fast to my decision that women were my constituency and would receive my outspoken support. Women, visible minorities, labour and the poor were all constituencies viewed by some party members as double-edged swords that could hurt the party if we were seen to be too closely allied with them. Since these very groups were my reason for entering politics, compromising my support for them would have been a betrayal of their trust, and would have rendered my participation in politics irrelevant and useless.

My victory signalled in some small measure the potential power of those groups, made me a national curiosity, and confirmed British Columbia's reputation for eccentric politics. For me, victory was also a vindication of my decision to reject

Rosemary (age five) and 'Junior'
(her brother) dressed in their Sunday best.

Back row: 'Junior' and Nana (Rosemary's
mother's Nanny) Front row: Rosemary,
Grace and their mother — all at Nana's
house, Jamaica 1936.

Imogene Wilson-James (Rosemary's
grandmother) in her early thirties, around
1900.

*Rosemary with her friend 'Rex' in the
backyard, Jamaica 1943.*

*Rosemary's Aunt Gwen and Uncle Stanley
at the Queen's Garden Party, Buckingham
Palace, London 1953.*

*Rosemary and Bill on
their wedding day in
August 1955.*

First day on the job — 1972 — as member
of the British Columbia Legislature.
Photograph by Jim Ryan Photo, Victoria, B.C.

In the British Columbia Legislature, 1973.

Leadership convention, Winnipeg 1975.

*International Women's
Year Conference,
Australia 1975.*

*Leadership convention in
Winnipeg 1975. L to R:
Gus Wedderburn,
Rosemary, Robin Geary,
Jane Covington.*
Photograph by Photo Features Ltd.,
Hull, P.Q.

Family portrait, Vancouver 1975. L to R: Gary, Cleta, Jonathan, Rosemary and Bill.

Peace march, April 1983.

First honorary doctorate, Mt. St. Vincent University, Halifax, Nova Scotia .

Four generations get together in Christmas 1985. L. to R: Marina, Katherine, Rosemary, Cleta and Rosemary's mother.

Ed Broadbent and Rosemary in 1986.

Rosemary with her grandchildren — Katherine and Ashton — in the summer of 1988.

Rosemary and good friend Shirley Mann on the dock at Lasqueti Island.

A new beginning at Match International, Ottawa 1989.

the Uncle Tom role that is often touted as the best route to success in society for Blacks and women.

When I awoke on August 31, my stomach was queasy and waves of nausea washed over me. For the second time in my life (the first being my wedding day) I was facing a future that was truly unknown, and I was scared. In a panic I realized that I had no idea what a politician actually did, day after day, other than make speeches and run in elections. I was sure that I lacked the ability to live up to the expectations of the electorate and I felt like a fraud, as though somehow I had managed to fool everyone into thinking that I could be a politician. The voters had called my bluff and now I was about to be unmasked!

My immediate reaction was to get into the shower and just stay there. That proved impossible because the phone calls and telegrams promptly came pouring in. It seemed that every Black person in Canada had been following the campaign and had had a personal stake in Emery and in me. They were celebrating right across Canada. Like Lincoln Alexander's before us, our victory gave them hope that the individual could rise above racism, and their outpouring of love, pride and awe added to my torture.

Feminists were ecstatic. Judy LaMarsh, a dear friend and role model, who was at that time a radio broadcaster on CJOR, could not conceal her joy as she reported the NDP win and the election of "two feminists—Phylis Young and Rosemary Brown." She analyzed and speculated and commented throughout the evening of the election and the day after on what those two phenomena would mean to the province in general and to women in particular.

I lay in bed in a near catatonic state while Bill and the kids, boisterous and ebullient, handled the phone calls and raced around—happy, stunned and amazed. From time to time Cleta or Gary would come into the bedroom just to stare at me. Then they would give me a hug and with a wild whoop race out of the room, adding their noise to the increasing din in the house.

Jonathan had no idea what the excitement was all about, but he was enjoying every minute of it. Lying there, I could hear Gary and Cleta asking Bill what it would mean to have a politician for a mother and speculating on how this would change our lives. They were euphoric, but I was terrified and tried to escape thoughts of the future by reliving the campaign from the night of my nomination to the present.

I recalled how, immediately after the nomination, we began the difficult but necessary task of forging links with my running mate, Norm Levi, and his supporters. Before the nomination, the Dodge-Brown committee had been careful not to be outspokenly critical of Norman, nor to speak ill of him during the nomination campaign. We had used the 'damn with faint praise' technique, commenting on his large number of election tries and failures, but adding that he was an able person and perhaps the voters would ignore his past and vote him in this time. We were also careful to express gratitude for his many years of service to the party.

We were not so kind, however, to his running mate, Ray Parkinson. The strategy was that, if only one of the opposing camp could be defeated, then it should be Parkinson, since he was the more vulnerable. So we played on the resentment and anger that party members always feel towards an elected member who loses a seat once held by the party. We hammered home the fact that he should not be given the opportunity to lose that seat again.

The Levi supporters had not been generous with our ticket. They had been determined to defeat both Pat Dodge and me, pulling no punches in criticizing my lack of political experience and party history, as well as Pat's youth and extreme radicalism.

Although our workers were angry about the hard-hitting and hostile nature of their campaign, we stuck to our strategy, knowing that coming from behind we had to break their ticket and isolate Ray Parkinson. If we were lucky, Norm, as a carpetbagger, would go down to defeat as well. In any event there was not the history of bad blood between Norm's supporters and mine as there was with Ray, so in the campaign we focused on accentuating our positives while gently stroking and seducing Norm's supporters.

It is not true that, when a political fight is over, the warring factions in a party close ranks. Although members of a political party like to refer to themselves as a family—a family without blood ties—they have memories stretching beyond lifetimes, and sensitivities more fragile than a butterfly's wings. Pacts are built on loyalties, cemented over real or imagined acts of betrayal, and often internal hostilities will distract a party from pursuing its goal or defending itself against a common enemy. Today, for example, many years and many conventions after a particularly bitter NDP provincial leadership campaign in 1969, the label 'Berger person' or 'Barrett person' (identifying supporters of Tom Berger and Dave Barrett) still sticks, and gives promise of remaining with some members until their death.

In 1972 my campaign committee was made up almost exclusively of Berger people and Norm's committee almost exclusively of Barrett people. We distrusted each other; but Vancouver-Burrard was a double-member riding, and we knew not only that we needed each other's coattails to win but also that voters had been known to split their loyalties, an occurrence that neither of us wanted to risk since the outcome was not clearly to our advantage.

So both committees were determined to apply whatever adhesive was necessary to keep our organizations working together throughout the election. The consensus was that we had a genuine outside chance to recapture the riding, and we were all resolved not to blow it.

Despite our determination and effort, the forging of the Levi and Brown campaigns into one unit never really happened. Norm and I respected each other, recognized our interdependence and, to some extent, even liked each other; some of our supporters liked each other very much. An uneasy truce existed between the two camps, and the tension never erupted into open hostility. We came to accommodate the depth of our division, and in time settled for a cooperative, holding effort rather than a united one. The credit for this compromise goes to

June Jensen, a gifted conciliator respected by both sides, whom we wisely and happily chose to be our campaign manager. She was a calm and unflappable woman who spoke quietly but firmly and was clearly in control of the campaign at all times.

The day the campaign office opened its doors at Broadway and Maple Street in Vancouver, volunteers began streaming in. Before very long we had exceeded our need for workers. Energy levels were high and everyone plunged into the fray with enthusiasm and optimism.

At that time, no one entertained or even spoke about the possibility of the NDP forming a government. We knew that the rural areas of the province as well as the affluent Vancouver constituencies of Point Grey, Little Mountain and Vancouver-South would never support NDP candidates. We were buoyed, however, by the knowledge that the Social Credit government had driven educators, trade unionists, seniors, feminists and the poor beyond the point of helpless rage, and across the province members of these groups were volunteering in unprecedented numbers to work in NDP campaigns. Teachers and trade unionists were organizing their own parallel campaigns to fight the incumbent government with ferocity and passion.

At the same time we could see that the NDP slogan "Enough is enough!" had struck a respondent chord; and our platform of public car insurance and increased financial and social benefits for seniors and the poor was winning us new voters among young drivers, senior citizens and other groups with traditional loyalties rooted in the Social Credit Party.

Social Credit supporters were mildly anxious but retained their arrogant stance, confident that, while British Columbians had always criticized their government, they had nonetheless re-elected it rather than risk the unknown and mythically detrimental politics of an NDP government. This time W.A.C. Bennett took to the hustings with his historic cry that 'the Socialist Hordes were at the gates' of the province, and only a Social Credit government could protect free enterprise from sure death. The deafening silence that greeted this led him to become more shrill as it became obvious even to him that, wherever the 'socialist hordes' might lead them, the people of B.C. felt it would be an improvement on what the Socreds had achieved.

The results brought in by our canvassers were so outrageously positive that we discredited them on the grounds that people were just not being truthful about their intentions. However, the parallel 'Apple' campaign being run by the teachers and the canvassing conducted by trade unions among their membership both supported the findings of our canvassers. In disbelief we checked and double-checked the results as support for the party seemed to grow at a phenomenal rate.

The Vancouver media kept referring to Vancouver-Burrard as a 'swing' riding: the voters could go either way, and indeed the riding's history was of swings between the NDP and Social Credit in alternate elections. Dave Barrett visited us from time to time, and on each occasion expressed pleasure at our organization and canvass results. However, June Jensen, the campaign manager, worried that all the speculation on victory might distract and lull me into a false sense of euphoria, and so she insisted that I should ignore all rumours and predictions and just concentrate on discharging my specific tasks to the best of my ability.

One such task involved participation in all-candidates meetings. These meetings were large and raucous; hostility towards the government was loud, open and generally took the form of ridicule. But for the absence of music and the fact that they were held indoors, they reminded me of Jamaican election campaigns. The weather was hot and wonderful, there was a definite carnival air about, and many of the audience obviously attended the meetings for their entertainment value.

Although I was not a stranger to public speaking and had participated in debates on other occasions, I was nonetheless petrified as I awaited my turn to speak at the first meeting. However, Norman was relaxed, and he managed to lower my anxiety level somewhat by teasing me that the NDP had never lost a candidate at an all-candidates meeting. He proved to be correct. The bias of the audience was clear and vigorous from the start—we were preaching to the converted. The outburst of applause greeting our introduction erupted with every comment we made and was equalled only by the catcalls prompted by every reference to or by the Social Credit candidates. In no time at all, Norman and I were convinced that we were clever, witty and knowledgeable; we handled hecklers with aplomb and we grew sassy on the applause. All future all-candidates meetings proved to be similar 'love-ins.'

The only hostile questions directed at me concerned the hypocritical fear that my children would suffer as a result of my political activities, and accusations of their impending neglect. At first the question made me defensive because I shared those concerns myself. I felt guilty about spending a lot of time away from the children, aged fourteen, twelve and five, so I handled the question badly. In time it became clear that the Socreds realized they had found my Achilles' heel. I was not fooled. I knew that the questioners cared not one whit about my children, but they saw that their questions wounded me and so, smelling blood, they kept tearing away, heckling, questioning and accusing me every chance they got.

My committee became alarmed and I became concerned about my obvious vulnerability and about the ease with which my opposition were using my guilt to undermine me. Norman and the committee offered me extensive advice on how to handle the matter, primarily that I should resort to humour as a means of diffusing the discomfort. But guilt and fear curled up tight in the secret recesses of my mind and I knew as I tried to dislodge them that in this instance, humour was impossible; I was no equal to the demons that whispered to me that I was placing my selfish ambition ahead of my children.

I raged against my guilty feelings, roared silent curses about the unfairness of the fact that in a similar situation Bill would not be plagued by any such emotions or considerations. I knew my feelings were irrational; that, far from being neglected, the children were thriving in the care of their father, a house-keeper and me. I knew, in addition, that they loved the excite-ment of the campaign and revelled in all the attention they were getting from their peers and mine. I argued and fought with myself in an attempt to destroy the assumption that some-how my physical presence protected my children and stamped me as a good mother, while my absence automatically branded me bad and placed them at risk. Finally, exhausted and enlightened by the struggle, I came to accept that I would not lose the feelings of guilt, and that I had a choice: either quit the campaign or accommodate and adjust to reality.

I forced myself to mock my fears and to incorporate my guilt into the humour that then came easily. I began my speeches by first thanking all the Socreds in the audience concerned about my children for their caring, and reported that the children were asking for their assistance in sending me to Victoria. After a few more throw-away lines, I would launch into the body of my presentation, from time to time referring to my experience as a mother and a wife and to the added dimension those two roles gave to my perception of the world, emphasizing this as one more asset that I would bring to the political sphere. Questions about my parenting responsibility and abilities soon disappeared.

I learnt a lesson from that experience that I used throughout my fourteen years in public office—namely to be the first person to identify my own weakness, my own Achilles' heel, and then to deal with that weakness before it becomes a public issue. Doing so is a task that calls for clearsighted and brutal honesty, but it is essential, not only because the opposition always seems to have an instinctive knack for ferreting out a politician's weakness, but more importantly because the fear of the public exposure of a hidden fear, or concern about the fear itself, is a problem that is better prevented than cured.

There has always been order in my life and the election campaign did not change that. My days began early so that I could spend some time with the children and Bill before they left for school and work respectively. After they were gone I would settle down with the coffee-pot to study the campaign briefing notes, eager to be well-informed on every issue. At noon I would go to the campaign office and eat lunch with any workers or volunteers who happened to be there, then I would return telephone calls and receive instructions concerning appointments.

The afternoon was spent canvassing, appearing on TV or radio, attending meetings with special-interest groups or participating in media events. I would have dinner with the family; after their homework, the children would come to the committee room where Cleta and Gary would stuff envelopes, lick stamps and make themselves generally useful while Jonathan would be petted and spoilt. Bill, who hated canvassing and so had happily taken on extended parenting responsibilities, picked them up later and took them home to bed.

My early evenings in the committee room were spent talking with the volunteers before going out canvassing or to all-candidates meetings. I would try to be home by eleven o'clock so that Bill and I could watch the news on TV together and I could unwind, then retire for the night. I had come to realize that, unless I had this time for reflection and relaxation, I would toss about for a sleepless night.

Although I am confident that I have a talent for persuasion that is outstanding, I hated and still hate to have to sell myself, whether for a job or for public office. I know that many politicians love knocking on doors, making promises, talking about themselves – and I have always envied them that gift. One of the great joys for me on retirement was that I would never again have to ask anyone to vote for me, to give me money or to work in my campaign.

I am a very private person, even a little shy; contact with racial hostility has left me wary and hypersensitive to the point that I found political canvassing excruciatingly painful and repugnant. In NDP politics, however, canvassing is mandatory so I had to do it, and do it with a smile on my face and a bounce in my step. To achieve this I had to use the process of displacement: I thought of myself and often spoke of myself in the third person, speaking of Rosemary Brown as a person I respected, loved and knew to be honest and dependable and to have integrity. I also used heavy doses of denial, so that the hostile response was always rationalized as being directed at the party, the ideology or the policy, but never at me personally. I canvassed through that first election campaign internally tense, uptight and focused, almost completely unaware of anything outside my immediate tasks. I later learnt that wearing the smile and the composure that masked this fact was behaviour that earned me the title of 'ideal candidate.'

True, I had been careful to develop a pattern to my days and nights but, as I lay in bed on the morning of August 31, I realized that I had been so totally wrapped up in the fate of my own riding and oblivious to the province as a whole that I was unprepared for the defeat of the Social Credit government; and my panic returned as the knowledge dawned that much as I had wished it, I had not prepared myself for victory and consequently was at a loss as to how to handle it.

I had time to panic at my leisure, because two weeks passed before I heard from the premier. When word came it was in the form of a memo announcing a caucus meeting in Victoria and requesting my attendance. By that time he had named his cabinet and the caucus meeting was really just a chance for the socialist hordes to preen and indulge in the inevitable photo opportunity.

Neither Emery Barnes nor I was named to that first cabinet, which consisted only of those elected members who had served in the legislature prior to 1972. Nor were we included in any subsequent cabinet appointments. Although I was disappointed by my exclusion, I was not really surprised. The response in the Black community, however, was immediate and negative. They interpreted the premier's action as an insult to the Black race. They felt that they had been duped by commitments made in the party's excellent policy on racial equality into supporting promises that proved to be false and without basis. Prime Minister Diefenbaker's act of appointing Lincoln Alexander to his federal Conservative cabinet increased the belief that the NDP's statements on race were just empty rhetoric.

In time the NDP did regain some credibility with the small percentage of Black people in B.C. who espouse the ideology of social democracy. But for the most part they remain cynical and pragmatic, playing the opportunistic politics of going where the power is, and the loyalty that Emery and I enjoy in the Black community has not been translated into widespread support for the NDP either here or across Canada.

Liberal and Conservative feminists greeted my exclusion from cabinet with a mixture of disappointment and relief; relief because for them my exclusion was proof that sexism was as alive and well in the New Democratic Party as it was in their own parties, a fact that gave them comfort. Most other women who had worked for the election of the NDP saw my exclusion as an ominous sign. They believed that they had been used by the party to gain power, and that their issues would be ignored now that the election was over.

As a member of the government caucus, I knew that inside the caucus women's most stubborn enemy was not misogyny but paternalism. The premier, as well as a number of male colleagues, held fast to the belief that they knew better than women themselves what our needs were and how best to meet them. Consequently they would disregard the demands articulated by women, substituting their solutions based on their particular beliefs of what was best for women.

This condescension was galling and extremely difficult for me to deal with, especially since caucus confidentiality prevented me from revealing these facts to the women's community and sharing with them the burden of this indignity. An example of the most glaring paternalism centred on the introduction of a women's ministry. The Women's Rights Committee of the NDP had embarked on a very long and analytical search for a way to implement and monitor policies to attack the systemic inequalities in women's lives. After many hours of research, consciousness-raising, exploration and debate on this issue, it was decided that the solution lay in the careful crafting of a ministry designed to do this job. The debate was not confined to B.C. All across Canada, feminists were searching for the best structure through which to address their political goals.

A women's ministry had the unanimous support of the B.C. feminist community. The hope was that such a structure would serve as a pilot that could be copied by the federal government and other provincial governments. A resolution was approved at the 1971 convention of the party and adopted as part of the 1972 election platform. After the election Dave Barrett, the new premier, publicly rejected the policy of the women's ministry on the ground that he did not believe in giving any group special status. He did at the same time, of course, appoint a minister of Indian Affairs.

In repudiating the women's wishes he repeated ad nauseam the cliché that he supported "human rights, not women's rights, because human rights include the rights of both women and men." The depth of his ignorance about women's condition was profound and equalled only by his belief that the women's movement was a temporary aberration, a blip in history supported only by a few discontented women. His mind was closed. He failed to appreciate the significance of the experiment in gaining and using power which that ministry represented; nor even to appreciate that it was part of what Herbert Marcuse referred to as the most important revolution of the twentieth century.

This attitude unleashed the fury of the women's movement across Canada against Dave personally and, by extension, the caucus, since for the most part the other members remained silent in the face of Dave's chauvinist pronouncements. The rage of the women was almost unbearable. Even many years later as I write about this, I can feel the knot forming in my stomach. Like the character in the Charles Atlas advertisement, Dave kicked sand in our collective face, and we felt helpless to reverse his intransigence.

The disillusionment and the speedy demise of our high expectations of the government, coupled with the knowledge that the Socreds were an even more regressive option, was the cruel and bitter trap in which we found ourselves. We fought the injustice of the situation with every weapon at our disposal. But even after the NDP provincial convention of 1973 reaffirmed its overwhelming support for the establishment of a women's ministry, Dave immediately informed the press that the resolution was not a priority and would not receive his support. Many of the tired, exhausted and angry women delegates dissolved into tears as a retreat from the violence that raged through our heads and battered our brains. Dave's action was not a B.C. peculiarity, but represented to women within and outside the NDP and the province the never-ending oppression, disrespect and contempt men have meted out to women since the beginning of time. We were determined that he had not heard the last of us; it was left to women outside the party, however, to respond by working for his defeat in 1975.

The Vancouver Status of Women Committee bestowed on him its first Male Chauvinist Pig award and presented him with a large plastic pig. It sat in the centre of our caucus table until the party's defeat in 1975.

The ease with which subsequent federal governments have appointed ministers responsible for women's matters makes us wonder what Dave was afraid of, and why women had to fight so hard and so long for a simple act of recognition. The tragedy is that the very public tension that existed between Dave and the Women's Rights Committee, backed by all B.C. feminists, as well as that between Dave and me, overshadowed the excellent programs, policies and laws supporting and enriching women's lives that were being introduced and implemented by his ministers of health, education and economic development, and the attorney general.

In 1975, when the government went to the people once again, one feminist group, the Vancouver Women's Health Collective, withheld its support. A number of other women's groups, though not prepared to support the return of a Social Credit government, reluctantly accepted that the Women's Rights Committee and the convention of the New Democratic Party were unable to force the premier to implement his own party's policy on women's issues. They too decided to sit out the election and explore options other than electoral politics in the search for equality and justice for women. Feminists were trapped between the two political parties in the province, both of which viewed them and their demands with hostility and distrust.

I have been asked on many occasions to express my own feelings about being left out of the cabinet, but my loyalty to the party prevented me from being publicly critical of Dave Barrett while he was leader, and my personal pride prevented me from publicly admitting to pain, hurt or anger about what was probably no more than an act of pettiness on his part.

However, I must confess that I have given the matter some thought and probably more importance than it deserves; in any event I have arrived at some conclusions and observations.

Although I am sure that Dave's decision to exclude me from cabinet was not based on any assessment of my intelligence, integrity or ability, I am equally sure that a male with similar qualifications, experience and community support would not have been treated as I was. I also concluded that being excluded from cabinet could be interpreted as a compliment to me—it meant that my outspoken feminism and my close ties with the radical wing of the party placed me in a position of being thought too independent to be relied upon for total allegiance to the leader at all times. At the same time I lacked the depth and strength of support within the party to raise any prolonged outcry against my exclusion.

Cabinet-making gives a leader an opportunity to exercise power over a caucus. It is a whip to punish, a wand to reward, and the enforcer that ensures and sustains the paramountcy of the will of the leader. In this instance Dave had the chance, if he chose, to punish me for running in nomination against Ray Parkinson, for enjoying the support of Ray Haynes and the B.C. Federation of Labour, and for defiantly calling for a women's ministry despite his firm opposition.

He also had the chance to place my skills, experience and talent to good use in one of his ministries. In the end, the nugatory reasons that he had for excluding me outweighed the valid ones that argued for my inclusion.

How do I really feel? There is power, prestige, influence and money attached to a cabinet appointment. In cabinet I could have done more for women, visible minorities and other disadvantaged groups who made up my constituency. The Black community would have been proud and it would have been a clear and positive message to feminists about the NDP's support for women's rights. On the other hand, I have often wondered whether the post of cabinet minister, with its heavy workload, would have deterred me from grabbing the once-in-a-lifetime challenge to seek the federal leadership of the party in 1975, with the opportunity that particular experience gave women to make feminism the topic of political debate on a national scale. On balance, would a provincial cabinet post have been more important than that? Who knows? I only know that, given the choice, I would not have traded the experience of seeking the federal leadership for a cabinet appointment.

There is an old Jamaican saying that when "yu tief from tief, God laugh," implying that God is amused whenever a malicious act backfires. I like to think that in Winnipeg on July 4, 1975, as the voting for a federal leader was forced into a third ballot and Dave Barrett anxiously trod the convention floor desperately stalking support for Ed Broadbent's leadership campaign, anyone listening closely would have heard a chuckle escaping from God's lips.

Once I had overcome the initial shock of being elected part of an NDP government, I plunged into political life with impatience and anticipation. I believed in the power of governments to create change and I believed in the commitment of the NDP to improve the quality of life of all British Columbians. Over the following three years I learned the hard lesson that often political power is more imagined than real, and that sometimes expectations can be so high that they surpass the bounds of possible achievements. Those two lessons were so painful that, by the time of our government's defeat in 1975, I was almost wishing for my own electoral defeat.

In the beginning, however, my goals and tasks seemed very straightforward and uncomplicated. I had two major items as well as a number of lesser ones on my agenda. First and foremost, because of my personal experience with discrimination, I wanted tough, ironclad human rights legislation, legislation to plug every loophole through which any individual or organization had ever been able to discriminate against a person because of her or his race, gender, religion, disability or marital or economic status. I wanted to be sure that all persons, regardless of those factors, would be free to live, work, eat and worship wherever they desired or could afford to.

Again because of personal experience, I was concerned about the discrimination in housing that was aimed at people with children. I was prepared to explore the possibility of legislating against such practices, without infringing on the right of senior citizens to exclusive and separate accommodation if they so wished.

I was tired of the old 'race, religion or creed' prohibition in existing law; it left institutions, businesses and individuals free to pursue discriminatory practices against women because of their marital status or against any individual because she or he was physically disabled. I accepted that human rights legislation has to be broader and more encompassing than the four points on my agenda, but, for me, those four—gender, disability, and marital and economic status—were non-negotiable items. I also knew that human rights legislation by itself was only half the struggle; that to be truly effective it had to be coupled with equally strong affirmative action legislation, and that was the second item on my agenda.

My work with the Ombudservice of the Status of Women Council as well as with the BCAACP led me to conclude that it was the double blow of discrimination coupled with blocked access that locked women, the disabled and visible minorities into low-paying jobs, high unemployment and poverty in old age. My social work training helped me to understand that equality is best interpreted and earned by people themselves, that it is not a gift that can be bestowed on an individual by someone else.

My theory, therefore, was that people should be empowered to pursue their own liberation, and one step on the road to such empowerment, one external service we politicians could provide, was to remove the hurdles and open the doors to opportunities.

I use the term external service deliberately because I know that, although liberation is hampered by low self-esteem, one must be realistic about the limits of one's influence. People wrestle with internal and personal demons born of years of negative socialization; these cannot be defeated by provincial legislation alone, although it can remove the practices on which much of that socialization rests. Provincial legislation can state quite clearly 'thou shalt not discriminate,' and introduce special measures to right the historical imbalance that has victimized any one group in a profession, trade or other type of employment. Human rights legislation and affirmative action were my immediate, concrete, pragmatic goals; empowered women and men working for their own equality was my dream; political process was the route through which I hoped to make it happen.

My reality became disillusionment. I learned that effective human rights legislation violates the unfettered right of the individual to choose to whom to rent accommodation, whom to hire or whom to serve in a place of business, as well as to whom to grant membership in an organization or club. It places the right of the individual in conflict with the right of a group, and consequently engenders controversy, hostility and backlash. It creates contradictions and challenges, discomfort and rage.

The task of formulating perfect, loophole-proof human rights legislation involves political risk-taking in its more dangerous form, a fact that often terrifies politicians. David Vickers, the courageous and brilliant Deputy Attorney General of the day, was, however, equal to the task. He earned my respect and gratitude as he hammered out a Human Rights Act that was too strong for the more timid members of the caucus; nonetheless, with the navigational skills of Alex MacDonald, the consummate Attorney General, it survived to become the best piece of human rights legislation ever introduced in this country. Its only weakness was its failure to include sexual orientation as a protected right, but in British Columbia in the 1970s not even an NDP caucus was prepared to risk such a revolutionary act, and Alex MacDonald was willing to leave debate and decision concerning that issue to the murky interpretation of the courts.

As I followed my agenda day by day, it became increasingly clear that nothing in politics would happen the way I had expected or envisioned. The hostilities between Dave Barrett and me raged unabated and affected my relationship with most of my colleagues.

For the three years that we were the government I existed as a multi-personality. I endeavoured to be a full-time mother and wife, an active feminist and outspoken advocate, a public figure and the fun-loving member of a small clique in the caucus. Needless to say, my immune system was thrown into turmoil and before the three years were over, I experienced a series of eccentric and grotesque ailments. During that period I developed symptoms of brain tumour, gall bladder ailments, angina and hemorrhoids. I had problems with my teeth, my eyes, my skin and my bladder. I nearly doubled my weight in the first year, lost the added weight in the second and gained it back in the third.

Much of the time in Victoria I was desperately lonely; I began eating and drinking too much. Despite this, I continued to overwork and over-extend myself on behalf of my constituents, women, visible minorities and my family. It was a nightmare, relieved only by my return to Bill and the children in Vancouver each weekend, and, after the evening sessions of the legislature on Tuesday and Thursday, by dancing with a small group of colleagues until 2:30 a.m. at The Forge.

I survived those three years in part because, by sheer blind luck, Robin Geary had walked into my life during the election, because the women's community remained supportive and nurturing, and because my family remained a haven and a secure oasis. But, unrecognized by me, a shift was taking place in my life. Imperceptibly and in subtle ways, I was becoming less dependent on my family, and more dependent on my political and feminist friends—almost stealthily they began to replace my family as my source of guidance, advice and succor. Despite my determination to prevent it, the erosion of my family life had begun.

Different people influence a person's life at different times. Soon after August 30, Robin Geary volunteered to help me handle the massive flow of mail that resulted from my election. When I learned that she was a better spinner and weaver than she was a typist, I struck a bargain with her to supply me with spun wool for my weaving and crocheting, in exchange for which I would do the typing. She remained to become the politically astute constituency representative who organized and administered my constituency office in Vancouver throughout the seven years that I represented Vancouver-Burrard. She was beside me throughout the 1975 federal leadership campaign and the Social Credit gerrymander in 1978 that wiped out Vancouver-Burrard and created 'Gracie's Finger.' She was there through the battles of the NDP government years, and in 1975 almost single-handedly forced many feminists who planned to boycott the election campaign to rethink their position and to work for my re-election.

Primarily, she was the buffer between me and the disappointed and disillusioned constituents who felt betrayed by the government's failure to deliver on their expectations. At the same time she insistently focused their attention on the positive aspects and actions of the government. Her efforts contributed greatly to my re-election in 1975, the election that saw twenty-six New Democrats go down to defeat — including the premier himself.

Despite my own disillusionment with the government I was saddened by the defeat in 1975. I was proud of the government's achievements and believed that an honest and impartial investigation of its record would show that, despite some of the premier's words and pronouncements on women's rights, the introduction and increase in services for women and the poor were phenomenal.

Through our Minister of Health, Dennis Cocke, we were the first provincial government to fund rape relief centres, women's health collectives and shelters for battered women. Publicly funded daycare spaces were increased. A guaranteed minimum income as well as extended medical benefits that included the cost of prescription drugs for seniors were introduced by Norm Levi, our Minister of Human Resources.

The Ministry of Education struck a task force to begin the job of identifying and eliminating school textbooks that were sexist or racist. The Ministry of Economic Development established a Women's Economic Rights Branch. The human rights legislation introduced by the Attorney General prohibited discrimination based on sex or marital status, and a Royal Commission headed by Mr. Justice Tom Berger examined the dual area of children and the family. Its report included many sweeping and fair recommendations in the area of division of property in the event of divorce.

Those women's groups that identified and worked with specific ministries were satisfied that the government was moving slowly, but clearly in the right direction. In time even the premier came to modify his position, and in 1974 permitted the appointment of Gene Errington as Coordinator on Women's Affairs, with a small staff and nominal budget.

All these positive acts proved unable to reverse the early sense of betrayal experienced by labour, anti-poverty groups, women's groups and other of the traditional supporters of the NDP. Moreover, this disenchantment was exploited and publicly highlighted by the NDP's traditional enemies. In addition, the mining and real-estate developers and other corporate groups found that, once they had been able to convince the Liberals and Conservatives to subsume their principles and crawl under the Social Credit banner to form one anti-NDP party, the defeat of the NDP government was assured—hastened and abetted by the large numbers of those previously supportive groups that simply refrained from voting in the 1975 election.

This, of course, is the narrow perspective—the global one is that social democratic governments in Australia and Jamaica were also under attack and the weapons of rumour, misinformation and criticism used against them bore a striking similarity to the ones used against the NDP in B.C. Nonetheless, there can be no doubt that our government's action added to and hastened its speedy demise.

Whenever anyone asks me what I achieved during my years in politics, I think of two things, one an obsession—namely the introduction of legislation for mandatory use of seatbelts for children in a moving vehicle, which was passed in October 1983 – and the other a sobriquet. I am reminded of the day when Michael Humphreys, my friend on Lasqueti Island, referred to me as a 'dithering device.' Not being a scientist, I had no idea what that meant, so I asked: he explained that in the case of politics it meant that I was an irritant. I like to think that he was right, that I was an irritant who kept the attention of both government and opposition members focused on the concerns of women and disadvantaged groups.

I like to think that Socred backbencher Pat Jordan's suggestion in the legislature that I 'go back where I came from' was triggered by my 'irritant' qualities, that the Socreds wiped out the riding of Vancouver-Burrard in an attempt to rid themselves of at least one of the 'irritant' members.

One of my proudest moments was being called upon to second the Speech from the Throne on January 26, 1973, at the beginning of the first full parliament of the first NDP government in British Columbia. It was a government that had achieved a number of firsts by just being there: led by Canada's first Jewish premier, it included Frank Calder, the first Native person to be a member of a government cabinet, and it was the first caucus to include two Black members: Emery Barnes and me, the first Black woman to be elected to political office in the country's history.

So, as I looked about the magnificent legislative chamber with its intricate carvings, domed ceilings and red carpeting – at Bill and my three children in the gallery, looking pleased and a little bit nervous, hoping that I would do well; at Robin, June Jensen, my campaign manager, and the many women who had slipped away from their jobs to be there; as my eyes passed over the press gallery, with my old nemesis and friend Allan Fotheringham sitting there waiting to be impressed – I began to speak of my history and my hopes, and to plead with the government to live up to our expectations of it. As I spoke I could feel the presence of women, Black women, Native women, slaves, immigrant women, poor women, old women and young women – I could feel their support, encouragement and hope envelop me, sending a surge of energy through me, empowering my words and my voice. I tried to convey their sense of urgency and their struggle, and I hoped fervently that the premier and his cabinet were hearing my words.

Graham Greene's observation about writers being born with a sliver of ice in their veins could apply equally to at least one of my political obsessions. Although my experience in politics often has left me feeling as vulnerable as a child playing in a minefield, afraid to continue and too terrified to stop, I remain totally dedicated to the goal of increasing the number of women who enter the political life of this country.

I have some feelings of guilt about this pursuit, knowing the hurt that could await these women; nonetheless because I see the political arena as one of the important theatres in which the struggle against our inequality takes place, I persevere in the task of enlisting women to seek public office. I attempt to assuage my guilt by drawing an honest picture for these women of life in the political lane, even as I endeavour to be as persuasive as possible in encouraging them to take up the challenge.

"Electoral politics touches our lives," I tell them, "in a sufficient number of profound ways that no matter what the cost, it cries out for the presence and involvement of women." Because both the hierarchical structure and the patriarchal history and nature of politics make it a hostile profession for women, it has for too long been the private and exclusive domain of men. They presume and try to convince us that they make and administer laws that are in the best interest of all people, including women.

Catherine McKinnon, the feminist theoretician, reminds us, however, that laws were originally formulated by men to protect them from other stronger and more predatory men, and that the concerns of women never entered these considerations at all, since the assumption was that women were the property and therefore the private concern of men. Canadian parliaments have been developed according to the 700-year-old English tradition of knights riding off to London for extended periods to attend to the nation's business, leaving their wives, children and serfs at home, and so reflect the clear presumption that the nation's business is men's work and beyond women's sphere of interest, capability or influence. Indeed the seating in our legislative chambers was originally arranged so that two sword-lengths separated the government members from the opposition. The arrangement was a protective device against the inflammatory nature of male tempers. And the ultimate symbol of authority, the mace, was originally a weapon of war.

In 1972 when I entered the B.C. legislature, I discovered that all the washrooms in the building meant for the use of elected members had been built with urinals in them. In the particular washroom being used by female politicians and staff, the urinal had been concealed behind a temporary box-like wood structure – a clear indication that our legislative forefathers had not conceived the possibility of women one day serving as elected members in that building, and that our presence there is still accompanied by the hope that our sojourn will be temporary.

On a more pragmatic level, many male politicians still view the entry of women into politics as an unwelcome intrusion and invasion of their privacy. Many of them are annoyed at the prospect of being expected to clean up their language and their jokes in the presence of female colleagues; they are threatened by having their prejudice and distorted beliefs about women challenged by female colleagues, and dislike having to defend or justify the bizarre or sexist positions they take on matters affecting women.

An example of one such incident was the snickering in the House of Commons in 1982 when MP Margaret Mitchell raised the question of spouse abuse. It showed that some male politicians remain defensive and embarrassed by having to participate in public debate on such issues as family violence and child abuse. Indeed, many of them express fear that the chances of their re-election are jeopardized by debate and votes on such controversial issues as abortion and sexual orientation. And others barely conceal their belief that there is something obscene, repulsive and illegitimate about women with power. Feminists take a whole different agenda into the political sphere; they have a different set of priorities and demands. As well, they are committed to dismantling and redesigning the patriarchal and hierarchical structure of the political system. This intent and this goal destabilize and frighten male politicians and invariably trigger resistance and hostility from many of them.

I was such a politician, and I was aware at all times of the impact that my assertiveness and radical demands were having on my colleagues both in caucus and in opposition. As with other New Democrat members, there was a sense of urgency about me; like theirs, my election had raised expectations; and, like them, I wanted to get on with the business of delivering on my promises.

I believe that the ideology of feminism blended with the experience of life as a woman creates the kind of politician necessary to balance what Darlene Marzari, an NDP provincial politician, refers to as the "testosterone-driven house" that is our Parliament. That is the reason why I am concerned that women who seek political office be aware of the full consequences of their presence in that arena, and that they seek office only in order to improve the condition of human life. I urge them to reaffirm their commitment to the goals set out by the women's political platform designed by the Council of Women at the beginning of this century; it declares that "truth, honesty, purity, justice and righteousness should be the foundation for women's involvement in politics."

While the women's movement in B.C. was battling the indifference of government, the movement in other parts of Canada, faced with similar roadblocks, began to explore other avenues of pursuing the goal of equality. Guided and encouraged by the Report of the Royal Commission on the Status of Women, there began an explosion of activity by feminists in the academic, business, religious and cultural communities. Many non-profit organizations that sponsored shelters for battered women, rape relief centres, women's centres, health collectives and status of women groups began to network and link up into national organizations.

Although all recognized the importance of political action, they also concluded that consciousness-raising and change was necessary in every public and private area of women's lives before the goal of equality could be achieved. So almost concurrently the National Action Committee on the Status of Women (NAC) was born, as was the federal government's Advisory Council on the Status of Women, with its regional political appointments, the federal women's office in the public service, and the Canadian Research Institute on the Advancement of Women – a brainchild of Naomi Griffiths, a professor of history at Carleton University – headed by Pauline Jewett.

Once the movement to national organizations began, it gathered momentum and in turn fuelled the demand for women's studies departments in universities, status of women studies in public organizations such as the CBC, and changes in law regarding situations that oppressed and discriminated against women. The recognition that the women's movement in Canada had taken on a life of its own and had become virtually unstoppable heartened the women of the B.C. NDP Women's Committee. Although we despaired of achieving any important changes in the lives of women at the provincial level, because our commitment to feminism was both global and national, we were able to look beyond our local experience and to become involved in national action and to support international initiatives.

To have been a woman in Canada during the late 60s and early 70s was to have had the great fortune of witnessing and participating in one of the important struggles for personhood. Not the most important, of course, because that had been won for us by the early feminists of the women's suffrage movement. But after the interregnum that followed the Second World War, the 60s marked an awakening. Those were heady, exciting and challenging times for Canadian women who chose to view them as an opportunity to be independent and equal persons.

Those were my double-life years, when I straddled the feminist revolution and political demands at the same time and burnt my candle at both ends: I served on the board of a number of national feminist organizations, and as the B.C. Participation of Women representative on the Federal NDP Council, while sitting as the MLA for Vancouver-Burrard.

CHAPTER EIGHT

"Why did you work so hard to defeat my bid for the leadership?" I asked David Lewis.

"Because you were a genuinely dangerous threat to the party," he replied.

A year had gone by since the federal NDP leadership convention in Winnipeg in July 1975. David was a guest at the B.C. provincial NDP convention, and one evening a small group of us were sitting around in Dave and Shirley Barrett's hotel room, talking and relaxing after a strenuous day of meetings. For the first time, David Lewis and I were completely relaxed with each other, so I felt free to put to him the question that had bothered me throughout the federal leadership race to replace him. I had never understood why he worked so hard against my candidacy because before my challenge, he, Tommy Douglas and most of the establishment of the federal party had treated me with affection and respect. The passion of their opposition to my attempt to win the party leadership was intense and forceful; and as the campaign progressed and my strength grew, their efforts seemed to take on panic proportions. Because this was so contrary to what was happening in the party as a whole, where my support was growing, it confused and puzzled me. I knew that the fact that I had never served as a Member of Parliament was a serious deficiency, that my lack of bilingualism was a handicap, and I recognized that not everybody in the party agreed with my views on every issue. However, I could not see that these shortcomings, important as they were, warranted the fervour with which the party establishment opposed my candidacy.

David Lewis's response did very little to enlighten me; I could not believe that he really thought I would be a threat to a movement and organization for which I had so much love, respect and admiration, and to which he knew I was so completely committed. In retrospect, of course, I now realize that his perception of my threat sprang from his observation that my leadership campaign attracted the support of party members who wanted to change the direction of the party in profound ways, party members who were the survivors of old internal struggles waged around the Waffle and other factions in the party, long before my arrival.

Indeed he and many others of the party leadership credited my almost spectacular level of support to the fact that, like a magic wand, I awakened every dormant discontent in the party; I appealed to people who saw in me hope for their cause and so flocked to my side. I attracted people who presented new challenges to the party based on a determination to expand its ideological parameters, people who demanded that it address the specific concerns of those new and emerging groups for whom democratic socialism was the means to the end of their oppression.

Although I had never considered myself more ideologically radical than either the leadership or membership of the party, I did feel that the party was not living up to its potential for women, visible minorities and some of the commitments made in the Regina Manifesto. So in the age-old debate about whether the NDP should be a 'movement' or an electoral machine I invariably came down on the side of movement, although I did not see the two sides as mutually exclusive. It must have been clear to David Lewis and others of the party leadership that in the event that a choice became inevitable, I would have chosen to see the party remain a social movement rather than sacrifice any commitment in order to achieve political power.

It was the cause of women, however, that catapulted me into

the leadership race, and it was the cause of women that seemed to engender the most hostility to my candidacy. The decision to place a feminist candidate with a feminist agenda in the leadership exercise was seen as divisive and a public embarrassment and betrayal of the party. It was described as a slap in the face to all those women who had toiled in the party over the years, confident in the assumption of their equality, and of all those men who had always affirmed and reaffirmed the truth of that assumption.

My decision to support the Women's Committee and to be its candidate resulted in a marked change in my relationship with certain party members. I can remember being with Bill on one occasion when I was greeted very coldly by Tommy Douglas. This surprised Bill because in other instances Tommy had always been effusive and warm in greeting me. Bill commented with a chuckle, "Oh, you must be slipping." "No," I responded, "I'm running."

Although the hostility to my running hurt, it never at any time threatened my decision to stay in the race. I was sure that running a feminist for the leadership of the party was necessary at that time and that such an endeavour would in the long run strengthen and benefit the party.

In 1974, angry, frustrated and hostile, the Women's Committee of the party prepared for International Women's Year.

Some of the more radical feminists in the province taunted the Women's Committee with the fact that our NDP government was no different, no less patriarchal and sexist than liberals and conservatives were in their relationship to women. They scoffed at the efforts of the B.C. government as puny and reluctant, dismissing any positive measures taken on behalf of women, preferring instead to repeat ad nauseam the one or two sexist comments Dave Barrett had uttered publicly at one time or another.

So, when David Lewis announced his retirement and the members of the Women's Committee realized that a new federal leader would have to be chosen in 1975, International Women's Year, the opportunity for rebellion blew our minds. Once we identified the leadership race as an opportunity, the coincidences seemed to tumble into our laps.

The first of these was a national NDP women's conference scheduled for Winnipeg in July 1974. This had been planned before David Lewis's federal election defeat and resignation announcement. The B.C. NDP Women's Committee decided to send as large a delegation as possible, to continue the debate on the relationship between feminism and socialism that we had begun and carried forward since earlier conventions.

The second coincidence was that I was scheduled to be one of the keynote speakers at the conference and so would be able to probe gently and canvass the question of a feminist challenging the leadership.

Robin Geary first raised with me the suggestion of a woman leader to replace David Lewis, and added in the same breath that I should seek to be the Women's Committee choice as the candidate for that position. I was genuinely shocked by her suggestion. I know that myth has it that all politicians dream of one day being the top boss, dictator, prime minister, president, king or queen. But whenever I had thought of NDP leaders, it had always been with amazement that anyone would want to compete for the job of leading a group of people I perceived to be fractious and cantankerous, albeit dedicated and committed to very strongly held views. The challenge of holding the multiple and diverse parts of this group together through a shared vision of justice for all seemed to me nothing short of herculean. I had always admired the leaders, but never envied them.

I said as much to Robin and although she agreed with me, she persisted that many of the ideas and policies we wished the party to espouse and support would be accepted more readily if we had a leader who upheld and promoted those convictions. Of course I agreed with her, but I just did not want the hassle that would accompany that particular job. Indeed, as we recalled the gratuitous harassment to which political leaders were subject, we concluded that a person needed a deep and broad streak of masochism to voluntarily seek out such positions.

Nonetheless we allowed ourselves the luxury of imagining what the government of B.C. would have been like if instead of Dave Barrett we had had a feminist premier in our province. We concluded that although we might not have achieved much more in concrete terms, our struggle would not have been so difficult and time-consuming and the atmosphere of the province would have been more positive and accepting of women's ideas, suggestions and requests. In addition, women's groups would have been prepared to fight to the death to protect and re-elect such a government.

Stimulated by this flight of fantasy, we went on to imagine the federal party with a feminist at the helm, and the wonderful policies and programs that a truly egalitarian social democratic party would spawn. We were not deterred by the thought of those few women who, having achieved leadership in other parts of the world, had not exercised their power to terminate the abuses of women and children but instead had ignored or continued to perpetrate them. We reminded ourselves that they had not been feminists, but had risen to power through the traditional, predominantly male social and political system and had been forced to come to terms with that system in order to ensure their progress and their survival.

She and I held firmly to the belief that there was and is a clearly qualitative difference between the way men and women wield power. During the process of our own consciousness-raising and growth, we had both read much of the research in this area, including John Kenneth Galbraith's Harvard study of 1973. It indicated that "women are less likely [than men] to go to war for the sake of honour, that they are more pacifist, care more about protecting consumer interests and are generally less hardened to the suffering of other people."

Our belief was supported by the findings of feminist scholars and researchers, as well as through the work of mainstream pollsters such as Lou Harris, who in 1972 concluded that women "are more inclined now to vote and to become active not only in their self-interest, but for the interest of society, the world and most of all out of compassion for humanity." Which is not to say that we said even to ourselves that all women were the same and that therefore any woman would be a better leader than any man. But we had come to the conclusion that although men and women share the same world, due to a combination of genetics, history and socialization women do inhabit the world and experience it differently from men. Personal experience, as well as study and observation, had led us to conclude that the world community of men and that of women are different; consequently the priorities of the two are different, and this difference is reflected in their political agendas.

For Robin and me, consciousness-raising helped us to accept these differences without feeling that we were diminished by them. We were more disturbed by the weak and unbalanced representation of women's point of view in the political arena, and by the inadequate and inappropriate methods used to address this, than we were by the absence of women per se.

We rejected the belief that a group acting 'in the best interest' of another did so as effectively and passionately as a group acting on its own behalf. And we observed with some cynicism that 2,000 years of living under the protective control and tutelage of men had not only left women their dependents and subordinates, but had also engendered men's contempt and disrespect.

We were convinced, therefore, that for women to continue expending time and energy on educating male politicians, in the attempt to help them represent us better, would only legitimize and bolster their belief in their inherent supremacy and superiority to women; and would further entrench women's position as dependents and subordinates to them.

We preferred to regard the education of men about the life and experiences of women as preparation for their acceptance of the inevitable equal sharing of the world between both sexes. We concluded that the full responsibility for the political representation of women's agenda should be assumed by women themselves. Consequently, we rejected as self-defeating the task of grooming a man, no matter how willing he might be, to assume the job of making a political party more accountable to women.

Although a feminist leader would be a welcome gift to any party, the job of deciding the direction and goals of the NDP rested not with the leader but with the membership. So for the Women's Committee, the primary purpose of participation in the leadership race would be to use the national debate around feminism and socialism in the party as a consciousness-raising catalyst to our definition of true democratic socialism.

Our priority therefore would be to find a strong feminist who was also a gifted teacher and communicator to take on the task of making this debate happen. Robin thought that, despite my myriad imperfections, I came pretty close to fitting the description. However, after further thought and much agonizing we both agreed that, exciting as it was to contemplate, the existence of insurmountable barriers made my candidacy an unrealistic objective at that time. The youth of my children, the stress that such a job would place on my marriage and my inability to speak French all seemed to add up to 'insurmountable barriers.' In addition, we recognized that if my bid were successful, the questions of my race and sex could prove to be so distracting that *I* could become the issue in future campaigns, rather than the party's message of equality, justice and peace. These all clinched the decision to sit this opportunity out.

Robin, a New Zealander by birth, agreed with me, a Jamaican, that the Canadian attitude to democratic socialism was truly disheartening. Although we were at a loss to explain why, we were fully aware that the ideology was so loaded with negative and threatening connotations, and so shrouded in fears, myths and distortions, that it would take the safest, most acceptable and bland of communicators to be its messenger to the Canadian voter. With a chuckle, we decided to change the criteria for a candidate: instead of a feminist teacher-communicator, it should be a person who combined the safe qualities needed to win with the qualities of a radical left-wing feminist who would take risks on behalf of women. Relieved that we had clarified our leadership prototype, we decided to go in search of such a creature.

On July 25, 1974, the B.C. delegation arrived at the Federal Women's Conference in Winnipeg, determined to secure both the support of the other delegates for a feminist leadership candidate, and the endorsement of the conference for this goal.

Our initial exploration revealed that delegates from the other provinces had not considered the possibility—nor made the serendipitous connection between International Women's Year and the federal leadership campaign. The B.C. women were neither daunted nor deterred by this fact, and set about to convince them of the efficiency and necessity, as well as the symbolism, inherent in placing the name of a woman in nomination for leader in our designated international year. In my keynote address I hinted at the gift that this opportunity represented, and ended with the wish that:

> . . . out of this conference will come the decision to have as our goal the convention of 1975, International Women's Year, be the convention at which women's policy, rewritten and redesigned to ensure true equality for all, will be endorsed by all members of this party . . . and that the convention of 1975 will be the convention at which in the election of officers . . . the power of the women's vote will be clearly reflected in the choice of those designated to serve as our leaders. . . .

The victory of the B.C. delegation was complete when the 132 delegates voted on July 28, the final day of the conference, to "establish a nationally representative committee to seek a woman candidate for the leadership of the party at the 1975 Federal Convention—one who supports socialist policy on Women's Rights."

The immediate and unanimous choice of the women at the conference as our candidate was Grace MacInnis. She had served the party long and well in both the B.C. legislature and the House of Commons, and for six years sat as the sole female member in the House of Commons, "working away like a mole on Parliament Hill," as she described it. Although she had not adopted the title of feminist, she had been an early and passionate fighter for human rights and justice, a staunch supporter of choice in reproduction, and a worker for many social and human services that were of particular benefit to women and children. Grace had been a witness to and a participant in the development of feminist policy at conventions since the early 1960s; and although she had not initially supported the development of a separate women's caucus within the NDP, she had certainly supported the strengthening and expanding of the role of women at all levels in the party. We loved her, respected her, were in awe of her vigour and commitment, and wanted her to be our leader. However, she was very gracious but firm in declining our invitation. She made it absolutely clear that she believed we should seek out and support the best candidate for leader without regard to that person's gender.

The search committee very regretfully turned its efforts elsewhere. The next choice was Nancy Eng of Alberta. At that time Nancy was the chairperson of the Participation of Women Committee of the NDP, and as such was a member of the Federal Council. (This committee was established by an earlier federal convention and was one of the small victories we had won; it ensured that the Federal Council of the party included at least one woman, elected by the women delegates at convention, who was directly accountable to the women of the party.)

Because of failing health and because she was not completely comfortable with the idea as a form of affirmative action, Nancy Eng declined the invitation of the search committee.

These two rejections signalled to the search committee the unpopularity within the party of the task on which they were embarked, but the determination of its members never wavered, and they continued to invite women across the country either to volunteer or to submit names of suitable candidates to be placed in nomination.

Meanwhile, back in Victoria, I continued my work in the legislature, relaxed and comfortable that my decision not to seek the nomination had been accepted, with regret, but accepted nonetheless, by the search committee. I would not have been nearly so confident had I known of the activity of Merran Acaster and the Victoria women's committee.

The Victoria NDP women's committee was a powerhouse among the B.C. committees. It referred to itself as the Victoria Socialist NDP Women's Caucus and its membership was drawn largely from the ranks of feminists who were employed in various branches of the public service. Because of their strategic placement they were of invaluable service to the other provincial committees in the introduction and acceptance of feminist ideals into government policy, programs and decision-making. They were also helpful in assisting women's groups to prepare briefs and presentations for legislative commit-tees. Their intimate knowledge of the workings of the public service made them a valuable resource to the entire women's community.

One day in the late fall of 1974, Merran Acaster, who had been a tireless worker in my election campaign, came to visit me in my Victoria office. She explained that the Victoria Socialist NDP Women's Caucus wanted to support my bid for the federal leadership. I trotted out all the arguments as to why I was unable to entertain the idea of seeking the leadership and, as I did with Robin, spent some time describing the profile of the person best suited to be our candidate. She agreed that my radical image would be a problem with the rank and file of the party as well as with the leadership, but felt that it would be balanced by my communications skill, and the opportunity it would give the party to prove its racial tolerance by voting for a Black person. She believed that my primary role was not to win the leadership but to be the catalyst for the debate around feminist issues. In the unlikely event of a win, however, she thought we could confront my concerns about family, race and sex at that time.

It was very difficult to say no to Merran; she was one of that small, very close circle of women friends who had assumed the role of family when I entered politics. Like me, she had small children and often we would compare our tasks, she as a single mother and me as an absent mother, and wonder together what impact our career pursuits were having on our children. I often spoke to her about my fear of missing some important milestone in my children's life, and about the loneliness of living away from Bill so much of the time. However, I remained adamant in my refusal to be persuaded by her. I had decided not to be a candidate and informed my family and constituency of my decision, and I decided to stick by that decision.

She accepted my refusal and left. Merran's visit was just the first of many, however. Members of the women's committee here and in other provinces began a concerted attempt to convince me to rethink my decision. The Vancouver-Burrard constituency members assured me of their complete support should I decide to run, and the women of the women's committee met with me individually and as a delegation to discuss the reasons why my candidacy would be important.

After a while it became clear to me that one of the main reasons that I was not seeking the candidacy was that I was not comfortable with the idea of deliberately running to lose. I had never done that before and I was reluctant even to consider it. During one of Merran's numerous phone calls, she suggested that Robin and I meet with a small group of women who had always been my mentors and guides to thrash the matter out once and for all. I called Robin and she rearranged her schedule, got on a plane and arrived in Victoria later the same evening. We met at Merran's farm in Victoria for dinner and soul-searching. John Twigg, Merran's new husband, volunteered to prepare a gourmet Chinese feast for us, and to handle all baby-sitting chores.

John was a pragmatist. He was Premier Dave Barrett's executive assistant, and he knew that the party leadership would close ranks against my candidacy and that I would lose no matter who the other candidates were, so his recommendation was that I should not run. He was very articulate and clear in his attempt to dissuade me from being seduced by the arguments of his wife and the other women. I loved and respected John, so I listened carefully to his words.

We had a marathon session that night. The group took each of my concerns separately and examined, analyzed and debated it in detail. I learnt that the search committee had done an unofficial, superficial poll across the country and had unearthed surprisingly strong support for my candidacy among groups other than women's committees in the party. The women felt that there was a real possibility that I could win, so that added another dimension to the debate. Most of the evening was spent, however, reiterating that the importance of the campaign was the message and the process, not my candidacy.

The message was that since feminism embodied justice for women, socialism was not possible where sexism in any form existed. The process would place women in positions to develop the skills in planning and running all facets of a campaign, and would be invaluable to all those women whose only previous experience in campaigns had been following instructions.

It became increasingly difficult for me to deny the committee and myself the opportunity that seeking the leadership presented at that time. Family and personal considerations remained as barriers, however, and I was not prepared to allow the committee to decide on those matters for me.

After a very long and exhausting evening I agreed that, if a successful resolution to my personal and family concerns was possible, I would allow my name to stand in candidacy for the leadership.

Robin and I returned to my apartment on Dallas Road; she planned to spend the night, then return to Vancouver with me on the following day. We heard the phone ringing as we approached the apartment and ran to open the door; it was Bill, he had been phoning since midnight to find out the results of the marathon. I gave him as detailed a report as possible, then asked him to think about us and about the children and about what a leadership race, even a losing one, would do to our family.

His immediate response was that the family would support my decision whatever it was, but that he would indeed give the matter serious thought. Neither Robin nor I slept that night—we argued, debated, agreed, disagreed, decided and undecided till daybreak.

At 6 a.m. Bill called again. He had not been able to sleep either. Fortunately, since it was Friday, I would be returning to Vancouver that afternoon for the weekend, but we agreed that he should tell the two older children what the possibilities were so that we could all discuss the pros and cons over the weekend.

The women with whom I had met the night before had extracted from me a promise of a speedy response, so I hoped there would be a resolution one way or the other before I returned to Victoria on Monday.

I was totally ambivalent about the leadership. Although I welcomed the opportunity that it would give us as women to rearrange the policy priorities and direction of the party, I was terrified of the responsibilities inherent in the job; I disliked the competition of the campaign and hated the idea of placing more space and time between my family and myself.

Serious thinking led me to acknowledge my secret feeling of always being underqualified for any task that confronted me. Whether it was the decision to seek public office, to apply for a job or to enter graduate school, there was always self-doubt. Because I realized that these feelings of inadequacy were in my head, and that they persisted despite the fact that from childhood I had always been told that I could do anything that I set my mind to, I was forced to conclude that negative messages had somehow infiltrated my socialization, and that these resulted in very deeply buried feelings of inadequacy.

I could not blame these feelings on Canadian racism, because I knew that they had been with me long before my arrival in this country. Some of them no doubt stemmed from growing up under colonialism and learning at a very early age of the existence of barriers, often invisible to the naked eye, but real nonetheless; learning that one had to be careful and test the future before moving beyond a given point, because these barriers had a recoil mechanism that caused pain and shame when bumped into. How could I have developed feelings of inadequacy as a woman despite the strong role models and positive reinforcement I had known long before the advent of TV, and before billboards and magazines with sexist images penetrated my awareness? Why did doubts about my ability to achieve linger in my head and increase as I grew older and more observant of the world around me?

Part of the terror I felt about the strong women in my family was the fear that they would discover that I was not as bright, as smart or as capable as they kept reassuring me I was. Part of the conspiracy we shared and the secret I carried through adolescence was that I never admitted to them that I recognized that there were barriers around them too, and that they could not always do anything that they set their minds to. And even though I had always signalled agreement when they assured me that I could be whatever I aimed to be, deep inside my consciousness somewhere I had always doubted the veracity of those protestations and had always sensed that they knew of the existence of my doubts.

Over the years I had developed a 'swimming plunge' technique to deal with challenging situations. I would first imagine the worst possible thing that could happen to me if in fact I had reached beyond my grasp: I would live through the embarrassment, humiliation or pain in my imagination. Then I would hold my nose, back up, take a run and, with eyes closed, leap. I must confess that each time that I survived the leap, my confidence soared, and in time fewer and fewer challenges triggered my 'sense of inadequacy' mechanism.

The idea of being the federal leader of the third largest political party in Canada sent my entire sense of inadequacy mechanism into convulsions. When I tried to visualize the worst possible scenario in that situation, it was so terrifying that I terminated it and came up gasping for air.

Once the debate, the analysis and the intellectualizing were over, only the terror remained. How could I possibly explain to anyone that I was simply afraid of the job?

Because to think was to inhabit a nightmare, I stopped thinking and talked. I talked to Bill, I talked to Robin, to Gene Errington, Hilda Thomas, to my constituency president, my executive, to women of the women's committee, my aunts, my brother, my uncle, friends, neighbours, my children. In short, to everyone who would listen, and each time they responded with assurances and reassurances as to my ability to handle the task, my terror increased.

I was overwhelmed by all these people with their exaggerated perception of my capabilities, and torn between recognizing the importance and necessity of running, and the fear of being exposed as a fraud in the process.

In the end I did face up to the nasty little toad in my head who kept reminding me of my inadequacy, and decided to discuss my fears first with Bill, then with Robin. In a nutshell, I confessed that I was just not fit to be leader of Her Majesty's Loyal Opposition, nor was I prime ministerial material. I believed that I could lead a movement, or even the third largest political party in Canada, but if there was the slightest chance that the status of the party would change, then I would be out of my depth.

Bill was very pragmatic. He pointed out that leadership was not a tenured position and I could resign at any time, that if I felt I could handle the job as it was presently constituted, that was good enough.

Robin's position was different. She was absolutely certain that I would not win the leadership – but that if I did win, the status of the party would change and we could find ourselves in the position of official opposition. Despite this she saw no necessity to worry, however, because her reading of the party hierarchy was that they would force David Lewis out of retirement and back as leader if there appeared to be the slightest chance of my victory. So she gave me her personal guarantee that my campaign would be successful in every respect except making me leader.

Cleta and Gary, my two older children, were beside themselves with excitement, and since Jonathan had responded at an earlier date to the question of what he wanted to be when he grew up by saying "Gary," he was excited and happy because Gary was. Bill assured me that our family was in safe hands with him, so after more talking and agonizing I held my nose, backed up and, with eyes closed, leapt.

On February 12, 1975, a press conference was called at the Vancouver-Burrard constituency office, 2485 West 14th Avenue, at which I made the following statement:

> I am declaring as a candidate for the leadership of the Federal New Democratic Party. I am committed to a campaign in which there are no deals, where I will

work hard and stay in until the end. My platform is based on a commitment to socialism, feminism, the preservation and development of our natural resources, the protection of the environment and for the rights of all workers and people.

As soon as I notified the women's committee of my intention to seek the leadership, I felt as though a load had been lifted from my shoulders. I knew that I had done the right thing and that my grandmother would have been pleased.

A campaign committee was constituted immediately to begin the very important task of designing the campaign. That committee consisted of sixteen persons, eleven of them female, and most of them either members of the Vancouver-Burrard constituency or the Women's Rights Committee. It was composed of Gail Clague, Jane Covernton, Mark Bostwick, June Dunlop, Teresa Ferguson, Carolyn Gibbons, Marianne Gilbert, June Jensen, Ed Livingstone, Jim MacKenzie, Joey Schibald, Stu Savard, Hilda Thomas, Candace Hanson, Leni Hoover and Robin Geary.

Rumours and public speculation that I might seek the leadership had begun with a *Vancouver Sun* article on January 23, 1975, headed "Leadership Pondered" and a *Times-Colonist* article of the same date titled "Rosemary eyes NDP leadership." Those two articles triggered an avalanche of phone calls and letters of support. Enigmatic musings by Allan Fotheringham in his February 7 column in the *Vancouver Sun*, as well as my response to a question by a UBC student newspaper reporter on February 6, in which I stated that I would make a final decision about running by the end of February, all fuelled speculation about my plans. So by the time the formal press announcement was made, resolutions of support had already been passed by the Woodsworth-Irving Socialist Fellowship in Alberta, and 'Rosemary for Leader' cells were actively organizing in constituencies in Saskatchewan, Manitoba and Ontario.

The committee decided that I should make a formal declaration as soon as possible — they wanted me to be the first in the race so that our platform could be placed before the party for discussion and debate before the hype and hoopla began, and they wanted our platform to receive maximum coverage from the media before they became distracted by other, presumably higher-profile candidates.

Our strategy worked; since I was the only declared candidate until Lorne Nystrom and Ed Broadbent entered the race, on March 24 and in early April, respectively, I had nearly six clear weeks during which the press divided its time between covering my status, speculating on which other candidates would challenge me, and discussing various aspects of the platform. Party members also had that much time to read and digest the policy papers and organizational material emanating from my campaign.

On the other hand, my early entry gave my opposition the time needed to pressure Ed Broadbent, who had earlier declared that he would not be seeking the leadership, to change his mind and re-enter the race.

We had gambled that this would happen, but since the priority was in getting out our message, we decided that having Ed re-enter the race, especially if it could be proved that his decision was the result of my challenge, would only serve to focus more attention on our platform and give our policy statements wider coverage.

Since the process and model of the campaign had also been the deciding factors for me in participating in the leadership race, many hours were spent hammering out clear ground rules about how it was to be run. We were determined that by its very structure and design it should serve to demonstrate the difference between me and the other candidates. Moreover, because we wished it to be our opportunity to test as well as illustrate the viability of our feminist beliefs concerning leadership and power, we built into it much that we had learnt through our involvement in the women's movement.

We established five rules:
1. The campaign was not going to be star-personality oriented.
2. I was going to stay in until dropped from the ballot, and not be the stalking horse for anyone.
3. There would be no deals, such as first ballot support.
4. All decisions were to be arrived at collectively.

5. The campaign would be run on the issues of feminism and socialism.

Our campaign issues were developed collectively by a group of feminists headed by Hilda Thomas. They were presented in a paper called "Feminism and Socialism" that I delivered to the Learned Societies meeting held in Edmonton on June 4, 1975. In it, I referred to the 1910 statement of August Bebel that "there can be no liberation of mankind without social independence and equality of the sexes." The argument was then developed that both socialist commitment and feminism were rooted in the struggle for "social independence and equality." The conclusion of the rather lengthy presentation contained two observations that clearly stated the rationale for the campaign:

> 1. If we accept socialism as a philosophy which is committed to the removal of all barriers that make one human being dependent on another, and further if we accept that the oppression of women is based on social dependence as well as on economic dependence, on social exploitation as well as on economic exploitation, then we see that socialism, although quite capable of dealing with economic dependence, has so far not really been successful in dealing with social dependence.
>
> 2. It is becoming increasingly evident that socialism, feminism and anti-racism, because they share a common enemy, would be short-sighted indeed not to pool their resources and experiences in a common struggle, and that when the collective goal is achieved what we will have is a more ideologically socialist society than presently exists anywhere in the world.

As the campaign progressed, other patterns emerged. The emphasis of our actions was on education through the discussion of issues. We relied very heavily on volunteer labour to prepare and distribute policy statements on major issues.

Children were encouraged to play an active part in the process, from donating their art work for a fundraising poster, to working the Gestetner, stuffing envelopes, stapling material and staffing the information booths at both provincial and federal conventions, to adding their ideas and suggestions to fundraising plans. Indeed Vanessa Geary, Robin's nine-year-old daughter, an inveterate and experienced political worker, on one occasion single-handedly ran off 1,000 copies of the discussion paper on women's rights for mailing; with no one around to consult, she decided to do so on pale pink paper, throwing her mother into a state of apoplexy about whether pink was the politically correct colour for a paper on feminism!

The campaign was also intended to be the laboratory where women could experiment with ideas and learn from experience about preparing policy statements, designing leaflets, making speeches, dealing with the media and organizing meetings, tours and fundraising events.

Anyone who has ever worked in a collective knows of the time, frustration, aggravation, turmoil and joy that go into hammering out each and every decision. On the other hand, she or he also knows how supportive such a structure can be, because although all responsibility is shared, so are all victories and all losses.

In the B.C. collective I can remember only one incident of serious tension, and it occurred at the very beginning of the campaign. It concerned the time that I would spend away from the legislature. It consumed hours and days of discussion, and actually threatened the solidarity of our committee. In a nutshell, the problem was that in the B.C. legislature there is a rule governing attendance. It states that any elected member who is absent from the precinct for more than ten days during a session, except in the event of illness or other disaster, will be fined $100 per day. Presumably the intent of the rule was to assure that the level of absenteeism condoned in the federal Senate not occur in the provincial legislature, and presumably the rule had been made necessary by the election of large numbers of men with competing business and professional interests.

Obviously one cannot seriously run for the leadership of a large political party in ten days. A few of the committee members suggested that I should absorb the cost of the fines for the days that I was absent from the legislature. I refused. I argued that the fines were a legitimate campaign expense and as such should be part of the campaign budget.

Feelings ran high, relations became strained, but I held my ground and by so doing received the support of the majority of the committee members. However, since we were a collective, majority opinion was not good enough. We had to stay with the issue until the whole committee arrived at a consensus, which they did, and $1,100 was added to the campaign budget to cover an additional eleven days' absence from the legislature. Furthermore the committee agreed that it would move heaven and earth to schedule my travel so that my total absence would not exceed twenty-one days, which my ten days permitted and eleven days covered by the campaign would allow.

Since the legislature sat from 2 p.m. on Mondays to 1 p.m. on Fridays, that meant that my travel would be scheduled whenever possible between 11 a.m. on Fridays and 5 p.m. on Mondays. That way there would be no unnecessary loss of time, and it would permit time to cover the national tour or other scheduled travel over which we had no control. It also meant that all my weekends between February 13 and July 1 would be spent on the road. Fortunately no other issue ever arose in the committee that created such disagreement or disruption. But my heart sank and an ache developed in the pit of my stomach as I realized that I would be seeing less of the children and of Bill as a result.

We did run into trouble with the party, however, when in the first letter we circulated we spoke of a "new, open and honest" approach to issues in the party. The Federal Caucus was furious, stating that this cast doubts on the integrity of all previous leadership campaigns. We agreed and withdrew the letter, and I issued a statement of apology. The matter did not end there, of course. All the other leadership candidates at one time or another referred to it as an example of the incompetence, inexperience and stridency of my campaign committee, and as proof that I was just a helpless puppet being manipulated by the malcontents in the party.

Writing in *Priorities*, the magazine of the B.C. NDP

Women's Committee, in July 1975, Hilda Thomas, one of our committee members, described the campaign very accurately:

> Support for the Brown campaign came from three broad groupings within the party. First there were the feminists who recognized in Rosemary the embodiment of the struggle for the rights of women that has been going on in the party since 1971, and who insist that socialism and feminism are inseparable. Then there were the people who are unhappy with the party structure, and who want greater participation and more openness at every level . . . the third group was the left — those who were primarily concerned about articulating a strong socialist position on policy questions, and who agreed with the Brown campaign positions on such things as labour, public ownership, Quebec and international affairs. There was, of course, considerable overlapping among the three groups.

These groups were compatible and worked very well together, and by the time the convention occurred, although it is true that most of the female delegates were supporting me and working for me, aside from Ed's campaign, the same thing could be said about the male delegates as well.

Our campaign was a successful collective built up of independent, autonomous provincial groups. Because of our ideological commitment every aspect of the campaign was decentralized, with each province responsible for its own fundraising and for conducting its own campaign.

Since each committee had participated in drafting the principles that guided the campaign, there was no fear that any of them would develop and assume policy positions that were contrary to our platform. In addition, people in each province developed a packet of information specific and particular to their area, arranged tours and meetings, covered all costs attached to my activities with them and contributed as much as they could afford to the central campaign.

No attempt was made to monitor or dictate to the provinces, but all committees were encouraged to keep in close contact with B.C. and with each other. The harmony and bond that grew out of this process was very energizing.

Between February and July of that year, I visited all ten provinces and the Yukon, covering nearly fifty towns and cities. On many occasions I would arrive at an airport unsure about what to expect, only to find a large welcoming committee, a packed meeting and an active and high-spirited 'Brown' committee, which had tied up the support of many of the delegates in that riding.

The travel across the country was exhilarating. The flight attendants all knew me and were concerned that I be very comfortable—the airport porters refused to allow me even to pick my baggage off carousels; cab drivers, hotel workers, in short, every working person with whom I came into contact tried to make my travel as easy and stress-free as possible.

Conservative and Liberal women turned up at my meetings just to wish me luck and to make financial donations to the campaign. Parents brought their children out to see me. I was invited to visit schools, daycare centres, seniors' homes. From coast to coast my travel was one great high! It just did not tally with my earlier perception of a country of people with cold faces, slammed doors and hate in their hearts—between February and July 1975, it seemed that with the exception of the NDP hierarchy, everybody loved me.

There is as little similarity between an NDP leadership campaign and a leadership campaign for the Liberal or Conservative party as there is between a 1975 leadership campaign and one happening today, thirteen years later.

In 1975 the proposed budget for the campaign was $7,283. And although we actually spent $13,147.04, because we had raised nearly $15,000 we had probably the only leadership campaign in living memory to finish with a surplus.

The raising of that much money was a major accomplishment and imbued the women in the party with an incredible sense of achievement, because, unlike Ed Broadbent and Lorne Nystrom, we did not have the support of the party's traditional large donors.

What we did have was the imaginative and innovative fundraising ability of women in the party. They designed activities that were a combination of fun and politics built on and emphasizing traditional female events such as craft sales, raffles, auctions, music, a festival and the sale of a poster designed by our children, their friends and Leni Hoover, one of our very talented artists who also happened to be a member of the committee. To this was added the financial donations of many women and visible minority people, most of whom were not known to me, and were not members of the party, but who desperately wanted to see my campaign succeed. These donors were many and far-flung, including an elderly Black gentleman in a nursing home in Alberta who donated a lottery ticket, and women in the United States, England and the Caribbean who had read about the campaign in their newspapers.

The campaign touched and excited women everywhere in Canada, and donations poured in in denominations of five, ten and twenty dollars. Many two-dollar bills were received from seniors, some of whom identified themselves as old suffragists, who promised to send two dollars each month until the campaign was over. Larger donations were received from those women who could afford to give more. There were never any strings attached, just a confession of excitement at the prospect of a woman leader and a desire to lend support. There were so many donations that in time they added up to more than we needed and gave the lie to the myth that women in politics are unable to generate financial support.

The role played by the press in my campaign was an interesting one. As I confessed earlier, I had known and liked Allan Fotheringham long before I entered politics, had come to know Lisa Hobbs at the *Vancouver Sun* and Kay Alsop of the

Vancouver Province through my work on women's issues, and had managed to avoid the strange love/hate relationship with the legislative press gallery that seems to exist between so many public figures and the media.

I had always found the media's treatment of me to be fair bordering on generous. Indeed, Barbara McClintock of the *Vancouver Province*, who handed out ratings of the MLAs each year, had assigned me an A+ rating consistently since 1973. I was curious therefore as to how they would handle my challenge of the leadership.

Their response was immediate, and it took the form of disbelief mingled with amusement. However, they were intrigued by the gall of my ambitious move to shoot for the top job in the party after only two and a half years of electoral employment.

I would probably have disappeared from the news after the initial press release and the flurry of amused speculation except that on February 13, when questioned by a reporter, Dave Barrett referred to me facetiously as "B.C.'s favourite daughter." I chose to ignore the derision implied by the statement and decided to treat it as an endorsement.

When Dave realized that his attempt at a put-down had been turned against him, he hastened to clarify in the *Vancouver Sun* of February 15 that in the NDP, "we need the kind of strength and leadership that Ed Broadbent has shown." The *Sun* reporter, who was by that time beside himself with glee at having breathed new life into a dying story, then confronted me with that report. Happy to keep the issue alive, I replied and they printed that "I'm not the first favourite daughter who has had to make it on her own, so I'm just going to have to make it on my own."

As the campaign continued and it became obvious that I was not a stalking horse for any other candidate and that my support was sufficiently alarming to the party leadership for them to pressure a reluctant Ed Broadbent back into the race, the press found that they could neither ignore me nor continue to trivialize my campaign. There was a subtle shift away from superficial discussions of my 'elegance,' 'private school education,' and 'home in the fashionable Point Grey district of

Vancouver' to more thoughtful and serious speculation as to the potential effect of my candidacy on the New Democratic Party and on Canada. The late, great Jack Scott wrote in the *Victoria Times Colonist*, "I have become convinced that her aspirations to head the federal New Democratic Party are not nearly so unlikely as they may have appeared a month or two ago. . . ."

And Nick Hills of the Southam News western bureau, writing in the *Winnipeg Tribune*, said:

> Rosemary Brown is a pain in the neck to the power brokers of the New Democratic Party. If anyone causes trouble at the national leadership convention in Winnipeg next month it will be her . . . none of this nastiness, of course, would have happened if Ms. Brown's campaign for leadership had gone where it was meant to go – down the plughole. It was launched to the accompaniment of a good deal of mirth and derision from people who didn't really know her. Today, although it seems impossible that she can win, there is enough support across the country to make her candidacy a real headache for the brokers who wanted a nice comfortable contest between Ed Broadbent, Lorne Nystrom and John Harney. . . .

When the convention opened in Winnipeg, the members of the press corps found to their delight and surprise that, because our campaign continued our practice of open meetings, they were free to sit in on all but the most private strategy sessions. They were horrified by what they considered to be the political naiveté of some of our decisions. However, because we refused to fudge or play games, they were impressed by the integrity, honesty and forthright manner in which we conducted our business with them, and they trusted us.

The result of including them in many of our deliberations was that their coverage of our activities was accurate, clear and unbiased. Some of them even ventured to offer advice from time to time, especially when they thought that we were going overboard with our purity – such as when we returned unopened the bottles of rye and scotch that arrived at our committee room as a gift from a local distiller.

They were, however, driven to distraction by our refusal to issue puffed up figures of delegate support. One of our commitments to the campaign's integrity was the decision not to participate in the ancient and traditional numbers games used by contenders to wage psychological warfare on each other, and we stuck by that decision. In time, press people began doing their own counting of delegate support, and they would report to us their findings of what our standing was, assistance we found very helpful in maintaining our tally.

It is possible that they worked harder, spent more time with, and had more fun with our campaign than with the others. What was obvious, however, was that in the end they seemed genuinely sorry that their predictions of my eventual defeat had proved to be so accurate. I know that it is folly to attempt to probe the collective mind of the media, but the opportunity to do so is irresistible. I believe that the reporters attached to our campaign were ambivalent throughout the entire period. I believe they hoped that I would win so that they could conduct endless research on 'the impact of a Black female immigrant socialist on the political landscape of Canada,' and they hoped that I would lose to demonstrate the accuracy of their political forecasting.

I imagine that even as wild and bizarre headlines were zipping through their heads – 'White Canadian Party Elects Black Leader,' 'One of the World's Largest White Countries Led by Radical Black Feminist Socialist,' 'Shocked Canadians Appeal to the World for Help After Black Leader Elected,' 'White No More,' 'Brown is Beautiful says Black Leader to White Country,' 'Country Falls to Feminists' – tantalizing them, they were hoping that in the end the party would choose a staid, sensible leader in the Canadian mould.

At the same time it was obvious that the campaign was challenging for them, as they bent over backwards to be critical of its content and style without appearing to be patronizing, paternalistic, racist or sexist.

They succeeded remarkably well, and if one day a student of journalism does a serious analysis of how the campaign was handled by the media, I believe that she will be able to trace the slow growth and maturation of that profession through its superficial ignorance of the will and power of feminists to a grudging admiration and respect for our commitment, integrity, wisdom and ability.

One incident during the campaign highlighted the fact that the penalty Canadians pay for living in the western provinces is not just levied by the federal government.

During a leadership campaign, the arranging and funding of the cross-country tour of the leadership candidates is the responsibility of the federal party, specifically of the federal party secretary. In March of 1975 my campaign committee received a memorandum pertaining to the tour that clearly indicated a failure of the organization to take into account that I was a resident of Western Canada, and so had a farther distance to travel than the other candidates. Since our history as a party includes more than one leader from Western Canada we were more than a little surprised by this oversight.

At that time I was the only declared candidate from the west and the committee actually discussed the possibility of accepting the discriminatory treatment, but rejected it. So on April 10 a letter was sent to Clifford Scotton, the federal secretary, protesting the inadequate allotment to cover my travel costs. On April 11 another more detailed letter was sent, explaining that the proposed itinerary further penalized me, because it was geared solely to fit into the schedule of the federal parliament and ignored the B.C. provincial government's timetable and its idiosyncratic financial penalty for time spent away from the precinct. Carbon copies of both letters were sent to Ed Broadbent and to Lorne Nystrom, the only other declared candidates at that time. They supported my protest, and an agreeable compromise was eventually worked out.

By the time the cross-country tour began, John Harney and

Douglas Campbell had declared their candidacy, thus swelling our ranks to five.

The tour was extremely valuable for a number of reasons, the main one for me being that it gave me an opportunity to observe and to become better acquainted with the other aspirants. By the termination of our journey I had come to like and respect them all for their love and their vision for the party.

I found Ed to be a very thoughtful and courteous person who always took the time to ensure that I was being taken care of before he went off to dinner, meetings, or to relax with friends at the end of the evening sessions. He always behaved with quiet, old-fashioned chivalry without embarrassment or show of self-consciousness. He was relaxed, displayed no anxiety about the possibility of losing and seemed to genuinely enjoy meeting people and talking and listening to them.

His supporters, on the other hand, were people who seemed to be obsessed with the fear that he might not win and who equated that possibility with the end of the world.

John Harney did not seem to be enjoying the trek one little bit. Although he was sometimes witty and funny, he often gave the impression of being bored and wanting to be somewhere else. Lorne was such a consistent source of annoyance to him that sometimes he could barely conceal it from onlookers. I liked John and I was curious about the fact that Dennis and Yvonne Cocke, whom I respected deeply, had chosen to support him rather than me.

Lorne Nystrom was like a high-strung thoroughbred; he was restless and hyperactive. He hungered to win so badly that the desire oozed from him like sweat. He had very little time for the rest of us and was always off somewhere closeted in deep and important consultation with one or more of his advisers. None of us ever witnessed him in a state of relaxation, and his constant anxiety was painful to observe. He was always courteous and polite when he was aware of my existence. I liked him; I saw him as one of the bright young men in the party and accepted his impatience as a sign of his desire to drag us all into the twenty-first century.

We all agreed that neither we nor the party would ever approach or achieve Douglas Campbell's criteria of true socialism, so we didn't try. He attacked the four of us and the party mercilessly from the platform and mercifully ignored us once he left it.

We each developed a basic speech that we delivered with slight variation and modification from one place to the other, and halfway through the tour we could all deliver each other's speeches verbatim. I always ended my speech the same way:

> In closing, I would like to suggest that the final choice for a leader must be made on the basis of one's concept of this party, how you see it. It must be made on the basis of how we can achieve our goal, of a socialist Canada, of who can best strengthen the roots, who can best foster participation and communication with the rank and file membership of the party, with our constituency, of workers, women, farmers, the poor and the disadvantaged.
>
> I recognize in the party the need for a leader with a commitment to a new kind of politics, both in a personal and collective sense. For a leader able to rebuild, educate and exemplify the ideals of this party, for a leader able to erase the wrongs caused by the discriminatory policies of a federal government bent on the alienation of the west.
>
> As you know, there is an old saying, that if you hang on to something long enough, it will go out of style, then it will come back, and that I think is where the Regina Manifesto is today. It is the new kind of politics, both in a personal and collective way, that we have to address ourselves to.
>
> I am dedicated not to patching up or reforming this system but to changing it.
>
> I am dedicated to the development of a socialist society in this country.
>
> That is my commitment and if elected leader, that is the goal to which I will lead this party.

The tour was very exhilarating for me. It was obvious that many undecided votes were swinging to my campaign and that I was picking up momentum as we progressed. I was meeting a number of the members for the first time and some who attended out of curiosity became supporters and committed workers. Gradually I became less tense, and by the time the tour rolled into Vancouver I was having fun.

Certain incidents linger in the mind—the enthusiasm of the Newfoundland members, who not only attended the meeting but brought all their relatives and friends along regardless of their political affiliation. The surprisingly sympathetic and encouraging response of the Quebec members to my pathetic attempt to speak French, and the large number of them who confessed that because of our platform, they would support me despite my linguistic incompetence. The way Nova Scotians accepted that, like my brother, who had run in a federal election against Robert Stanfield, I too suffered from a touch of political insanity, which endeared me to them. The absolutely awesome strength and talent of the Ontario Brown Campaign Committee. The energy in Cape Breton, hospitality and hope in New Brunswick, the Woodsworth-Irving Fellowship and the trade unionists in Alberta. The feminists in Manitoba and the determination in Saskatchewan. And everywhere Black parents bringing their children out to meet me, not caring about my politics, only that what I was doing gave them pride.

By the end of the tour my campaign committee was almost euphoric. The level of committed support had increased dramatically; campaign expenses were expanding to keep up with donations. The media were beginning to sit up and reassess their earlier pronouncements, with one columnist, Nick Hills, even going so far as to report that "Rosemary Brown is running second . . . to the point that Nystrom, who thinks he's second, is beginning to invent delegate support."

By the time the campaign committee arrived in Winnipeg two days prior to the convention, I was no longer intimidated by the job of leader. I had grown so much during the campaign and been so impressed by the talent within the party that I had become confident that no matter who the delegates chose as leader, the NDP would remain a force and influence in Canadian politics.

I was completely caught up in the excitement and enthusiasm

of the committee and hung between a state of exhaustion and exhilaration most of the time. By then I had stopped eating and had lost twenty-three pounds.

We knew that we would be arriving at the convention with me sitting in second place. The goal of all the provincial committees was to lock their support in tight, and then to work on picking up additional delegates as other candidates were dropped from the ballot. We knew that my strength was from the B.C. and Ontario (where I was running second) delegates, and that I was weakest in Saskatchewan, most of whose delegates were committed to Lorne Nystrom and where I was running third or possibly even fourth behind John Harney.

CHAPTER NINE

Just for one second as the plane touched down in Winnipeg, Robin, Hilda and I looked at each other in a moment of silent panic—this was it. All the months and hours of hard work would end in three days. The party would have a new leader, and no matter who was chosen, we knew that we had achieved at least one of our stated goals: the national debate on feminism had occurred, the consciousness-raising had happened, the shift towards full equality was taking place. The battle we faced over the coming days was for socialism. This was going to be a tough one. The party had become skilled and experienced through its wars with the Waffle. It had also become paranoid about the intentions of people it dubbed 'the Left.'

We were under no delusion. The hierarchy had interpreted our feminist position as just a cleverly constructed mask to hide our true left-wing intent. Grudging as they had been in espousing many of our feminist demands, they had done so in the hope that, satisfied, the women would abandon 'the Left,' split the coalition and allow the Brown campaign to die after a brave showing on the first ballot.

We were determined that this would not happen. We had come to our feminism through socialism and to us the two remained indivisible. We quickly shifted into overdrive and hit the tarmac running.

Regular meetings of our national campaign committee had been occurring prior to our arrival in Winnipeg. The first one had been called on June 30. At that meeting the Manitoba committee had been joined by Bob and Barb Beardsley of Toronto, as well as Gayle and Clare Powell from Saskatchewan, and they had constituted themselves the national 'Brown is Beautiful' campaign committee.

The 'Brown is Beautiful' slogan, a modification of the phrase coined by the Black movement in the United States, was first introduced by Clare Powell into the Saskatchewan campaign. It proved so successful that it was adopted by all the other committees and became our official slogan. No one seemed to be concerned about its links to the Black Panthers or Malcolm X; all welcomed it as a symbol that we were radicals without being extremists in the American way.

As a symbol, for me it went beyond a play on my name. It linked me to the American Black struggle and gave me an opportunity to be identified with it. I was really pleased with the committee's decision and with the use of the colour brown (with its root and earth connection) in the design of the logo.

I am reluctant to write about the convention itself, because I realize that such reporting will be one-dimensional and even egocentric. My experience of the convention in reality was limited by the very small role that I played as a candidate. Experience in subsequent leadership races in which I have been involved as a worker taught me that the real work in such campaigns is done far away from the limelight and from the candidate.

Indeed, the candidate is usually sent out to play in front of the public and the media so that the workers can complete their important tasks without interference and distraction. An accurate and complete description of a leadership campaign, I have concluded, can only be achieved through the collective remembering and recording of all of the participants in the scenario. So, what I am about to record is just a glimpse, the small remembering of my part in the historic events that took place July 4 to July 7, 1975, in Winnipeg, Manitoba.

I was assigned four tasks by the campaign committee. I was to meet and talk with the delegates, participate in the floor debates, deport myself well in the 'bearpit' session (the public forum in which questions are hurled at the candidates, as TV lights glare and the audience surrounds you in a circle so close that you can almost feel the warmth of their breath), and excel in the final candidate's speech.

The time between my arrival on July 3 and the bearpit session on Friday, July 4, were a blur of delegates' meetings, policy briefings, press interviews, receptions and greetings. I was too rushed to be anxious or nervous. I tried to escape to my hotel room whenever possible to study the policy kits from the various provincial committees in preparation for the bearpit session. I felt the weight of my supporters' expectations and I was terrified of failing them. Everyone was on a high. Our support continued to grow, and, although our second place position never changed, we were widening the gap between ourselves and Nystrom and closing the gap ever so slightly with Broadbent.

The bearpit, when it arrived, proved to be easier than I had feared. I lost no supporters, gained a few more, and the consensus of the committee was that I had conducted myself well.

The next hurdle was the final speech; however, the committee insisted that some time had to be spent participating in the policy debates on the floor. They believed that my involvement in that aspect of the convention was more important than any more media events or delegates' meetings. They were determined that my position as a thoughtful participant in the debate and discussion of party policy should be emphasized, and that I should not be seen to be the kind of leader who would only turn up at conventions to deliver the keynote address and socialize with delegates.

Bill arrived at the convention on Friday. He decided that it would be impossible for me to get any rest so long as I lived in the convention hotel, so he booked into another hotel and I moved in with him. I turned my room over to Clive Lytle, Hilda Thomas, Mark Bostwick, Jim MacKenzie and June Jensen, so they would have a quiet place to work on my final speech.

Saturday morning I arrived at the convention relatively rested, but tense. I was anxious to be with the speechwriting committee; however, since I agreed with the committee's decision about my participation in the floor debates, we consulted and agreed that two interventions would be sufficient.

The first time I spoke, loud and sustained applause broke out from the delegates as soon as I identified myself. I found out later that I was the first of the candidates to participate in the floor debates. My committee was ecstatic at yet another demonstration of how I differed from the other candidates. By the end of the day, of course, all the candidates had spoken, and all had been warmly greeted, even Douglas Campbell.

On my second trip to the mike, my brain slipped into reverse, and speaking in support of a party motion I said, "when I say that women should hold at least fifty percent of the elected positions in the party, I mean that if there are four vacancies on a committee four of those vacancies should go to women." I realized the mistake as soon as I had made it and joined in the laughter that greeted my obvious Freudian slip.

I spent the rest of the time until the evening session closeted with the speechwriting crew. I had never been comfortable with the idea of delivering a speech written by someone else. I had only done so once before, when Robin had prepared a speech for me to deliver at a meeting. Since our speaking styles were different, my delivery was abominable. She was furious at my destruction of her masterpiece, I was embarrassed at my poor delivery, and we agreed that we would not repeat that experience. Throughout the campaign, my pattern had been to take the speech notes that were prepared for me by Hilda and Mark and to translate them into my own style of speaking.

However, I recognized that the talent of this particular group of speechwriters was so formidable and this speech so crucial that I dared not even dream of tampering in any way with their creation. Since it was a collective and I was a part of it, I was able to have enough input so that I hoped I could be comfortable with the style, but I was not sure. I was desperate, therefore, for the speech to be completed so that I could go off to a quiet corner and rehearse it. Time, alas, did not permit this, and as the time for delivery approached, my anxiety level rose almost to the point of immobilizing me. I suddenly remembered how much I hated public speaking and I just wanted to chuck the whole thing and disappear.

At 5:30 p.m. Robin came to collect me. It was time to dress, to be in the committee room relaxed and smiling to give a boost to the workers, and to reassure them that I was ready for the fray. There was no time to return to my hotel, so I dressed in the committee room behind a sheet held up by two workers. I calmly applied my makeup while Hilda read the speech to me. At that point, true to form, my stomach shut down and I could neither eat nor drink. However, I forced myself to give a brief pep talk to the workers and to look to all the world cool, calm and relaxed. Only Bill and Robin knew that my heart was pounding, that my hands were freezing, my breathing laboured and my mind a blank, and that my legs would soon begin to tremble.

After my little pep talk, Bill led me to a corner behind the stage. He held both my hands in his very tightly and said in a calm voice, "breathe in, breathe out, breathe in, breathe out, breathe in. . . ."

Muriel Smith had completed her gentle, personal and very moving nominating speech, and Clive Lytle, my second nominator, had begun his. Clive has a speaking voice much like Paul Robeson's singing voice. It is deep and rich and, combined with a beautiful mastery of the English language, makes him a joy to listen to. I became completely caught up in the magic of his delivery and was walking towards the stage before I realized that my nervousness had evaporated.

The loud, long and sustained applause, the bright lights, and Clive and Muriel's words all lifted me and carried me through my first words, "I'm here today to ask you to select me to be the new leader for our party, a party whose traditions we love . . . and whose future we trust . . ." As I continued to weave the vision we had for the NDP of the future, the number of interruptions by applause continued to grow.

And as I spoke of ending poverty and creating equality, I was emboldened and strengthened by the hopes and dreams we had for this country; my voice was clear and my words firm, and I knew that I was doing as good a job as my supporters would have wished and a good job as well for all the women, Black people, poor and voiceless who had inspired me to champion causes and enter public life in the first place. At that time it was more clear for me than ever before that getting the message across by being there was indeed the most important justification for our campaign.

If I am elected leader of the New Democratic Party I make this solemn pledge to the 1.6 million children in Canada who live in poverty, without adequate food or clothing or shelter and with little hope for the future; to the poor of this country, especially the parents who suffer the despair of knowing that their children, like them, will be caught in the economic snare of want and misery and pain; to the workers who struggle to maintain the pride that comes from knowing that it is their hands that turn the machines and produce the goods and build the buildings that make this country; to the farmers who cling to the land in spite of all the pressure of rising costs and diminishing rewards, because they know that what they do is the most important job of all; to my socialist comrades in Quebec to whom I say: come with me, work with me, so that together through the NDP we can rid Quebec of the grip of Power Corporation, ITT and Douglas Aircraft; to the Native Indians whose century-long struggle for simple justice in their own land is soon, with our help, going to be won; to the women, whose understanding of these struggles has grown through their own struggle, and whose example and support and love have given me the strength and the courage to stand here today and to take on this task.

To all of you I make this pledge: That I will never forget that our party has its roots in the Prairie soil, where it grew in spite of dust and Depression, fed by sweat and tears and the passionate hatred of injustice;

that I will never forget that we are the party of the working people, and that our task and our duty is to bring them legal and moral justice in the face of attacks from power and privilege; that I will be unbending in my stand against every form of oppression which deforms and crushes people and prevents them from the fulfillment of their lives; and that as leader of our New Democratic Party, I will be answerable to the members of this party as we go forward to become the government that will build a truly socialist, truly humane society—here in Canada.

I did not hear the applause at the end of my speech because by then my brain and my hearing had collapsed under the combination of exhaustion, tension, anxiety and relief, but I have been told that it was deafening. My task was over, I wanted to go home and go to bed.

Because of the time constraints on all candidates' speeches, I had to delete parts of the complete speech, so it was decided that I would give it in its entirety in the committee room at the end of the evening. When I arrived there, the room was packed. All the committee members were spinning with excitement. Even the calm, steady Bob Beardsley was taking little hopping steps up and down. My speech had picked up support, votes were shifting our way, the delegate count was rising.

When I looked around the convention floor on Monday, my workers seemed to be everywhere, huddling, speaking to delegates, conferring. I had no task to perform, no role to play. I sat beside Bill and across from my brother at our constituency table and worried.

What if we had been able to pull it off? What if, after the votes came in, I was indeed leader of this party? What would it really mean to the chances of the party ever forming the government in Canada? What if the pundits were right and I was the 'kiss of death' to this party, which for so long had acted as Canada's conscience? Would my leadership increase open racism and sexism among Canadians? What were Canadians thinking? Did they care that I was within hours of leading the third most important political party in this country? What were women really thinking about this? How would my leadership benefit the Black community? What effect would it have on Bill and on our marriage? Where were the children? I wished that they were here! My brother reached across the table and touched me. "Smile," he said, "you're on candid camera." I looked up and sure enough there was the camera trained on me. Just then someone walked up and delivered a rose, which had been sent by an anonymous admirer in Vancouver. The press, who were bored with waiting for the vote to begin, milled about asking questions about who I thought had sent the rose.

Tension on the floor mounted as we awaited the results of the first ballot. When it was reported, our committee breathed a sigh of relief. Their count had been accurate, I was in second place, 413 votes to Broadbent's 536 total.

One of our more controversial decisions, and one about which our opposition had chuckled with glee, was the decision not to accept 'part-time' support. We demanded of our supporters that they stay with us through to the end. We argued that their support should be based on our platform and position on issues, and that they should remain faithful to me, so long as I remained faithful to the platform. The political veterans saw this position as proof that we were both innocent and doctrinaire.

We began the day with 395 ironclad committed votes that we hoped to build on, and clearly they were all there on the first ballot. Before the beginning of the second ballot, Svend Robinson came to visit me. He pointed out that, if I delivered my 413 supporters to John Harney, he would then have 726 and the surprise move would stun both Broadbent and Nystrom into immediate defeat.

I told him that this would be a bold move, which would work even better the other way around since I was sitting in second place and John was down in fourth. "In any event," I added, "even to contemplate such an action would violate two of our ground rules concerning making no deals, and not dropping out until defeated." Svend decided that as the candidate I had very little say anyway and went off in search of Robin or some other committee member. He never returned and John Harney was defeated on the second ballot.

The third ballot plunged our committee into a momentary state of gloom, for although I was still in second place, Ed was widening the gap between us, and some of the unexpected votes we had received on the first ballot had deserted us. We were now down to our core vote of 397, Ed had 586, Nystrom was still in third place with 342. As I looked around I noticed that the Broadbent workers were beginning to look less anxious. Panic hit them, however, when Nystrom was dropped after the third ballot, leaving a clear two-way fight between Ed and me. Although Ed had a comfortable lead with 694 ballots to my 494, Nystrom's exit meant that 413 ballots were up for grabs.

The gloves were off. Dave Barrett, Bill King, Allan Blakeney, Tommy Douglas, all the big guns were running around the convention floor twisting arms, calling in chips, working at an energy level hitherto unheard of. My committee was doing the same. It was fascinating to behold. A life-and-death struggle for the party seemed to be taking place there on the convention floor that Monday morning.

I sat detached and watched it all. Bill, as a psychiatrist, was enthralled. He had never seen or experienced anything like that before. My brother concentrated on his responsibility, that of maintaining my smile for the benefit of the TV cameras that now encircled me, and which I'm sure also encircled Ed. The camera people wanted to catch the instant reaction, the immediate response to the results of the final vote.

Marilyn Roycroft, chairperson of the Brown Campaign balloting committee, came and knelt beside my chair. "Keep smiling," she whispered, "but listen carefully." Something in her voice forewarned me, so I found my smile, beamed into the cameras and listened. She explained that we needed seventy-five percent or 307 of Lorne Nystrom's support to win. Everyone had worked the Saskatchewan delegates, but Blakeney, Nystrom and the powers that be had a tight rein on them. "We are just not going to make it," she said. We smiled at each other one more time for the benefit of the camera and she stood up and left. Bob Beardsley came over, patted my shoulder and slipped a note into my hand. "Move that it be unanimous," it read, and I knew that Robin was off somewhere weeping.

The press was very generous. "Brown Last To Be Defeated—Leadership Race Tight To The End," headlined the *Winnipeg Free Press*. "Brown wins believers in defeat," read *The Province*, where Nick Hills wrote, "with Rosemary Brown the end was full of grace and eloquence, and even some humour; but particularly honour in pledging all her support to the man who had beaten her."

In the end Ed had garnered the support of 948 delegates; I had 658.

I waited for the predicted letdown, anticipated the inevitable depression that must follow such a long and sustained level of activity and anxiety—but it never came; instead, there was only bone-deep weariness.

Bill had greeted me with an embarrassed smile after my speech on Saturday night and a query as to where I thought he had planned to take me as a gift and a treat when the campaign was over. I suddenly remembered that his dream had always been of one day being able to afford to have us stay at the Banff Springs Hotel. But, as the room rates had kept increasing faster than our budget, it had become part of the family fantasy and dream. Each year on our summer trip to Banff with the children, we would visit the hotel, saunter through the lobby, admire everything and then leave, to imagine what it would be like to be guests there sometime. So it was as a joke that I responded to his question, "To the Banff Springs?" Then I blanched, for the look on his face revealed that that indeed was the wonderful surprise he had planned for me.

I felt sick at the possibility that I might have ruined his gift by my attack on the CPR owners of the hotel in my speech at the convention. He reassured me with a chuckle that it was most unlikely that the management of the Banff Springs or any of the CPR brass would watch an NDP convention on TV or would be aware of my attack on them. We were wrong.

We boarded the train in Winnipeg later that night and, not

surprisingly, the Black attendants all came to greet me and congratulate me on what they felt was a successful and proud moment for the Black community. However, to our surprise and embarrassment, when our cab arrived at the Banff Springs Hotel the following morning, the manager was on the front steps to welcome us and to thank us for choosing their hotel in which to rest. In our room we found beautiful flowers and a large bowl of fruit with a card of greeting and good wishes from the management. Throughout the three days that we remained there, we were given the most exceptional red carpet treatment. Although my opinion of the Canadian Pacific Railway didn't change, I admired the grace with which they handled my public castigation of them. I returned to Vancouver relaxed, still tired, and convinced that the CPR had not even been slightly wounded by the fact that my big guns had been trained on it.

The Brown campaign committee waited until my return to Vancouver to hold its final meeting. It was one of many post mortems during which we analyzed and dissected and rethought and recalled every aspect of the campaign, and 'wondered if.' In the end we decided that we probably had succeeded beyond our expectations. We hoped that our impact on the party would survive; that the doors we had opened to feminism and to socialist commitment would remain open. We hoped, but we were not sure, because at the end of the campaign the same persons were in control of the party as were there when it began.

We wound up the committee's financial affairs, and disbanded, and I turned to the task of responding to the hundreds of letters and telegrams of congratulation, and thanking the many workers and supporters who had put so much into the campaign.

Dear Sisters,
    Just a note to thank you – thank you for believing in me and encouraging me to run for leadership of our federal party. Thank you for supporting me with your financial donations to the campaign.

Thank you for all the work and energy that you gave me so willingly in the campaign. Thank you for the words of hope and encouragement.

Thank you for the love that sustained me.

Thank you to Hilda and Robin in particular who carried the brunt and supplied the word when the word was needed.

To those of you who came to Winnipeg, thank you for your votes.

It was a long battle, a tough fight, but it was worth it—feminism and socialism both moved forward. The NDP moved forward. Your strength, your courage helped make it happen.

Sisterhood is powerful. You proved this.

Thank you, thank you, thank you and love.

Yours in Sisterhood,

Rosemary

Marianne Gilbert suggested that maybe one day I would write about the entire experience. "Never," I assured her.

It has been thirteen years since that convention. It is now clear that the choice of the party was a sensible one. Ed Broadbent has been a solid and reliable leader who went into the federal election in 1988 ahead of both the Conservative and Liberal leaders (according to the polls) as the person the Canadian people would most like to be their prime minister. Although the party lagged far behind him in public support, it now seems that this rejection is based more on dislike of the unknown, and of the NDP's links with labour, than on fear that Ed's leadership would unleash socialism on the land.

The 1988 election results left us where past elections have left us, in third place, except that we won more seats than ever before. Who knows, maybe that is the way a federal NDP government will come in Canada, inch by inch, one election at a time.

The leadership convention of 1975 remains a political milestone in my life. It opened up the country and showed me another, more friendly and caring face of Canada. It caused me to travel farther, dig more deeply and learn more about this country of my adoption than if I had been born here; and for that I'm truly grateful.

I'm grateful also that the campaign came and went before Canada began to measure the success of political campaigns by the extent to which they ape and resemble the American model. It was good to know that the primary concern, of the media as well as all other Canadians, was about the quality of service I would give to the country rather than about any aspect of my or my family's personal and private lives. Politically I was pleased that the New Democratic Party reinstituted a tradition, older than the party itself, and even predating suffrage, of national political debates on women's issues, a tradition which had disappeared in modern times, and I am grateful to have been the conduit through which the first trickle flowed.

The one aspect of the experience that gives me my greatest joy, however, is knowing that on July 7, 1975, all over this country, Black people, children as well as adults, eyes and ears fixed on TV and radio, waited for the results of that final ballot, and for that short while, dared to dream of the impossible.

CHAPTER TEN

All in all, 1975 proved to be a mad round of highs and lows.

Our eldest child, Cleta, graduated from Magee High School, and her choice of graduation gown triggered a family crisis. She had made her purchase unassisted by me and was very proud of the beautiful buttercup yellow dress she had chosen. When she modelled it for us, I complimented her on her choice. Her father hit the roof when he noted that the 'spaghetti' shoulder straps left most of her back, front and shoulders exposed. He issued an ultimatum that she had to cover herself in some way or wear another dress. Tears and hysteria followed.

I was busy trying to balance my legislative constituency work with the demands of an accelerating leadership campaign. Nonetheless, something had to be done to resolve the impasse. Cleta would not hear of wearing some other dress. So I volunteered to crochet a short jacket, just long enough to cover her shoulders.

I must have been crazy, or else responding to what Helen Levine, a remarkable Canadian feminist, social worker and teacher, refers to as making myself "indispensable to family." As graduation day approached, it became clear that the jacket would not be finished in time. I tried to work and crochet at the same time. Since I was now flying between Victoria and Vancouver in order to save travel time, I lost the hour and fifty minutes that I could have gained by travelling on the ferry. I prepared Cleta for the worst by suggesting that a sleeveless or one-sleeved jacket might be an innovative approach to her problem, but she rejected my daring approach to fashion.

Graduation day I boarded the plane in Victoria: the jacket had one and three-quarter sleeves. I crocheted frantically in the car as we drove to the graduation ceremony, and hooked the last stitch just before it was time for the class to march into the auditorium. When Cleta showed up with her jacket on, a cheer went up from her classmates—it seems that the whole class had been following the saga of the jacket.

Cleta was beautiful as she walked up to the podium for her diploma, and her father beamed at her modestly covered back, front and shoulders. She kept the jacket on through the required father and daughter dance that followed the ceremony. I have never seen her wear that jacket again.

It was also the year in which I had the unhappy necessity of having to vote against my own government not once, but on two occasions. Both instances were caused by legislation that I interpreted as weakening trade unions.

I had always believed that the problem with trade unions was that they were not strong enough to be the equal of management in a dispute, and that it was management's recognition of this weakness that triggered their intransigence in bargaining and the responding strike action on the part of workers. I believed, therefore, that to ensure equality and balance, a government had to strengthen the position of organized labour, not weaken it. For this reason I had no option but to join Colin Gabelmann and Harold Steeves, two other backbenchers who spoke eloquently and convincingly in opposing Bill 84, an act that clearly weakened the Labour Code of B.C.

In October of that same year, I found myself once again in dispute over a matter pertaining to trade union workers. My government, concerned about the potential for tragedy in the small town of Nanaimo when propane workers, who were members of the Teamsters Union, went out on strike, decided to legislate them back to work.

Unsubstantiated rumour has it that a prominent trade unionist telephoned the premier and pointed out to him that such action would be patently unfair. The International Woodworkers of America and Retail Clerks, two unions actively supportive of the NDP, were also out on strike at that time and were not being subjected to government intrusion in their dispute. So any failure to legislate *them* back to work would be a clear case of political bias and favouritism. The premier definitely did not want to be accused of favouritism in his dealings with the trade union movement, so his minister of labour drafted and introduced the necessary back-to-work legislation and made it applicable to all three unions.

There was some debate as to whether the labour leader who called the premier was voicing a genuine concern for the well-being of the government or whether he was a participant in the strategy of the right-wing forces to destabilize the government and bring about its eventual downfall. In any event, he was successful on all counts.

Again Colin Gabelmann, Harold Steeves and I saw the legislation as violating a working collective bargaining process and weakening the rights of workers to bargain as equals, and decided that we could not endorse or support such action. Today, thirteen years later, I still believe that the government was trapped into moving against its own best interest and sealed its defeat by the introduction of that Bill.

Buoyed by the public response to the decision to legislate the striking workers back to work, Dave Barrett began to talk about the possibility of riding the public's good feelings about us into an election. Most backbenchers in the caucus were opposed and argued strenuously that the euphoria was not even paper-thin and would deteriorate at the drop of the writ. It was clear from these long, heated discussions that the cabinet was also split on this issue. The consensus was that, as a first-time government, which had innovated and introduced so many new policies, we needed the time to consolidate them, and that we should take our full five years to do so. Dave Barrett and the most influential member of the cabinet disagreed. They were confident of our re-election, and sure that the voters, recognizing what an outstanding government we were, would give us another mandate.

Most of the caucus remained unconvinced, so political pundits, pollsters and gurus were brought in to map and chart and measure and illustrate through scientific and scholarly presentations that our fears of defeat were unfounded.

I said then, and I maintain now, that nobody knows better than a politician who lives and works closely in her or his riding how constituents will vote in an election. I needed no technology to convince me that our rating among the people in Vancouver-Burrard was low and getting lower. I had had two years of being invited to every christening, graduation, golden wedding anniversary, hundredth birthday and other significant celebration in the riding: the invitations stopped. After two years of being greeted, hugged, touched, smiled at and stopped continually when I walked along any street in the riding, I was now being greeted with slight nods, averted eyes or angry berating.

I felt the lowering of the approval temperature wherever I went. Women's groups were disillusioned, anti-poverty groups were disappointed and labour groups were enraged. Whatever anyone else might be finding, I knew that if the government went to an election, my geographical as well as ideological and community supporters would work to ensure its defeat. I heard my story repeated over and over again by other backbenchers and even some cabinet ministers.

The government was determined, however, based on information that it had and was unwilling to share with us, that the time had come to go the polls. So our reports on the situation in our own ridings were dismissed as the over-sensitive overreaction of inexperienced members. The government proceeded with its agenda and on December 11, 1975, the first NDP government of British Columbia went down to devastating defeat, losing all but twelve of its sitting members. Norm Levi and I survived the battering. The premier did not.

The close vote in Vancouver-Burrard necessitated a recount.

As soon as my re-election was confirmed, I flew to Jamaica, where for two weeks I tried to erase all memory of the nightmare campaign. While there, I received a call from Robin telling me that the first act of the new Social Credit government was the closing down of the office of the Coordinator of Women's Affairs by the new Provincial Secretary, Grace McCarthy. Gene Errington, my friend and women's friend and defender in the capital, was fired; the fragile beachhead that so many women had fought so hard and so long to establish was eliminated with the stroke of a pen. It was a lesson in vulnerability that would be repeated years later when the Meech Lake Accord made an empty mockery of Sections 15 and 28 of the equality provisions of the Charter of Rights and Freedoms.

The only ray of light in that whole experience was that Robin, who had been a scrutineer at the recount, reported that a consistently large number of voters had jumped party lines and voted for the two women candidates in the riding, and that it was this very clearly biased 'women's' vote that had assured my victory. Sisterhood *is* powerful – the gender gap was emerging.

I returned from Jamaica as angry about the calling of the election as I had been when I left. When I attended my first caucus meeting I was in no mood to endorse the motion of the caucus that Dave Barrett remain leader. I remained silent throughout the caucus discussion about his future, speaking only briefly, once to support the sentiments of the one caucus member who counselled Dave to resign as leader so that the party could call a leadership campaign, and the second time to oppose the suggestion that Eileen Dailly should step aside so that Dave could run in a by-election in her riding.

My first intervention was ignored, my second accepted because happily Eileen's margin of victory was so slim that a by-election victory for the leader could not be guaranteed. It fell to Bob Williams from Vancouver East, the minister who had been the staunchest advocate of an election call, to surrender his seat to his leader.

I dreaded the return to the legislature, fearing that the new Socred government, under the leadership of Bill Bennett, the son of the original Socred premier, would exercise every option and opportunity to humiliate us. However, I was buoyed by the belief that our sojourn in opposition would be temporary since the voters of the province would soon come to recognize what a bad bargain they had struck in exchanging an NDP government for a Social Credit one.

The first day that I returned to the legislative sitting I thought would surely be the worst day of my political career, but I was wrong. The humiliation and insults hurled across the floor at us by government members never let up, so that in time we became inured to them and began to respond in kind, earning for our legislature the reputation of being the crudest, ugliest and most unpleasant provincial parliament in all of Canada.

In time, Dave won his by-election and returned to the Assembly. He immediately began to plan for the next election. He filled us with hope and enthusiasm, and convinced us to hold on to our seats so that we could be the foundation on which a new, wiser NDP government would be built. He was evangelical in this zeal, and so open and cooperative that I was seduced by his dream. And so when the opportunity I had always wanted presented itself to me, I rejected it.

Bill and I were relaxing one Sunday morning, listening to the CBC, when the phone rang. It was Ed Broadbent. He asked me to run in the anticipated federal election. He explained that NDP polling had shown that with the right candidate they could beat Simma Holt, the sitting Liberal member in Vancouver-Kingsway. I explained that Simma was a friend and that I would have to give the matter serious thought.

Bill's immediate response was that it was a gift and I should grab it. He was particularly impressed that Broadbent, whom I had challenged for the leadership less than a year before, now wanted me in his caucus. Bill had assumed that, as in other political parties, NDP leadership races leave irreparable hurts.

I was sorely tempted. I wanted to be a federal member more than I wanted any other job, with the possible exception of High Commissioner to Jamaica. I agonized over it all day and half of that night, as Bill kept encouraging me to go for it. The following morning I phoned Robin, told her of the offer and suggested that she prepare to talk me out of it, because I really wanted to accept.

In the end, Dave convinced me, when I discussed the offer with him as a courtesy and indicated that I wanted to accept it, not to do so. He was convinced that we had a chance of forming the government provincially after the next election, but only if we all held on to our seats. He asked me to give the provincial party this one more chance to return to power, after which I would be free to stay and be a part of the government or leave to seek a federal seat. He was certain that there would be other federal opportunities for me, but that there would be no other opportunity for us provincially, if we lost the next election. It boiled down to my selfish federal ambitions versus the provincial New Democratic Party. It was no contest: the party won.

So in the end I had to phone Ed and decline the offer of his support in securing the nomination. He was disappointed, but I was so much more so that I wouldn't allow myself to reopen the idea once it was closed.

Two years later, a government gerrymander eliminated my provincial seat of Vancouver-Burrard. The next time that an opportunity beckoned me to a federal seat, I had retired from politics and was too busy and too weary to heed its call.

The year 1977 is sealed in my mind by two acts—one a surprising honour bestowed on me by my elder son's high school graduating class; the other, a slip of the tongue that got me talking and kept me talking for more than fifteen hours over a period of five days.

When Gary told me that his class had voted to invite me to move the toast on behalf of the parents to the graduating class, I was pleased. When he explained that it meant I would have to give a speech at the graduating banquet on behalf of the parents, I realized that an honour had indeed been bestowed on me. I was very moved by the accolade and was determined to make every parent feel that I was truly speaking from the bottom of her or his heart. I also decided to be brief:

On behalf of the parents, I would like to propose a toast to the realization of an eighteen-year-old dream.

I know that eighteen years ago when each of us met you, our own child, for the first time we were convinced that by some incredible stroke of luck we had been blessed with one of the most beautiful and most perfect of creations—full of incredible potential and destined to achieve great things.

I also know that there have been times over those years when we have wondered what manner of aberration we had parented.

Throughout those years, however, as we watched with wonder the miracle of you learning to walk, then to talk, and finally to think, we never ceased to be excited, amazed, sometimes enraged, often challenged and always educated by you.

We watched you grappling with the reality of a school which taught you a seven-day week did not necessarily begin on Sunday or a 12 o'clock class start at 2 p.m. while demanding of you the best that you had within you academically as well as personally.

Along with our love we developed a sense of pride in you and respect for you, because we could sense, emerging out of the mass and tangle of those confusing years, mature, compassionate, tolerant and generous adults—willing to accept responsibility for your actions, your decisions, your mistakes—and even for some of ours, too.

And so today, on behalf of all the parents, I would like to say to you as one of the most fortunate and privileged groups of people who inhabit this earth— moving out into an imperfect world, a world that in many ways is not even ready for you, that we, your parents, recognize the burden and responsibility with which you travel.

We also want you to know that we have no fear for you or for your future. For you have taught us that love and understanding and humour are positive and powerful forces. You have taught us to respect gentleness and to recognize the necessity for and the excitement of being flexible at all times.

With patience you have helped us to meet the challenge of change, and to be tolerant of difference. You have opened our eyes to the beauty of simplicity and our minds to the value of all life.

We have grown and matured together, you and I, and I know that in the process we have become friends.

So, we want you to know that you face the future surrounded by our love and our admiration — accompanied by our respect and our support. And we rise to congratulate you and to toast you.

We do so still convinced that it was an incredible stroke of good fortune indeed which decreed and destined seventeen or eighteen years ago that we should be entrusted with your care and nurturing during your pioneer years.

May 27, 1977

Gary told me afterwards that my words had moved some of his classmates to tears, but not him, because he had known all along that I would make a good speech.

Norm Levi, who had been a social worker before winning a seat in the provincial legislature in 1972, was so committed to the idea of grassroots politics that one of his first acts as Minister of Human Resources was to set in motion a process that he hoped would eventually lead to more control of welfare spending at the community level. Because it was a new and possibly controversial idea, Norm asked Harry Rankin, a Vancouver city counsellor and lawyer, and me to co-chair a committee that would be responsible for receiving briefs and exploring the feasibility of putting such an idea into practice.

Norm proved correct in his assessment that the idea would be controversial. Our committee conducted hearings in the Vancouver City Council chambers, and the opposition to the idea immediately became very obvious. The top bureaucrats in the city's welfare system were opposed, as were the Socreds (now in opposition) and, for some strange reason that has never been clear to me, Jack Webster, a formidable and boisterous folk hero of the open-line radio shows. Norm recognized immediately his mistake in not securing Jack's support prior to launching the idea. Jack was a very powerful force because of his large and faithful following, and because he not only had a knack for putting his finger on the pulse of his listeners' concerns, but because once he got hold of an issue, he would rag it to death before letting go. He did not like the idea of community control over welfare spending and he never stopped attacking the concept in his rasping Scottish accent until the NDP government had been defeated and the Socreds re-elected, and their Minister of Human Resources, Bill Vander Zalm, had scrapped all the resource boards but the one in Vancouver. That board's demise was postponed for a year so that it could wind down its activities.

The committee had recommended that communities have the right to elect representatives to Community Resource Boards. These boards would be responsible for administering welfare services at the local level, a form of decentralization that would allow both local communities and recipients of service to be involved in policies affecting them. As in the introduction of any new policy and program idea, there were glitches, but by the time of the defeat of the NDP government in 1975, communities were happy with resource boards and supported them, especially those that had moved to the next step and administered both health and welfare services.

The dismantling of the resource boards proved to be surprisingly unpopular; when the government postponed its decision to move against the Vancouver board for a year, Vancouverites breathed a sigh of relief and hoped that their board would be spared.

This was not to be, and when Vander Zalm introduced Bill 65 to dismantle the Vancouver resource board in September 1977, community groups erupted in opposition. They formed a coalition with social workers and unionized human service workers that proved to be the forerunner of the great Solidarity Coalition of seven years later.

The coalition sponsored a public meeting at the Queen Elizabeth Theatre. As the Opposition critic for the Ministry of Human Resources, as the social service ministry was called, I was invited to speak on the Opposition's plans to stop the legislation. Without actually thinking through the full significance of my promise, I stated that I would debate the Bill until the minister withdrew it, no matter how long it took. I received a warm round of applause and left the stage. It was not until the press pounced on me as I tried to return to my seat in the audience that I heard the word 'filibuster.' It was not until they asked if that was my plan that I realized with horror that I had committed myself and my caucus to a course of action without discussion or their permission. I was overwhelmed by the enormity of my breach of caucus etiquette and prepared myself for the worst.

Social workers across the province hailed my action, and David Schreck, the outgoing executive director of the Vancouver Resource Board (VRB), pledged his support and assistance to what he enthusiastically endorsed as an act of bravery.

Robin, my constituency representative, and I knew that the filibuster would not happen. We knew that the caucus, led by Dave, would tear a strip off me, then demand that I retract my commitment. We would have been right in our expectation but for one thing: by the time I arrived at caucus on Monday, Dave and other members had been deluged with telegrams of congratulation as well as positive media support for my plan. I still had the strip torn off me, but the caucus now had the dilemma of deciding how to retreat from a position for which it was reaping so many accolades.

The NDP provincially had always had an uncomfortable relationship with welfare policy. As a party we believed very strongly in the role of the state in the delivery of social services, but at the same time we recognized that the public perception of us as a 'welfare' party hurt us at the polls. The struggle to maintain a balance between being true to our ideals without being victimized by them was ongoing, and the caucus was split on how best to handle this dilemma.

It was not a dilemma for me; I accepted welfare as a short-term tool to sustain the poor until the very necessary redistribution of wealth and services that would eliminate poverty. I saw no need to keep that commitment secret.

After a lengthy debate, during which I was often reminded, and rightly so, of the errors of my ways, the caucus decided to allow a limited filibuster. With relief and joy, I phoned Robin to tell her that the green light had been given. She had not anticipated this outcome and had been busily preparing a carefully worded statement for release to the press. With a whoop of delight we began to plan our strategy.

We decided that she would be responsible for the collection of debate material and I would concentrate on becoming physically ready for the ordeal. I immediately focused on three things: strengthening my legs so that I could stand for long periods of time, strengthening my voice so that it would survive long periods of speaking and increasing the ability of my bladder to retain fluid. My normal daily regimen had always included exercising on the mat and the stationary bicycle at the government fitness facility every morning that I was in Victoria, and walking briskly for an hour each morning on the weekends, when I was in Vancouver. Now I increased my exercising, reduced my fluid intake and tried to increase the retentive powers of my bladder. In short, I did some dangerously stupid things in preparation for the debate. My advice to anyone contemplating a filibuster would be to consult a physician before embarking on any kind of training regimen.

I decided that since the filibuster is part politics and part theatre, I should strive to make a visual as well as verbal statement. I decided to dress in black for the duration of the debate as a signal of the sombre nature of the occasion, and the sad impact the dismantling of the VRB would have on the quality of life in Vancouver.

Community groups organized to maintain a corps of supporters in the gallery for the duration of my speech as moral support, and Gordon Gibson, the Liberal leader and MLA, sent boxes of material to aid in the debate.

On Monday, September 19, I rose to begin debate on Bill 65. I entered the legislative chamber with a cardboard file box containing approximately six hours of debate material, a bottle of throat spray, throat lozenges and a packet of raisins. Robin was sitting in my office, ears glued to the electronic speaker, listening to the debate. David Schreck was sitting in the gallery surrounded by fifteen or twenty social workers, community activists and other well-wishers. It was the beginning of a debate that lasted five days of sitting, a total of fifteen hours and forty-eight minutes.

Bill Vander Zalm sat through it all, leaving, as I did, only in times of dire physiological need. My colleagues wandered in and out, monitoring my health carefully. Lorne Nicolson and Gary Lauk, our two volunteer constitutional experts, raised inventive and obscure points of order leading to procedural wrangles that sent the Clerks of the House and the Speaker into puzzled consultation, while I used those few precious moments to rest my voice and to take a break.

The debate on the floor was only part of the marathon, however, because each day in caucus there was lengthy discussion as to whether the time had come to end the filibuster. The press was being monitored carefully for any signs of hostility to my actions. After a while even my staunchest supporters came to accept that the filibuster would not achieve its goal and that my debate was merely a holding act, which would not deter the government from its action.

By Thursday my neck and shoulders were aching and I was beginning to experience periods of dizziness. Nonetheless, I continued my exercise regimen, as well as the curtailment of my fluid intake. The caucus was becoming increasingly concerned about accusations of holding up the legislature's business and of the cost to the taxpayers of my actions. Everyone was sensitive to possible public and media backlash, and the pressure on me to end the filibuster increased. I was torn between wanting to speak as long as humanly possible, worrying about incurring the wrath of the caucus further, and doubting whether I was in fact achieving anything. I believed that I could force my body to survive for much longer, but emotionally I was drained by the conflict in the caucus and the unrealistic expectations in the community.

At the caucus meeting on Friday morning I agreed that I would end the filibuster before the legislature rose at 1 p.m. I entered the chamber with a brave face, but I was disappointed, dejected and beaten. I was convinced that my emotional state aggravated my neck and shoulder pain and contributed to the episodes of dizziness. At 12:30 I gave up. I left the chamber and hurried to my office, closed the door and wept. Then I dried my eyes, powdered my face, repaired my lipstick and went out to meet the press.

When my doctor examined me later, it turned out that I was seriously dehydrated. The combination of exercise and reduced liquid intake had indeed been a very stupid and unhealthy one. Once I started taking fluids again and rested over the weekend, I was back to full health and ready to continue my assault on the government.

When the Social Credit government struck a royal commission on electoral boundary reform, headed by an ex-provincial court judge, Larry Eckardt, in 1978, we all assumed that this merely meant that the six double ridings in Vancouver would be split into single ridings, as would the double ridings in Surrey, Richmond and Victoria. I worried about the outcome of the investigation because Vancouver-Burrard, like most other double-member ridings, was a mix of small pockets of affluence and poverty, but consisted mostly of middle-class, middle-income earners. Although neither Norm nor I particularly enjoyed being part of a two-member riding, neither of us wanted to see it split, since it would result in one good NDP riding and one that could be either Liberal, Conservative or Socred, but probably not NDP.

Robin and I discussed the options almost daily. We finally decided that I would contest the nomination for the strong end of the riding, even if it meant going up against Norm. We were awed by the political organizing skills of Gloria, his wife, but we felt that we had no option but to take him on if he decided to go for the NDP end of the riding. We pulled out all the old voting results, studied them, and tried to second-guess Mr. Eckardt as to where the line would be drawn through the riding.

Bill was pragmatic. "Perhaps," he suggested, "it was time for me to leave provincial politics and explore other professional options." Briefly, I thought of trying once more to attend law school, then rejected the idea. There was still much that I wanted to do in politics.

We were not prepared for the results when they were tabled in the legislature. I was so nervous about the results that, when the report was handed out to the MLAs, I did not open mine. This proved not to be necessary. Norm left his chair, walked over to me and said, "Well, I guess they have found one way to get rid of us." "How?" I asked. "They have wiped out the riding," he replied. Norm has a very picaresque sense of humour, so I assumed that this was one of his jokes. To be sure, I nonetheless opened my copy of the new map. To my stunned disbelief Vancouver-Burrard was nowhere to be seen. I looked quickly across the aisle at Grace McCarthy, the minister responsible for the establishment of the commission, and the person who had introduced the report to the legislature. She looked back at me, a soft smile on her lips, triumph in her eyes.

It was a brilliant gerrymander but for one thing. In the carving up of Vancouver-Burrard, the more conservative part of the riding had gone to Grace's riding of Little Mountain; the rest was divided between the two NDP ridings of Vancouver Centre and Vancouver East. Pride made Mrs. McCarthy call the now-extended riding Little Mountain. Because of that, both Norm and I were free to seek seats elsewhere. If she had retained the name Vancouver-Burrard for the new extended riding, we would have been tempted to stay and challenge her for it, and we would have been defeated. Realizing that we were down but not out, I returned her smile, closed the report, left my seat, walked to the women's room and threw up.

Maclean's magazine reported in its 'People' section, "Bill

Bennett's B.C. Socreds recently stuck it to the NDP Opposition by pulling the riding out from under three of the party's strongest performers. Sent into the wilderness were former cabinet ministers Norm Levi and Bill King and Canada's best known Black feminist politician, Rosemary Brown."

The loss of a riding is a traumatic experience. It's like being thrown out of your home or robbed of a valued and cherished treasure. The sense of impotence and helplessness is profound. I never duck a fair fight, but a gerrymander is a low blow. We three NDP members lost our seats, courtesy of Mr. Eckardt's electoral boundary reform. I allowed myself to succumb to rage for a few days. Then I determined that I would leave politics when the voters rejected me or I decided to do so, not because someone played politics with electoral boundaries. Any thoughts that I might have had of retiring and attempting to study law evaporated.

While I had been wallowing in my rage, Robin, Mark Bostwick, Dennis and Yvonne Cocke had been poring over previous election results in existing ridings represented by Social Credit. Telegrams and phone calls were pouring into the office from NDPers around the province inviting me to run in their ridings.

Bill was angry, as he always was if it appeared that I was being ill-used by someone. He ignored Mr. Eckardt and directed his venom at Mrs. McCarthy. He encouraged me to fight back and insisted that I reject any idea of retirement. He wanted me to take on Mrs. McCarthy in her own riding. He was so angry he threatened to enter politics himself.

When I sat down with Robin and the Cockes, it was to explore two options, Burnaby-Edmonds and Coquitlam-Maillardville. I had been invited by both ridings to move in and run against their incumbent Socreds. We studied the profiles of both ridings carefully, looked at the voting record and decided that either could be won for the NDP.

I finally chose Burnaby-Edmonds. I liked the fact that it was an old and stable riding with solid labour and CCF roots. Norm later chose Coquitlam-Maillardville, as we were both determined not to compete for the same riding. I hoped that 1978 held no more surprises for me as I prepared to move my political base to Burnaby.

CHAPTER ELEVEN

The family greeted my decision to seek the nomination in Burnaby-Edmonds with some ambivalence. Once the initial rage about the gerrymander had passed, they had hoped that I would retire so that we could all return to a more normal family life. Jonathan was carrying on Gary's excellent record in track and field and he wanted me to be free to attend more of his meets. Everyone seemed to have a premonition that this move would prove to be more disruptive than what the family was ready for.

Immediately following my successful election in 1979, my supporters in Burnaby increased their pressure on me to live in the riding. The question of my place of residence had been an issue of contention raised by my opponents in the party during the nomination fight and exploited by both Socred and Liberal opponents throughout the election campaign. The residents of Burnaby are fiercely loyal to their community, and resented the idea that a person from outside the municipality would want to represent them in government, but not want to live among them in the community.

I sympathized with their sentiments. I had always believed that an elected person should live in the riding she or he represented. This belief has proved to be an old-fashioned philosophy that over the years has increasingly been 'more honoured in the breach than in the observance.' So for me it was a matter of honour. In addition, I felt that it was one way of expressing my gratitude to the riding that had opened its heart and welcomed me.

When I broached the issue with my family, the response was an immediate and firm "No," and so began one of the most painful and bitter disputes in which our family has ever been involved.

To this day, I am still not sure why in 1982, after serving three years as the Burnaby-Edmonds representative, I did not simply retire from politics and move on to other things. Instead I dug my heels in and waged an unpleasant and disagreeable feud with my family for two years over a matter that I myself supported with reluctance and resentment. I pointed out to them that if the situation were in the reverse we would all be expected to pull up roots and follow Bill to wherever his job took him — so that for me it was a matter of principle. The children reminded me that forcing a family to bend to the will of a family member was the type of situation they thought that feminism was trying to change. I felt anger and guilt at that reminder, but inexplicably persisted in my determination to move the family.

I had a special and particular love for the house to which we had moved when Jonathan was a baby less than a year old. I had fallen in love with it the very first time that I saw it, and I had spent months convincing Bill that we should purchase it, despite the fact that its upkeep might prove to be a financial strain on him as a young physician. The house was far from perfect, but it was situated in a quiet park-like garden of large trees and rolling lawns with a view of ocean and mountains from two floors. We had moved in, settled down, renovated, and planned to spend the rest of our lives there. Our children made friends, loved the schools, the proximity to the beach. In short it truly was the home of our dreams. Our immediate neighbours, the artists Lawren and Beth Harris, welcomed us to the neighbourhood and invited us to a number of their Sunday afternoon socials. Bill and Howie, their son, shared a passion for jazz and over the years became close friends.

In the end I won the struggle, but the victory was a truly Pyrrhic one, for, although the family agreed to leave 'Belmont,' only Bill really accompanied me to Burnaby. Cleta and Gary moved away and made homes for themselves elsewhere. Jonathan, who was still in high school, haunted the old neighbourhood. When one day he discovered that the new owner had cut down all the trees we had loved and cared for, he wept uncontrollably. After that we gave him permission to board at the home of his friend, Carl Loffmark, so that he could complete his education with the friends he had known since nursery school.

During those years, Bill was rarely home. He left for the office early every morning in an attempt to beat the traffic and returned very late every evening for the same reason. The family's support for my work dwindled to token gestures. We were all unhappy, and I felt guilty at being the cause of what I recognized as the deterioration of my marriage and the dejection of my family. The decision of Mount St. Vincent University in Halifax to confer an honorary degree of humane letters on me was welcomed as my first such honour, and the only happy thing that happened to me that year.

I plunged into my work in Burnaby, determined to ensure that the riding, which had voted NDP consistently for years before the debacle of 1975, would remain NDP for years to come. With my young and politically astute assistant, Diana Matheson, and a large core of hard-working, committed New Democrats, the task was made easier by the fact that the riding was represented federally by a brilliant, high-profile, hard-working MP named Svend Robinson. I was so confident that we could make the riding secure for the party that I took time out to develop and indulge my interests in international development and expand my work for peace, through visits to China on a women's tour and to Greece and Moscow for peace conferences.

In 1982, as part of a women's tour of Greece, I met Margareta Papandreou, wife of the Greek prime minister. At that time, she was president of the Women's Federation of Greece, and accompanied us on much of the tour, as we visited the places where women had performed acts of bravery or in some way influenced the course of Greek history. During the time that we spent together, Margareta spoke of her plans for an international women's summit on peace and asked whether I would be interested in participating in such an organization.

I indicated my enthusiasm for the idea and asked to be included in its planning. She explained that it grew out of the idea of Women Parliamentarians for Peace wanting to extend and broaden their membership and base of support. I became an enthusiastic member and participant, and in 1986 at a conference in Athens became the official representative for Canada, although by then I had resigned from the legislature.

Women for a Meaningful Summit, as the organization was called, functioned primarily to attend and monitor meetings of NATO, and the summit meetings between President Reagan and Secretary Gorbachev, or their foreign ministers. The whole point of the exercise was to let those gentlemen know that they were being observed and scrutinized by women of influence from the major nations, as well as some of the smaller countries of the world. We hoped that our presence, plus the sessions we were able to arrange with their aides after these meetings, would convey to them the sense of urgency women had concerning the future of the world.

We did not delude ourselves about the leverage or influence we had. We just knew that we had to intervene at the highest level of discussion open to us and to exercise whatever influence we could. I saw my membership in the women's summit as an extension of my involvement with the Voice of Women and other peace initiatives over the years.

Something happened, however, to wrench my attention back to my riding. In the Budget Speech of 1983 Premier Bill Bennett unleashed a barrage of legislation reflecting and paralleling the punitive right-wing economic ideology that was being adopted by conservative governments in Great Britain and the United States. Community groups as well as people employed in all areas of the government reeled before the onslaught, and the NDP caucus decided that it had no option but to dig its heels in and fight the government until it revoked some of those statutes.

This time, however, the community was not prepared to place their hopes solely on the efforts of the Official Opposition. Coming together, trade unions, churches and community groups united as one force to fight back, and the Solidarity Coalition was born. From July to November that year the Coalition directed a powerful and effective opposition to the government. It protested, picketed, demonstrated, held a sit-in, and, on October 15, 1983, marched 60,000 strong against the government. In the legislature the NDP divided the caucus into three teams and kept the debate going around the clock in an attempt to prevent passage of the bills. The Solidarity Coalition and the NDP: same goal, different arena, different methods.

In the end, the heroic effort was defeated, but it left a community more politicized and mutually supportive than anyone had thought possible.

The NDP caucus made a deliberate decision to stick to its legislative role and not to be involved or try to influence the actions of Solidarity. Solidarity was truly a people's movement, and those MLAs who participated in it did so as individuals rather than as representatives of the caucus. The Coalition created a critical mass of talent and ability beyond any group or political party's capacity to control. Its collective strength shook the province although it did not budge the government. The whole experience capsulized the struggle against economic conservatism, and perhaps signalled a new approach and form of community resistance.

Those were tumultuous years at home and abroad. The struggle in South Africa against apartheid was escalating and the international movement in support of it was growing. Bill and I redoubled our efforts and our financial contributions to this struggle, always frustrated because there was so little that we could really do to affect events there. We had been rocked by the Sharpeville Massacre of 1960, by the raw, murderous intent of the government directed against children and adults alike. We had desperately wanted to become directly involved, recognizing that it was not just Black people, but all humanity that was being dehumanized and degraded by the South African government's actions.

In 1986, when Bishop Tutu visited Canada to plead with our government to impose stiffer sanctions against South Africa, a dinner was given in his honour, hosted by the Toronto Arts

Against Apartheid group. I was invited to bring greetings from the women of Canada to the women of South Africa:

> Tell them
> that hundreds of thousands of women here in Canada love and support them. We know that despite the unrelenting brutality and violence of apartheid they will not be broken, will not be bent.
>
> Tell them
> we know that theirs has been a long struggle and a cruel one — but we know that since their first public act of opposition in 1913, when they campaigned against the pass laws, they have been growing stronger.
>
> Tell them
> that, as women, we recognize that their fight is our fight because we are all part of the common dignity of our sisterhood and of the human race.
> We mourn the loss of their children and weep for the senseless slaughter of their loved ones.
> We are angered when the rubber whips are used against them — but we are proud when they fight back.
>
> Tell them
> to keep on resisting, keep on marching, because we know that now the rock is struck, the boulder is dislodged.
>
> Tell them
> hundreds and thousands of their sisters here in Canada love and support them.

Peace remains the number-one priority in my life and in its pursuit in 1987, I attended another International Women's Conference on Peace, this time in Moscow. It is sometimes tempting to become so caught up in the minutiae of daily living that we forget how fragile the relationship is that keeps the great nations of the world in peaceful coexistence. That particular conference reminded me that we have to be constantly alert to that fact, because nothing that we work for has meaning in the face of a nuclear holocaust. The conference also gave me an opportunity to be with thousands of women from around the world who share the determination to 'give peace a chance,' and to realize a longtime wish to meet my special role model, Angela Davis. It was my great joy to find that she was as tall, as strong, as beautiful, and as special as I had always known she was.

As the tumult in the world outside escalated and spread, life at home settled into a more even pattern. Gary, our older son, had left to work with troubled adolescents in a program called Youth Unlimited in Regina. As a young teenager, he and another high school classmate had organized a social program for kids in the basement of a church in Vancouver; he remained involved in the program until his graduation. A person visiting from Regina had been so impressed with the program that she invited him to apply for a similar position with the Regina program. He accepted, loved his job and excelled at it. However, after five years the cold winters drove him back to Vancouver, where he was soon working with adolescents again, this time for the Vancouver School Board.

Cleta had graduated from law school and was completing her articling at the Ombudsman's Office.

Jonathan, while preparing to graduate from high school, threatened our sanity with the constant roll of drums, which Bill and I tolerated because of his promise that when he became rich and famous, we would never have to work again. Jonathan's droll and zany humour led me to suggest to him that he should become a rich and famous comedian instead, especially since that is a much quieter profession — until one of his concerts sent shivers up my spine. I believe that he is a truly gifted drummer and I hope that one day the world will come to share my very biased appraisal of his talent.

Katherine and Ashton, our two grandchildren, gave meaning to the words of the song "You Light Up My Life." None of my children were showing any sign of interest in a political career, although they were all politically aware and seemed to have inherited a commitment to social justice.

After ten years in opposition against an undemocratic, intransigent government, which continued to erode the rights of parliament and the opposition, I began to falter, so that when Dave Barrett announced to the caucus his intention not to continue as leader, my thoughts too turned to retirement.

Dave's retirement announcement triggered an immediate search for a new leader. There were inquiries from the Women's Committee as to whether I was interested in the job and pressure from many people to enter the race. This time, however, I was adamant that I was more interested in winding down my life in politics than in taking on new challenges.

At the same time that Dave informed the caucus of his decision to step down, he also proposed the name of Bill King as a suitable successor. That suggestion received our overwhelming support. I had been impressed with the manner in which Bill had conducted himself as interim leader during the 1975–76 period when Dave was out of the Assembly. He was a tall man of stately carriage and great eloquence. As the Minister of Labour in the short-lived NDP government of 1972–75 he had piloted through the legislature and defended the controversial, outstanding Labour Code of B.C. The appointments to the Human Rights Commission, which fell under his jurisdiction, had been thoughtful and appropriate, and his only discernible flaws were that he had a quick temper and was prone to be stubborn. He was about as sexist as the average caucus member, but demonstrated a willingness to have his consciousness raised. I liked Bill and assured Dave that I would give him my support.

Some time later, Dave reported back to caucus that Bill, who had retired from politics after his 1979 defeat, had declined the invitation to run for the leadership. However, Dave was confident that he only needed to be persuaded. Mindful of my own experience in the past, and knowing how arduous a leadership race can be, I declined to be part of the persuasion team, but still held to my decision to support his candidacy in the event that he agreed to run.

When a number of caucus members reported that Bill was firm in his determination not to seek the leadership despite their efforts, I reluctantly accepted his decision. I was convinced that he had the public stature and respect to ensure us a victory against the discredited Bennett government, but I disliked the idea of placing a person under duress without really knowing what personal and private reasons influence her or his decision; I withdrew my commitment and began to look elsewhere for a candidate to support.

The prospects were bleak. None of the three women MLAs, Eileen Dailly, Karen Sanford and Barbara Wallace, nor indeed any woman in the party, seemed interested in the challenge. Disillusioned with the experience of our government in 1972–75 and dispirited by the number of years in opposition, many of the original members of the Women's Committee had moved to carry the struggle on through the trade unions, community groups, the federal public service, electoral politics and the practice of law. Many others had coupled their feminism with the freedom struggles in Latin America and South Africa, expending most of their time and energies in that direction.

The result was that the Women's Committee was greatly weakened. It was being badgered about the need for its continued existence now that women's issues were widely covered by convention policy; and the struggle for its survival left the committee unable to develop or place a woman of stature before the party at that time.

One afternoon Robin came bouncing into my office, a wide grin on her face. "We've got a candidate," she beamed. Then, inviting Dennis Cocke, whose office was across the hall, to join us, she closed my office door and proceeded to extol the virtues of David Vickers as a potential party leader. I listened with interest, but some skepticism. I knew David and held him in high esteem. He had been an outstanding Deputy Attorney-General in the NDP government, excellent on women's issues, human rights and justice, and with an exceptional social conscience and concern for children and the disadvantaged in our society. I had always had a special admiration and love for David because of his dedication to the cause of mentally handicapped people. Because of my sister, I had always been sensitive to people with this disability and sympathetic to their families. But he was not very active in the party and had no history of long service to it. I considered those to be real and insurmountable barriers in the minds of party members.

Before I could respond, however, Dennis stated in a loud and clear voice, "No way, he's not well known in the party." Robin was crestfallen but determined. "Talk to Yvonne about it," she suggested to Dennis, and he agreed that he would but added that he was sure she would concur with his sentiments. Much as I hated to question Robin's political instincts, I had to agree with Dennis that David's chances in a leadership race would be slim. Robin insisted that he would bring new blood and new energy to the party and that we should at least agree to meet with him.

Dennis telephoned Yvonne and returned later to report that Yvonne thought there was no harm in meeting with David, but that she agreed he would be too severely handicapped by his low profile to win the endorsement of the delegates. Later that week, we had our meeting with David and we were impressed. A Committee to Elect David Vickers was immediately struck and we became part of an enthusiastic group of workers dedicated to raising David's profile in the party and ensuring his eventual victory as leader.

A week after our first meeting I received a call from Bill King, who informed me that he had decided to seek the leadership of the party. I told him that unfortunately I could not lend support to his campaign because I had given my commitment elsewhere.

Not many days after Bill's call, Hilda Thomas phoned to let me know that the Women's Committee had decided to endorse Margaret Birrell as their candidate for leader and needed my support. I was then faced with the task of saying to her as I had to Bill King that I was sorry, but my support had already been committed.

The decision not to abandon David and throw my support behind Margaret was a difficult one. It also drew a great deal of criticism from women in the party who had supported my bid in the 1975 federal leadership campaign and who had continued to support my political and feminist goals over the years. It proved to be confusing to younger members of the Women's Committee and forced me to examine my actions and my motives very carefully. In the final analysis, I had to accept that I did not believe that Margaret's leadership would have furthered the cause of either feminism or socialism in the party, or that it would have strengthened the party. In that case, to support her would have been contrary to my conscience and my beliefs.

I recognized David's shortcomings and imperfections, but believed that his record would survive the closest scrutiny and his leadership would have a positive and salutary effect on the party. I tried to say as much in a letter of explanation and support I wrote to the women of the party. Nonetheless it was for me one of those unhappy choices that I hope I never have to make again.

In the final analysis our efforts proved to be not quite enough. David was defeated by a campaign that focused on the brevity of his party membership and rumours that he was really a liberal, that depicted him as a pawn of 'the Cocke Machine,' and that finally branded him anti-labour for having worked as a junior in a law firm that represented management in a particularly bitter labour dispute in the mid-60s, and for being a participant in that action. Unlike that of 1975, this was a mean leadership campaign.

During the balloting, after three candidates had been defeated, leaving David Vickers in first spot followed by Bill King and Bob Skelly, the Vickers committee realized that by shifting some support to King we could knock Skelly off the ballot; this would leave the final vote to be decided between King and Vickers. We knew this would work to our advantage since many Skelly supporters were committed to Vickers as their second choice.

The committee, however, decided to reject the idea and allow the convention to run its course. We believed that in the final analysis a party chooses the leader that it deserves, and that to tamper with such a choice would be undemocratic. On the next ballot, King was defeated. He threw his delegate support behind Bob Skelly, thus ensuring Bob's election on the fifth and final ballot.

I accepted the decision of the convention and determined to work as hard as possible to support the new leader and win the next provincial election.

As the time for an election drew near, discontent and alarm at Skelly's inability to halt the party's downward slide caused rumblings of discontent and calls for the leader's resignation.

The leadership campaign had left deep scars, with one candidate, Graham Lea, leaving the caucus to sit in the legislature as an independent. When Premier Bill Bennett decided to step down and the Socreds elected the very pretty and charismatic Bill Vander Zalm to lead them, we knew that we were in trouble.

Four of us in caucus decided that we should approach Bob Skelly and suggest to him that he step aside as leader, so the party could call a quick convention to choose a leader who was better able to compete against Vander Zalm. The person we had in mind, although we had not discussed it with him, was Mike Harcourt, the extremely popular NDP mayor of Vancouver. He was the only person, in our opinion, able to beat Vander Zalm. Bob agreed to schedule a special evening caucus meeting to discuss our proposal.

We prepared ourselves very carefully so that we could place our ideas clearly, succinctly, and without prejudice to the caucus. However, when we walked into the caucus meeting that evening and saw that the president of the party, the past-president and a number of other members of the executive were present, we knew that we had a fight on our hands. I suggested to my colleagues that we chuck the whole idea: if the officers of the party felt strongly enough about Bob's leadership that they were prepared to fight to defend it, then we should let it be, especially since we were not prepared to make this a public challenge. The other members of the group thought we should speak our piece anyway, just for the record.

It was certainly one of the most discordant and contentious caucus meetings in which I had ever participated. When it was over I knew that although I would continue to work as hard as I could on behalf of the party during the pending election, I would not be a candidate myself.

When the 1986 election was lost, much was made of the fact that the leader's inability to perform consistently could be attributed to the actions of those dissident MLAs who had unsettled him prior to the campaign by suggesting that he relinquish his leadership. Knowing how divisive and destructive such an act is, why would anyone ever challenge a leader during her or his term of office?

I remember having thought as I followed the attempts of Dalton Camp to encourage John Diefenbaker to resign his leadership of the federal Conservative Party, how suicidal for the party such action was, yet years later I was willing to do the same thing myself. I believe that such actions are launched in desperation by desperate people. In our case, it was simply that loyalty to the party was stronger than loyalty to the leader. We knew that the party would lose under his leadership and we hoped there could be a chance of victory under another leader.

We were not interested in a public struggle, however, and we never spoke to the press, nor indeed to any persons other than our caucus colleagues. Once Bob Skelly indicated his refusal to step down, and the party reaffirmed its support for him, the matter was ended, as far as we were concerned.

In hindsight, and as I watched the Liberal Party struggle with the leadership of John Turner, I concluded that the Dalton Camp method is the only one that should ever be used. In other words, a leader should never be challenged unless the challengers are prepared to follow through to a successful resolution. Our challenge was weak and futile and in the end may indeed have hurt the fortunes of the party. I know that we would have lost the election anyway, and that by challenging the leader we only served to make ourselves the party's scapegoat. I also know that very rarely does a political party win an election while it is hemorrhaging internally.

CHAPTER TWELVE

I was awakened by the sun filtering through the sheer curtains; the sound of children's voices and the sounds of birds slowly penetrated my consciousness. I stretched and rolled, closed my eyes and pretended to sleep. For the first time in fourteen years, I was free to be abed, fritter my life away, do as I would.

The day before I had publicly announced my intention to retire and I felt wonderful. Barb, my constituency assistant, had been angry at my decision to leave; the executive of the constituency felt cheated that I had changed my mind and decided so close to an impending election not to run. I was sorry and apologetic, but suddenly I knew that the time had come for me to go, so I was leaving.

I called Mrs. Goad, the real estate agent who had sold me our house, and told her to put it up for sale. My children were ecstatic, and for the first time in years, the scowl disappeared from Bill's face. As I lay there with my eyes shut I thought of Sojourner Truth's "I will come to you no more."

As soon as the press announced my retirement, phone calls, telegrams and letters poured in, many saying "Thank you and good-bye," others with invitations to speak, write, teach. Within months, a series of testimonial dinners, banquets and parties was arranged. The most lavish was organized by the B.C. Congress of Black Women at the Pan Pacific Hotel and was attended by 500 friends and well-wishers. The Women's

Committee of the NDP presented me with a picture collage of the meaningful moments in my political life, which saw me enter politics with jet black hair in 1972 and leave it a 'silver-top' in 1986. The women's community groups had a fete at Isadora's, a popular co-op restaurant, and presented me with one of Persimmon's exquisite sculptures. Harambee, the national Black organization, inaugurated a generation fund in my honour, to finance the education of gifted Black children. Burnaby-Edmonds NDP gave a dinner in my honour and presented me with a crystal vase, and the B.C. Association of Social Workers gave a dinner to honour my contribution to the profession.

The round of farewell and testimonial dinners organized by the women's community highlighted for me the source of strength that the women had always been to me. From the very beginning of my political career, my goal had been to change the status of women, racial minorities and other disadvantaged groups in society; but I realized that I would not have been able to do any of the public things or participate in the political arena except that women identified me as their spokesperson and worked to get me into the position where I could place their issues on the public agenda. The Black and other racial minority communities in B.C. lacked the clout to do so. Much as they would have liked to elect a candidate of their choosing, they could muster neither the numbers nor the resources to do so. They had had to be content with supporting Emery Barnes and me, the person whom the women in the New Democratic Party worked to insert on the party ticket.

I have never lost sight of the fact that I was the women's candidate, that they nominated me, worked for me and elected me. Occasionally this brought me into conflict with the leader and the caucus, but I never compromised my commitment to women, and wouldn't, unless it came into conflict with my commitment to peace and social justice. Conservative women and women on the right continually reminded me that I did not speak for them; however, I did work for them. When I fought for fair family law legislation, pension reform and childcare, I was fighting as hard for women on the right as I was for other women. Although my base of support rested with radical feminists, they never limited my struggle to their particular concerns, and indeed demanded of me as they did of themselves that the freedom and equality of all women should be my mandate.

On October 22, 1986, the Socreds won yet another election, and the NDP in Burnaby-Edmonds very sadly were defeated. Two days later Bill and I moved out of our Burnaby house, and I received notice that I had been appointed to the Ruth Wyn Woodward endowed chair in Women's Studies at Simon Fraser University.

A retired moderator of the United Church of Canada had once responded to a question on the subject by describing retiring as the putting on of a new set of tires. That was certainly the way I regarded my exit from electoral politics. I was free at last to explore the interests and opportunities opening up to me in education, international development and peace; free at last to stomp the country encouraging women to enter the political arena. I would have time somehow in some way to place the experience and skills I had developed in Canada at the service of the women of my roots.

After fourteen years, I had time, too, to garden, enjoy my granddaughters and pursue even more intensively the passionate commitments that are the legacy left me by those older, stronger women in the family who continue to be my driving force.

Yet I wondered what life would really be like now that I was out of politics. For fourteen years, people had treated me as though I had power, as though I could influence events, change things. A mixture of awe and respect accompanied such a perception, and I suspected that, without realizing it, I had grown accustomed to the treatment. I have always been fascinated by power, by the speed with which it seduced some people and by the fact that others seemed immune to its blandishments.

I had also always been aware of the gap that existed between perception and reality, and the fact that the view from the inside of any arena looking out was so much more limited and narrow than the perception of those looking in from the outside.

In truth, I was actually very disappointed by how little real power I had and how often I failed to live up to the expectations of people who appealed to me for help.

At first, I thought that if I had been a cabinet minister I could have had some direct power, but even of that I'm not sure; often cabinet ministers were forced to introduce and defend legislation to which they were opposed, because it was the will of the leader, majority vote in caucus or recommendation of the party pollsters. On the other hand, they were sometimes refused permission to introduce legislation to which they were wedded because of opposition from the leader, majority vote in caucus or recommendation of the party pollsters.

In retrospect, I realize that it was power in the traditional patriarchal context that I lacked, rather than the more personal and compelling power that comes from collective decision-making and the mutual respect people of like mind share with each other. But when one works in a traditional patriarchal institution, it is necessary to have power in what I perceive as the negative context before one is able to redesign, re-form and redirect such power into a more positive force.

My interest in power had always stemmed from a belief in its potential as an instrument of change. As far back as I can remember, I have wanted to change the world, and I always knew that the use of power was essential to that goal. I was interested in entering the profession of law in order to change unjust and unfair laws. I entered social work because, as a young woman in Jamaica, I had seen it help people change their lives and empower them to fight the system. I entered politics convinced that it was indeed the root of and enforcer of all wrongdoing, and that any real change, to be effective, had to begin at and go to that root. I believed that politics could be a revolution without guns. I believed in it and in its potential to be power in a positive and good context. I stand before you wiser and sadder about the limits of politics as mould breaker or architect of a new social structure. Indeed if one is to accept Noam Chomsky's theory, there is no such thing as power in a positive sense.

Christina McCall, a writer and feminist, once described women as having influence rather than power. I was struck by the analysis and upon examination found it to be true of my political experience. It seemed that I spent most of my political years attempting to convince cabinet ministers, and their bureaucrats, and governments, of the need to address women's concerns, and the concerns of the poor and other disadvantaged groups, with at least the same level of seriousness and intent they afforded other issues.

The fact that my efforts resulted in failure many more times than they did in success reinforced my sense of powerlessness. I felt cheated; somehow the power that seemed to be promised by the position of 'legislator' was denied me, as though an open door slammed shut upon my approach, leaving me frustrated and bewildered outside. Conversations with other women politicians have helped me see that this too is a shared experience, rather than a personal once.

Throughout my time in office, I was able to observe the ease with which the men twisted each other's arms, to see that even when they opposed each other's views there was an underlying respect, a feeling of family, between them. My approach, on the other hand, even to those members I considered friends, was met with wariness. It was as though they were positioning themselves to defend against attack. A smile would always greet me, but it would only reach as far as the lips. Their eyes would be veiled – and on guard. I'm not sure whether this was a phenomenon peculiar to their relationship with feminists, or all women, or whether I was witnessing the way men would invariably respond to a woman they considered their equal.

On the other hand power, or the perception of having power, created a whole curiosity and myth about what kind of person I really was. On more than one occasion people would comment with surprise on my physical size. One day while I waited for the light to change, a woman approached me at a street intersection. "I thought you were six feet tall," she commented, "but you are just average." She viewed me with a mixture of amazement and disappointment. I have often heard this comment made about other public figures, "he was shorter than I thought," "she was smaller than I expected," as though as a society we endow people who hold power with height also, as though we expect them to be giants.

It is said that Henry Kissinger once remarked, "Power is the ultimate aphrodisiac." I found that for some men the idea of a woman with power was tantalizing. They were clearly curious about my susceptibility to seduction. I remember an occasion when I was at a party, and a well known roué decided to monopolize my time, to my delight and pleasure because he was a wonderful dancer and I love to dance. We were having a great time indulging in fancy footwork and light flirtatious repartee; it was fun!

"Who are you?" he asked, "How is it that our paths have never crossed before?"

"I'm Rosemary Brown," I replied. He was convulsed with laughter.

"Don't be silly! You couldn't be that man-hating battle axe — you are wonderful," and with that he twirled me around the room, laughing about my having tried to put one over on him.

For women in power, sexuality presents a dilemma concerning dress and behaviour. The struggle is to be true to one's wishes to be attractive and charming without being perceived to be seductive. Some women unconsciously place a layer of fat between themselves and this world, as an unspoken message that they are to be seen simply as powerful persons, rather than as women, as an attempt to hide their femaleness and blend into the grey anonymity of the male world. Clearly these women have come to believe that being female places them at a decided disadvantage in the power arena, and they would like to eliminate that factor. Other women try with varying degrees of success to maintain a balance between their femininity and their public life. These women believe that femininity can be a useful tool in the power arena and, if wielded with skill, can actually give them an advantage over their male colleagues.

Feminists, and here I speak for myself, recognize the fact that they are women as important to their job and position. Sexuality and femininity are rejected. They see themselves as pioneers in the attempt to open up arenas and to change them by their very presence. For feminists the whole point of moving into power arenas is to revolutionize them, rather than to use them as a stepping stone to personal and private advancement. This position, I believe, frees feminists to be, to dress and to behave in a manner defined by themselves, rather than in response to the possible consequence of the attitude and retaliation of their male colleagues or superiors.

Throughout fourteen years in public office, I was constantly running into the mythical Rosemary Brown, the creation of other people's minds, and invariably she was taller, tougher, smarter, sexier, and more powerful than I was – but she always was and remains even today the person that I wanted to be.

On one occasion I was shopping in a downtown department store before Valentine's Day when my eyes caught a display of men's jockey shorts, some with red hearts on them, some with cupids, others with red lips. I stood looking at them wondering which ones to buy as a surprise valentine present for Bill. I took my gloves off to check the texture and quality of the fabric. At that point a woman came up to me, "You look just like Rosemary Brown," she said, "but I know that you are not her. She wouldn't be here playing with these obscene shorts."

I was stunned; I blushed, though fortunately red doesn't show up well on brown skin, so she was unaware of my condition. I just smiled and walked away, leaving my beautiful warm kid gloves sitting on the counter, too embarrassed and flustered to return and retrieve them. So another lesson was learnt: that as a society we endow the people we respect with *our* values, *our* definitions of good and evil.

I never explored the extent of the power to which I had access, never tested its limits – Matina Horner, the feminist researcher who coined the concept 'fear of success,' might conclude that I was at least a little bit afraid of it. I don't think so; very early on I recognized that the power at my disposal would not meet my particular expectations and so concluded that to achieve the goals of feminism, election to the provincial legislature was just not enough. As an elected official I was able to participate in drafting legislation, but my power to influence was often not as great as that of high-ranking bureaucrats or ministerial advisers, who had more direct and effective clout than I did. From the inside, they could derail or indeed even put on track important, albeit low-profile, policy and program changes, and do it quietly, without fanfare. In this game, 'the Regulations' are more important than 'the Bill,' as well as less public and more difficult to access. I decided that in the next life, if I am unable to reincarnate as a premier or prime minister, I would certainly like to return as a deputy minister.

Yet I believed then and still do that elected politicians do have some power. This is why, despite my discontent with not having sufficient 'traditional' power during my term of office, I continue to encourage women to enter the world of politics. Shirley Chisolm said,"Politics is the only route to power, and even in the most democratic society, power is the name of the game. Power makes, interprets and enforces the law. It decides which interests shall flourish and which shall perish. It determines who will be educated and how much, who may work at what kind of jobs, where they work, what they may do and with whom."

Even the backbencher in opposition has power — power to speak with immunity on any issue, so long as it is done within the legislative chamber. To be listened to, to be reported in the media, is a form of power. All elected members, including the backbencher in opposition, have power to influence, to give information, to challenge, to state the case. It is the kind of power, however, that most politicians use sparingly unless it affects their constituency directly or touches on a crusade or project of theirs. For the most part it is wasted power, imprisoned by the fear of offending or alienating any voter or potential voter.

Politicians also have another kind of power, namely access. Very few people (other than other politicans), no matter how high their station in life, will refuse to meet or speak to a politician. It is as though there is a voice in the base of their brain that whispers, "Who knows, one day this contact may prove useful." "Who knows, one day I may need the intervention or influence of this political person." And this triggers a positive response, no matter how tepid, to the request.

All of these powers, of course, can be abused. And there have been so many instances of abuse that in fact politics as a vocation has become synonymous with the corrupt use of power. But this is not all; in addition to the expectations there are the responsibilities that accompany any person in public life. Although having to live as a public person was not an onerous burden, it was certainly stressful for the family, and for me. At the very beginning of my political career I explained to the children that although I was the only member of the family elected to public office, they too would be subjected to public scrutiny. I did not believe in being subtle with them about the stress my public life would put on them. I told them that there would be some persons who would want them to fail. That simply because they were Black it was expected that they would become involved with drugs, shoplifting or some other form of antisocial behaviour.

I told them that, if any of these expectations were fulfilled, their father and I would be saddened and my opponents would revel in our misfortune. I told them that since I was an outspoken advocate of women's rights, there were people who wanted me to have delinquent kids and a broken marriage in order to vindicate their opposition to the women's liberation struggle. I threatened that, if they embarrassed me, although I would continue to love them, I would be angry and disappointed because I too was searching for answers, I too needed to know whether it was possible for me to be faithful to feminist ideals and be successful as a mother as well.

The response of the children was that they were so proud of the achievements of both their father and me that they would never do anything to embarrass or hurt us; however, they made no secret of the fact that they found being our children in some respects a burden. As Gary, my older son, lamented, "If only we weren't the only brown Browns in Vancouver." In fact, the children found that my public life was a mixed blessing, which closed as many doors as it opened to them in this very polarized political province.

When she heard that I was writing this book, a young woman who spends much of her life in politics and contemplates seeking political office someday suggested that I should include a chapter entitled, 'Women and the effect of power on their relationships with their spouses.' She went on to say that it should be depersonalized and not be the story of my relationship with Bill, but a general discussion of the topic.

Her theory was that because society expects men to have the primary career in the family and to bestow the glow of the limelight on their wives and children, the reversal of this role must change the relationship these men have with their families, with other men, even with other women. She wondered whether such a man's value was diminished in the eyes of his family and society, and whether consequently he felt diminished in his own eyes.

I was fascinated by her suggestion, because it reminded me of the numbers of women who had told me that they could not pursue their political aspirations because to do so would be threatening to their husbands. I was also reminded of the delegate, a man in his late middle years, who explained that he could not support my bid for leadership of the federal NDP because he did not believe that a woman should hold a more important job than her husband, and who gave a solemn "yes" in response to my asking whether I would have to become a 'Black widow' in order to secure his support.

So I asked a number of male acquaintances whether they would resent their wives' entry into political life. Without exception they assured me that, on the contrary, they would welcome and support any such effort on the part of their spouses. At another time, I asked the wives of these men whether they would be assured of their husbands' support if they decided to seek public office. Without exception, they hesitated. They expressed the fear that, although their spouses would articulate support, and would probably mean it, the disruption in the family pattern would create tension, unconscious resentment and jealousy would develop, and the relationship would begin to deteriorate.

They all agreed that they were sensitive to the existence of an invisible line beyond which they could not step if they were to maintain an even keel in the marital relationship. Their conversation reminded me of women I had known who had retired after one or two terms in public office because of family tension and disintegration in their relationships with their husbands.

The reality is that as a society, we are still uncomfortable with any variation on the nuclear family. This discomfort is manifest in the teasing men indulge in, referring to men married to women in public life as 'Mister Jane Doe,' or looking deep into their eyes and asking, "What is it really like sleeping with a judge? A cabinet minister? A corporate executive? Ha! Ha!" or indulging in some other veiled but cruel joke.

Some men take this situation in their stride, plunging into their wives' careers and working beside them with genuine pride in their achievements. Others withdraw and concentrate on their own careers, taking the attitude that both spouses are equal in different ways, so no competition or jealousy exists.

My observation has been that often a more subtle power struggle ensues where, despite protestations of equality, the male demands the wife's collusion in supporting, in a clandestine way, society's assumption of male superiority. That is, she supports and reaffirms his public statements of equality while accepting his private practice of inequality.

I have observed that the husband will undermine the wife in subtle and perhaps unconscious ways, the most common method being through sexual control. He will begin to manifest signs of disinterest in any sexual activity with her; he will withdraw from former affectionate or erotic play. If she does not read the signals correctly and withdraw from public life, the next step will be for him to act out, perhaps through an affair with another woman, and he will go to great lengths to ensure that she becomes aware of this. Often this is accompanied by critical comments about her appearance and her work.

Most women who find themselves in this situation recognize this behaviour for the power struggle that it is, a signal that their spouse is hostile to the reversal of roles and has decided to end the marriage unless the situation reverts to 'normal.'

The choice is then the woman's as to whether continuation

of the marriage should take precedence over her career goals. Her struggle to arrive at a decision is painful, compounded as it is by all her latent fears, the most profound of which is the fear of being poor and alone in old age. I recall a friend who, mourning the end of a bad marriage, commented that despite the unhappiness in the marriage, it was the loss of someone to grow old with that terrified her most. Even in instances where women have professions that guarantee them a buffer against poverty in old age, they still share with many women the fear that some catastrophe might occur and plunge them into abject poverty in old age, and the belief that somehow a husband is guaranteed protection against such an eventuality.

I believe as well that most women have a genuine desire to combine family and career successfully, and search for the formula that can make this happen. I believe they yearn to break the cycle that decrees that although such a combination is possible for men, it eludes women.

As a 'role model,' I soon picked up that the message of feminism is doomed as far as young women are concerned, unless it is possible to prove that it is compatible with the traditional male/female relationship. I learnt that like me, young women want it all, the husband, the children, the profession; and they fear that feminism might be unable to deliver that package.

The result is that a large percentage of women continue to deny themselves the opportunity of pursuing public and professional goals; many others retire from public and professional life prematurely. Others persevere and accept the disintegration and termination of their marriages, and the lucky few manage to maintain both successfully. In my own case, when a crisis directly or indirectly created as a result of my political career, and certainly exacerbated by it, threatened our marriage, both Bill and I were forced to make some major compromises in order to ensure the marriage's survival. Whether we succeeded, only time will tell.

I am willing to assign seventy percent credit to husbands when marriage survives a woman's acquisition of power and ninety percent blame to them when there is failure. Because in the final analysis the success or failure of the marriage has less to do with how the woman behaves than with the man's ability to deal with the reversal of their roles.

Men have not been socialized to be equal partners in marriage nor to accept a status secondary to that of their wives. Women who place these demands on men are asking them to break the pattern in which they were moulded. Men either have to see some benefit to themselves or have to have a genuine commitment to equality between the sexes before they will willingly embark on such a course.

In any event, many of the women to whom I spoke stated that their spouses genuinely believed that they were being supportive of their endeavours, and denied that their sniping, critical observations, promiscuous behaviour or any other hostile act was in any way an attempt to sabotage their wives' careers. These men maintained that they were not affected by the teasing of other men, nor by the subtle and unconscious ways society demonstrates its anger at their acceptance of the role reversal.

On a more personal note, I would like to add that regardless of gender, marriage to a politician can be very stressful. I remember Yvonne Cocke being asked by a student at a panel on women and politics held at UBC to speak about the benefits that accrued to her as the wife of a cabinet minister; she replied she could not recall 'one single redeeming feature' in being in such a position. Politics, if practised properly, is a demanding full-time occupation that can take over all of one's thoughts, ideas and attention. It is difficult for anyone to compete successfully against such an abductor.

In retrospect, I now realize that retirement did not just free up my time, it released my mind, interests and preoccupations from fourteen years of being deaf, blind and unaware of anything outside of its political context.

So in reality for me even the word 'retire' is a misnomer. As I teach, lecture and speak to groups across the country, I now know that I carry on the same struggles – only the place and the date have changed. I haven't retired, I have simply expanded my modus operandi.

CHAPTER THIRTEEN

As soon as the doors of the plane opened, the heat carrying the strange smell of spice and sweat and musk rushed in, almost suffocating us, followed by the noise—raised voices, loud laughter, music colliding, separating, blending. The passengers, most of whom had been standing impatiently in the aisle, ready to disembark since the first sound of the bell had warned us to fasten our seat belts and prepare to land, jostled and teased each other good-naturedly as they rushed for the door out into the sun, hot, hot, hot.

I remained in my seat near the front of the plane, eyes closed, and anticipated the certainty of muscles relaxing, heartbeat slowing, and the tension draining away from mind and body and soul. "Welcome 'ome man . . . welcome 'ome," said the voice in the distance.

Thirty-five years had passed since I had left this island, planning to spend four brief years of study in Canada and return to marry my childhood love, Roy. Much had changed since then and I was returning a very different person to a very different Jamaica on a very sad occasion. Uncle Karl, the patriarch of the family, was dying, and this was my desperate rush to be on time to say one final "love you" and "farewell." With his passing, only my mother, herself aging, would remain of that generation.

My feeling of loss was heightened by the realization that with their passing, my brother, my sister and I – 'the children' – would become the old people, the wise ones. Well, my brother and I, anyway – because of her retardation the family had always considered my sister a child in need of care and protection, so although chronologically she was a mere two years younger than I, she remained a child in the opinion of our elders, us and our children. I wondered whether we could ever be the inspiration and guide to our children and grandchildren that our elders had been to us. Their fierce and uncompromising demand that we be the best that we could be had driven us to reach beyond our grasp and set goals beyond our reach. Their tough and nonnegotiable sense of right and wrong had been the compass that had guided us through treacherous times of changing morals and ethics, and had kept us honest in the face of the most exquisite temptations. Their firm conviction that we are all responsible for each other, and their insistence that we should care more about the needs of others than about desires of our own had protected us from indifference and greed.

And as my mind wandered in and out of memories, I recalled their overwhelming sense of pride in the family, their joy in each other's achievements, the love and affection that bonded them together and conveyed to us their sense of near disbelief in the luck and good fortune that had destined them to share each other's lives and be a family. They really were each other's best friends, and for the first time I realized that they were ours, too.

I also came to understand the tough rules by which my life had been shaped and formed and to appreciate that these rules had been transmitted across the generations more by example than by words. And I wondered once again how we, 'the children,' had measured up in the eyes of the old people, and how we would measure up in the eyes of our children and grandchildren.

"Merry man, hurry girl!" The impatient voice brought me back to earth. I opened my eyes, blinded for an instant by the harsh glare of the sun bouncing off the metal doorjamb; I waited for my eyes to focus. One of my young relatives was beckoning me to hurry. I was to leave the Air Canada jet here in Montego Bay and be whisked through customs onto one of the many small planes that, rumour had it, had once been 'ganja planes' used occasionally for the transporting of marijuana; it would fly me directly to the heart of Kingston, where a car waited, another relative at the wheel, to drive me directly to Uncle Karl's hospital bedside.

"Hi mi love how you do?" I replied effortlessly.

Merry, the diminutive of Rosemary, which my mother had said fitted my carefree disposition so aptly that when I was a child she had greeted me each morning with the song "Good morning, merry sunshine, how do you do today. . . ." Merry, the signal that I was safe, that I was back home.

My young relative steered me quickly past long lines of waiting arrivals, through the Montego Bay airport, with a bright smile and wave of her hand to the customs officer and a "this is my cousin from Canada, man, let her through." "Right," he responded, marking the X with chalk on my two pieces of luggage to indicate that I had been cleared to proceed.

We sprinted across the tarmac to the small plane, propeller twirling, door ajar, waiting. I turned, gave her a quick hug. "Thanks mi love," I said. "No problem," she replied.

Forty-five minutes later I arrived in Kingston; Rennie, who was married to my cousin Pauline and is one of my favourite men in all the world, was there to meet me. After a quick hug, he drew back, looked at me, shook his head slowly and drawled, "Man! Retirement agree with you!"

Actually, I had experienced such a resurgence of energy since retirement that I anticipated that it would cause my hair to recapture its black colour and my wrinkles to disappear. And as we fought our way through Kingston's narrow, crowded, noisy streets to Nuttall Hospital, I confided this to Rennie.

I also expressed my regret that, now that I would have more time to visit Jamaica and enjoy more time with them, none of the elders would be there to share that time with me. As we parked the car and walked towards the entrance of the hospital, I was engulfed with a wave of sadness so intense that my stomach ached, my heart pounded and my whole body seemed to be in pain. What if I were too late? What if he were already gone? I began to run. As I raced towards the door I heard singing, the voices of young girls in the distance. I stopped and listened, smiling as I recalled my own youth, the happiness of playing that ring game with my girlfriends, "There's a brown girl in the ring tra la la la la." I hummed as I walked slowly into the hospital. I would say farewell, I would miss him, but I would carry on strengthened, enriched and empowered.

> Then you show me you motion
> tra la la la la
> for she likes sugar and I like plum.
> then you skip across the ocean. . . .

INDEX